Floyd Patterson

VICTORY
OVER
MYSELF

VICTORY OVER MYSELF

by Floyd Patterson
with Milton Gross

PUBLISHED BY

BERNARD GEIS ASSOCIATES

DISTRIBUTED BY RANDOM HOUSE

Library of Congress Catalog Card Number: 62–15657

Manufactured in the United States of America

FIRST PRINTING

To Wiltwyck School for Boys,
which started me
in the right direction

VICTORY
OVER
MYSELF

Chapter One

I can never forget the dream. I sleep a lot and I dream a lot, but this was different because it was the night before I fought Ingemar Johansson the second time, and that made the difference.

You've got to understand how it is—being the heavyweight champion of the world and then not being the champion. You've got to be able to feel what it means to be somebody—to belong—and then suddenly you don't belong, and you wonder whether you were ever meant to be a human being other people could look up to.

That's how it was that night in my dream. I could see Ingemar throwing the jab and the hook. I could see him letting the right hand go and doing many things. I could see myself doing many things, but never once did I get to the end of the dream. I never wanted to see the end. I just wouldn't let it end.

The way I figured it, even while sleeping, was that if I let it go on to its conclusion and I won in the dream, then I might take it easy with him again and be carried out once more. If I saw him winning, then it would be a sign of my own weakness. I couldn't let either one happen—at least not until we were in the ring again, because I had been nothing and then I'd become something and then I was nothing again.

That dream haunted me all the next day while I waited in my

3

hotel room until we were ready to leave for the Polo Grounds for the fight. When they told me it was time to go, I excused myself from the others and went into the bathroom. I closed the door, turned on the light over the mirror, and looked at my reflection in it.

"When you look at yourself in the mirror the next time," I said half aloud, "will you or won't you be the world champion again?"

I turned out the light and left myself in the darkness for a moment before walking out into the brightness of the room and a new life into which I was reborn when I became the first man in boxing history to regain the heavyweight championship by knocking out Ingemar in the fifth round.

When I began to prepare this story of my life, I asked myself why I wanted to begin the story just at this point. Why not when I beat Archie Moore to become the youngest in history—I was twenty-one then—to win the title? Why not when I kayoed Johansson the second time, in March, 1961? Why not with my four-round knockout over Tom McNeeley on December 4, 1961 in Toronto or my decision to accept the challenge of Sonny Liston? Why not from the point of my earliest recollections as a child, where my story really should begin?

Well, I've thought of it all and I can only say that the second fight against Ingemar was the real crossroads of my life. If ever I was in danger of becoming the mixed-up kind of person again that I used to be as a kid, that was the point. Maybe I ought to tell you, too, what it was like the morning I awakened after regaining the crown. Maybe then you'll understand what it was like while I was still in doubt and all the frustrations of all my years tore at me.

I opened my eyes and the sun coming through the Venetian blinds dazzled me momentarily. Temporarily I was back again with the dream that I would not let end on the night before the fight. Suddenly I realized that the dream had ended. "I'm the champion," I said to myself. "I won last night."

Just as suddenly I appreciated the terrible load that had been lifted off me. It was as if I had been carrying a great weight that was almost too much for me to bear and finally I'd been able to put it down. I remembered the terrible anguish and shame at having been beaten the year before. I remembered the darkness in all the rooms I had sat in and the silence I'd allowed to press in on me and the many questions about myself I'd deliberately avoided answering.

I jumped out of bed. Somebody had placed all the papers on the floor at the side of it. I picked them up and began thumbing through them. The first thing that struck me was a picture of Johansson's sister Eva. She was holding her face in her hands, weeping. I said to myself, "Last year that was Sandra, my wife."

I pulled up the blinds and looked down into the street twenty-six floors below. The sun shone so brightly down there. I told myself I had to get out there and go for a walk, be among people, feel the warmth of the sun.

That's what I did later that day. "How about a walk?" I said to my attorney and friend, Julius November.

"Where?" he asked, because he knows that when I walk I generally do it alone or with some close friend, but in a quiet neighborhood.

"Right out there," I said, pointing to the busy street below.

We went out and it felt just right. We walked down busy Seventh Avenue, maybe about fifteen blocks, up one street and down another, and then back to the hotel. The people on the streets, they made me feel good. They recognized me. They wanted to shake my hand and asked me to sign autographs. They called me champ.

As we were nearing the end of the walk, one man came up to me and he was being real nice. "When you hit him that second left hook and knocked him out," he said, "I thought you'd killed him. He was out on the canvas for five minutes, at least."

That is the highest kind of praise a fan can pay a fighter and yet it sent sort of a chill through me. In my mind's eye I could see Ingemar lying there in the ring, his leg quivering, and I was scared. I thought I hurt him real bad. I never saw anybody shake like that. I was frightened.

It struck me then how much of my life I have been frightened by one thing or another. As a child I was never at ease at home or in school or in the streets. I was embarrassed most of the time, shamed at other times, smothered in a feeling of inadequacy. In school I was too frightened to speak. I had a fear of being inferior. When I first started to court my wife, I'd look at her and say nothing. I had few friends, no interests, nothing of which I could be proud, no clothes, no real talent except for making myself miserable. I was one of "The Lost Ones," which was the way they described me when I was first sent to Wiltwyck School, a farm for emotionally disturbed youngsters, at Esopus, New York, back in September, 1945, when I was ten.

When I first began to attract some attention as a fighter and the newspapermen wanted to know a little something about me, my manager, Cus D'Amato, said I was "kind of a stranger." What a strange way to describe a human being! And yet it was so true. Maybe it is still true, because as I think back to my first knockout of Johansson, I realize how vicious I was in the ring that night and know that I never want to be that vicious again. At the same time I know I must be, because I am in a business of violence.

The strangest part of it all is that I hate violence and yet I have found myself as a person in the ring. I look calm. People have said that I am poker-faced, expressionless, almost without emotion. But how many people know me? Maybe it's been my own fault or my own choosing. I haven't allowed too many people to get close to me.

That's an odd thing, too. Here I am, the world's heavyweight champion. As many words have been written about me as about any champion in the history of boxing. Not all of them have been accurate. Not all of them have been true, but maybe it's because I've been such a stranger to myself that, naturally enough, I've been a stranger to others.

I suffer a lot, but most of it is inside. I guess you could say I'm sensitive, maybe too sensitive, but that's the way I am. And in the last few months, while this book has been in preparation, I've been trying to figure out why it's been that way.

I'm a grown man now—twenty-seven—and I've learned finally that the world is a place in which to live, not a cellar in which you hide. There was a time when you could hit me and I wouldn't think much of it, but you could say something and it would hurt me terribly. In that respect, at least, I haven't changed much, although I know now that what is said depends upon who the person is that's saying it.

Now I'm saying it and I find it isn't easy. I have something special to say, but I don't think I'm somebody special. I came from poverty and now I'm a wealthy man, but many people were poor—just as poor as we were—and made their way. I have a beautiful home in Scarsdale, New York, and my children will never want. My folks have their own home in Mount Vernon, which is a longer way back than you can measure in miles to the Bedford-Stuyvesant slum in Brooklyn where eleven of us kids once lived in an old-law tenement railroad flat.

No matter how many headlines spell out my name today, I'll never forget what I used to be. My name was spelled out in a different way in the days when I was a kid. They wrote it down in truancy records and in the juvenile courts, and it was spelled out in the heartaches I gave my hard-working parents and the heartaches I gave myself.

It's a long time back, but it's a reminder to me of how far I have come. Maybe it isn't right to look behind you, but I've got to because there's a picture of me taken when I was two. My mother still has that picture, and for a long time it hung over the bed I shared with my two older brothers, Frank and Billy. They and another relative were in the picture taken at the Bronx Zoo, and so was I.

My mother tells me that when I became a little older I used to tell her over and over again as I pointed to the picture of myself: "I don't like that boy!"

When I was past nine my mother came home from work one night and the picture no longer was the same. Over my own face and body I had scratched three large X's with a nail or something. I can't explain why now. I wouldn't remember it at all if my mother hadn't remembered it. I guess maybe I liked myself so little that I wanted to eliminate myself completely from that photo. Or maybe the world was so hard to face that I wanted "out" from more than the picture. It was too harsh a reminder to me of the feeling I had inside that everybody was so much better than I.

Chapter Two

I can't remember ever having any fun at all, or even laughing, until after I was placed in the Wiltwyck School for Delinquent Boys. I hated laughter because it seemed no matter what I did everybody was always laughing at me. They'd laugh at the dirt on my face and the torn, shabby, over-sized clothes I wore, and the way I couldn't read or write or answer a question in school or even talk to somebody when they talked to me.

It got so that I wouldn't look anybody in the face or want them to look at me. I'd run and hide. Somehow I was always hiding and always running, and I guess maybe that's how I got to like the darkness. There was safety in the darkness for me. The day was a nightmare. When the light came fear came. I just naturally took to the night. That's when I'd prowl through the streets of Brooklyn, wander through alleyways and around dark corners. During the days there were cellars to hide in or the protection of the darkness in movie houses like the Banko, Regent and Apollo, and then there was always the subway when you played hooky from school.

First I'd ride the Eighth Avenue Subway Line from one end of it to the other, up and back, up and back, all day long, but then I discovered this little room just off the tracks past the end of the station at High Street.

It's hard to understand now how a kid of nine would have nerve enough to walk off a station platform along the tracks and find this space that wasn't bigger than a hole in the wall, where the subway workmen would keep their tools. There was a metal ladder to get up into it, and once you were in you locked the door behind you and there was total blackness. There was no noise except when the trains went by. It became my cave, my hideaway—a safe hole in the wall away from the bitterness of the world. I'd spread papers on the floor and I'd go to sleep and find peace.

Most of the time I didn't think at all about why I was there or what I was doing there. It was enough to be out of class where I was always afraid the teacher would call on me and I wouldn't even know what she was saying, much less know the answer. I didn't worry about what I'd have to do tomorrow because at such times every day was a day by itself. There was no tomorrow. The days would come and go and I'd feel myself safe.

Sometimes I'd daydream about what it would be like to have everything you wanted, clothes and all, food and candy, and how I'd feel if somebody gave me a tremendous amount of money. I'd think about going home and giving it to my mother and how she'd appreciate it. I'd think about my father coming home from work and finding all that money on the table and he wouldn't have to work any more.

These were the times I was happy. I wasn't happy at home, although my mother and father did all they could for us kids, but it was a hard life. Maybe it wasn't any harder than any of the other families who had to live the way we did. There were always too many mouths to feed, too many kids to clothe, too much time to work just keeping body and soul together to take care of the kids the way kids need. It wasn't easy for anybody, but somehow it seemed harder for me than it did for Frank and

Billy, my two older brothers, and the eight children who came after us.

I was born on January 4, 1935 near Waco, North Carolina, where my father worked as a laborer for the Seaboard Railway. When I was a little over a year old my folks moved north to Brooklyn. That became home, but home was always another place after a short while. I remember six or seven of the flats in which we lived, but maybe there were more. My parents moved from one to the other, always looking for a little more room for their growing family, always trying for something better, but somehow it always seemed to get worse.

The last one was under the Lexington Avenue El at Number 253. Before that there were 23 St. Andrews Place, 233 Macon, a place on Howard Avenue, but it was always the Bedford-Stuyvesant section of Brooklyn, which was the kind of place the writers mean when they speak of an asphalt jungle. It was always a cold-water, four- or five-room railway flat, sometimes with a coal stove in the front, sometimes with a small oil heater in the back. The only windows were in the rooms in the front and the back, and it was always too hot in the summer, too cold in the winter, and never big enough.

Frank, Billy and I would sleep in the same bed, the two of them at the head of the bed and I at the foot, but in between so that their feet were always all over me. I don't think that bothered me. I didn't know any better, but there came a time when I began to have terrible nightmares. I'd wake up in a dreadful sweat yelling at the top of my voice. My mother'd put cold towels on my head and hold me in her arms and comfort me.

Other times—we were living on St. Andrews Place then—I would just be starting to go to sleep after lying in bed awake with nothing special on my mind when I'd fall into a kind of a trance. I'd know what I was doing, but I just couldn't keep myself from doing it. I'd get up and start to walk. Once they

11

caught me out on the street just walking along in my pajama bottoms. Nobody knew when it was going to happen or why it happened. My mother took me to a doctor, but I kept it up all the time until I got to Wiltwyck and then these nightmares stopped.

As I look back on it all now, I guess everything I did then was my own rebellion against the way we had to live. Maybe rebellion's the wrong word because I wasn't rebelling against my parents. I wanted to do something for them and I didn't think I'd ever be able to.

My father, Thomas, was in his early forties then, but he worked so hard for so little. Each job he took seemed to me to take more out of him. He worked on construction gangs, as a longshoreman, in the Sanitation Department, as a truck helper in the Fulton Fish Market. He'd come home so tired and so frustrated that sometimes he wouldn't even eat. He'd lay down on the bed and fall asleep in his clothes. He'd even work at another job on Sundays to make a few more dollars. On Friday I'd watch him come home and put his hard-earned money on the table for my mother and I began to feel ashamed, even at that early age, of eating there. I felt like a freeloader.

It could be that's why I started staying away from home at nights. I know now how my mother worried, but at that time all I could think of was there'd be one less mouth to feed, one less kid to worry about. When I finally did come home after staying away a night or two, I'd always try to bring something, some fruit or some bottles of milk in a shopping bag, something like that.

Where'd I get it? Where do other kids get things in a neighborhood like that? You steal them. My mother would tell me how wrong it was, but I don't suppose I thought of it as stealing. I don't suppose I thought of anything correctly in those days. There wasn't bitterness in me or meanness. To me the real things were the things I saw in the movies when I'd sneak in, or the rare times I'd pay the eighteen cents to get in. I guess I envied the actors and actresses without realizing it. They'd have this big luxurious house—a man and a wife and one kid. The kid would always be dressed right and nobody laughed at him. I wasn't bad. I'd tell the truth. It's just that I couldn't see anything changing for me, or me becoming something.

I don't know which came first—not being able to look anybody in the face or becoming a truant. I don't think you can separate one from the other or put a date on when either started. After I grew up, started to box and appreciated that to get anywhere at all a man has to control his emotions, I learned that the school psychologists felt that once I fell behind the other kids my age in school it was like a wall being put up between them and me. But where was the start of it? I wasn't stupid. I've learned that my I.Q. was average, but why did I refuse to learn?

When promotion day came at Public School 25, or P.S. 93 or P.S. 3 or any of the six or seven others I attended when I had to as my family moved around, I never cared whether I was promoted or left back. I never knew. I just wasn't there on that day. I never bothered to find out. They say now that I instinctively wanted to escape, but was it because I felt rejected or was I doing the rejecting?

All I know now is that I was ashamed. I wasn't defiant. I couldn't read. I couldn't write. I felt like even if I tried I would fail. There was just no use in it. I couldn't see success in anything, but I went to school regularly until a gang of kids once chased me at P.S. 25 when I wouldn't fight with them. At first I thought of running into the school building. Then I realized they'd only be waiting for me afterward. I ran all the way home and stayed out of class that day. It seemed so easy to do. Nobody seemed to care whether I was there or not, and I certainly liked it better not being there and not being laughed at.

It seemed to me that's when I discovered how safe a cellar

13

was in which to hide away. Sometimes my mother was home taking care of the little kids. Sometimes she was at work as a domestic or in a bottling plant. She'd work until it was time for the next baby to come. So I couldn't always go home. One day I even went all the way to school, but instead of going into the class I went down to the dark basement and stayed there until the dismissal bell rang.

Fridays, though, were the worst. That was assembly day and all the kids had to wear a white shirt and tie. I would have liked to be like them, but in our home there was a phrase that was born of necessity. "Make do." If I heard it once I heard it a thousand times. It meant you wore what there was. What there was for me were my father's undershirts and shirts—hand-me-downs.

Picture the sight if you can. I was a big kid, bigger than most of the others in my classes, but my father was a big man, almost six feet tall with a big, thick neck. I'd put on his shirt and I'd look like something out of a comic strip. His ties—when I tried to wear one—would hang to my knees. No wonder everybody laughed the few times I tried to go to school on Fridays looking like a child playing grownup in his father's clothes. It's fun when it's a game, but no fun at all when it's real. It was real in my house, and I understood it. I didn't complain about it. I didn't own a new suit of clothes until I was sixteen years old.

I never wanted to bring this up. I don't think my mother ever realized the way I felt. Even if she did, there wasn't much she could have done about it, poor woman. The only reason I mention it now is that maybe it will help to clear up some of the misconceptions about me. I am what I am now because I'm a product of what I was.

I'm not ashamed of it now. I'm not sorry for it now. I was lacking then, but I believe I made up for it. All those years of torment gave me a kind of callus which helped me later on when I was able to find the thing I could do best. That is my answer for what some people may think is my dedication when I hide myself away in training camps. I haven't rid myself of

14

all of it. I know that, but some day I may. Even now when I'm training for a fight in a public place, such as I was at the Hotel Deauville in Miami Beach for Ingemar the last time, I'm embarrassed when I want to try something and miss a punch or get tagged by a sparring partner.

That's one of the reasons why I like to do my roadwork where the public will not see me. Even at this late date that would bother me—running and sweating when other men are going to work. It actually happened once, just that way, too.

I was between fights and was doing a little work just to stay in shape. I was living at home then in St. Albans. I'd come into town to work out, but I'd do my roadwork in the mornings about 5:30 in a park near my home. That way I'd be through before people started coming out of their houses. This one day, though, when I was supposed to be picked up by a car after I was through, there was maybe an hour's delay before the driver showed up. There I sat on a park bench waiting for him, a towel around my neck, the sweat pouring off me in the heavy clothes I wear for running and all those people going by me to work. They looked at me as though I was crazy. I took the towel off my neck and hid my face in it.

It wasn't much different in my younger days. Say my mother would take me to a medical or dental clinic. I'd never look at the doctor or nurse. I'd look at the floor or off into space, any place just so I didn't have to look them in the eye. If anybody spoke to me I wouldn't answer. I wouldn't even tell my name. If anybody touched me I'd run.

The one thing I didn't do was run with a gang. Maybe the reason was I couldn't make friends easily. Friends meant the other kids had to visit your house. I wasn't there enough, and even when I was, I didn't want anybody seeing the way we lived. The biggest gang around our way was the Fulton Street Bishops. I would have had trouble breaking in with them even if I wanted to, which I didn't. They remembered me and my brother Frank.

My mother had sent me to the store to buy something. Usually when you come from a store, you have change in your pocket. These kids knew it. They knew me. They knew I was from the neighborhood. You'd think they'd try to rob somebody they didn't know. But I wasn't giving up the money. They hemmed me in and started to beat me. Just then Frank came along. He grabbed a stick from the gutter and started to whack at them. Somebody pulled a knife, but Frank had that stick and kept switching it in front of their noses and they ran. I still had the money. That was the big thing.

Another time I wasn't so lucky. I was hanging around with some other kids, bigger than I was, maybe teen-agers. It was all big talk, I thought. But suddenly the police came and the next thing I knew I was in the police station with them. I had done nothing. The police found that out and let me go, but the other kids had broken into a store and stolen a bike.

That wasn't the first time I was in a police station or in a court, though, and it wasn't the last. My mother tells me that I would tell the truth where the other boys wouldn't. If I'd done something, I'd admit it. If I hadn't done it, I'd start to cry. That's how she knew I wasn't lying.

The truth didn't help me keep out of the courts or the police station. I never stole money, but I stole other little things. And of course, as a habitual truant, I was forever getting picked up Seems to me like I lived in court and should have had a room there. It was hooky, running away from home, getting caught stealing. It must have been thirty-to-forty times, and all the time I had the feeling now that I'm here they can do anything they want with me.

Once I got caught up in the hills in Staten Island. I couldn't have been more than nine or ten, but I'd taken the ferry there and was sitting on a big rock overlooking a highway at three in the morning when I saw lights coming up the road. At first I thought it was just another car, when suddenly a spotlight came on and the beam hit me. I started to run, but the road

16

turned in the direction I was running and they caught me. It was the police. What was my name? What was I doing there? The same questions. They kept me overnight and then sent me to a court in Brooklyn and my mother had to come and get me.

I couldn't tell her I didn't mean any harm. The cellars or the subways or the movies where sometimes I'd stay overnight and sleep, especially if there was a new show the next day, or going to Coney Island to watch the people taking the rides, or watching the animals in the Prospect Park Zoo, it was all the same to me. I wasn't looking for trouble. It seemed trouble always came looking for me.

I asked my mother many times to let me quit school. That way, I figured, I wouldn't have to be running away all the time and hiding from the truant officer. That way, I figured, I could get a job of some kind, do a man's work, bring something into the house.

As time went on before I turned to boxing, I did lots of things, worked very hard, but it never bothered me. It kept me busy, kept me from thinking about the things that confused me so much. When I was able to, later on, I worked as a laborer on construction gangs, as a longshoreman, a street cleaner, a truck driver, a handy man in a hotel, but as a kid my mother only knew one thing and it was drummed into our heads at home: If you went to school you kept out of trouble. Somehow it was never stressed that going to school mainly meant getting an education which would help you cope with the things around you. It was kind of a negative thing instead. It was a thing of fear. If you didn't go to school, "the officer" would come.

My mother must have kept word of all my trouble away from my father. He worked so hard just trying to put food on the table for us kids, it would have been unfair to add more troubles to those he already had. So I wasn't allowed to quit school, but I wasn't allowed to go to work either, except for building a shoeshine box and doing up shoes on the corner of Fulton and Kingston Avenues. Sometimes on a weekend I could make as much as five dollars. I'd bring most of it home. My mother would let me keep some of it. I bought candy, but somehow even that candy, that sweet thing, would get me into more trouble when I'd try to slip a piece of it into my mouth on those rare days when I would go to school. The teacher would catch me doing it and I'd be punished again.

After a while it got so it seemed there was no escape. There was no place to run, no place to hide, no one who would listen and understand the torment of a boy caught in a world that made so little sense to him. I couldn't think otherwise because somehow it seemed that I couldn't do right even when I wanted to. For instance, in school, during those days when I would attend. The teacher would be up in front of the room wearing what always looked to me like a new dress. I'd never seen my mother in something as pretty or as new. In fact, until after I became the heavyweight champion, I never saw my mother dressed up. The teacher would ask a question. Most times I didn't know the answer, but even when I did I'd be afraid to raise my hand, scared to attract attention to myself, certain everybody would laugh.

I can see now how all this would build up inside a boy, how the fear would turn to frustration and the frustration to anger and the anger, well, to a lot of things. Thank God, mine didn't go all the way. But I didn't know that on a day when I was walking along the street and another kid ran up to me and thrust a paper sack into my hands.

"Here," he said, excited-like. "Here's some soda for you."

I looked into the bag and there were several bottles of pop. I didn't know him. I couldn't understand why he would be giving me something that was his without my paying for it. I didn't know why I should be selected for a gift. People didn't usually give me something for nothing. I started to run all the way home with the bag. However, I hadn't gone half a block when a man put his arm on me and grabbed me by the shoulder.

"What you got there, boy?" he said.

"It's mine," I said.

He grabbed the bag and looked into it. "Where'd you steal these?" he said.

"I didn't. A kid gave them to me," I answered.

"You just robbed the factory down the street. I saw you. Let's go."

He was a plainclothes cop. He dragged me all the way back to the soda plant up the street. They tried to make me admit there that I had broken into the place and stolen the bottles. I kept telling them I hadn't stolen anything, but the cop started to slap me around and I started to cry.

Suddenly he picked up a wooden crate from the ground and hit me over the head with it. That made me crazy mad. I grabbed another crate and started swinging it at him. I tried to kick him and punch him. The cop later told my mother that I was like a wild man screaming and crying and yelling that I didn't do anything. Lucky for me my mother was home then. Luckier still that she was able to persuade the cop that she knew I was telling the truth because I was crying.

They let me go that time, but a couple of other times I wasn't so lucky. Once I broke into the back of a market because I was hungry and had no money. I grabbed two bags, filled them with fruit and went out the way I had come without anybody seeing me, I thought.

A couple of blocks away I sat down on the curb to eat. I didn't feel I had done anything wrong. In Bedford-Stuyvesant that's the way a kid gets to think. You get out of the neighborhood and you see so many with so much, but all around you at home so many have so little. The policeman, who came up the street before I had a chance to beat it, didn't think that way. So another line went down on my record along with the ones already there . . . "Runs away from home . . . Truant . . . Broke into store."

Fortunately, the authorities didn't add more. Once before I

had pulled what seemed to be a kid's prank that could have turned out to be much worse. Across the street from P.S. 93 at Herkimer and New York Avenues there was a lot where the Sheffield Farms Milk Company kept their trucks. We kids going by would see these trucks and everybody'd say to himself what a big thing it would be to be driving one of them. Some of the trucks even had the ignition keys in them. The other kids would do it occasionally, so one day I jumped up into the driver's seat, turned on the key, and started up the truck.

That was fun. You could imagine yourself zipping along the streets, delivering milk to the stores, and going up to the pay window every week to collect your salary. Sometimes I got bolder after I learned how to throw the trucks into gear. I'd inch out the clutch, drive the truck forward a few inches, then back a few inches. I felt like a pilot or something.

I never had a mind to do more, but a loud voice shouting at me interrupted that dream late one afternoon. The watchman in the garage must have come out of the office just as I was inching the truck forward. He scared me. I didn't know what to do. I stepped on the gas harder than I meant to and the truck jumped ahead. I didn't know what to do then. The man was chasing toward me. I just stomped down on the accelerator and kept driving the truck right out of the lot and down the street with the man running after me. I went down Herkimer Street, turned right on St. Andrews and pulled up to my house. I didn't even bother to turn off the ignition. I figured they'd find the truck there and everything would be all right. I jumped out of the seat and high-tailed it into my house.

Inevitably all this had to catch up with me. It did. It wasn't just one incident, but there I was in front of the judge again, and he was telling my mother that I was going from bad to worse.

"I know, Judge," she said. "I know something's got to be done."

I was looking down at the floor, but I heard it all. I felt this was the end. I heard the judge saying words like the law, pro-bation, juvenile delinquency and all it meant to me was one word: prison. I said to myself, "What difference does it make? Who's going to miss me? Who am I? Why is it so important if I'll be here or there?"

Then I heard my mother say: "The twig is bent early." I'll always remember those words.

Chapter Three

Looking back, I think how hard I felt toward my mother. It was her own choice. She could have said yes or no, but she agreed to send me to a jail. It was like a stone inside me. I didn't realize then that she had made the only choice a mother could have made who knew her son was heading for real trouble and was determined to keep him from it.

As we were driving in the car up to Esopus, New York, I kept my eyes closed, thinking about it. Mr. Cooper, he said his name was, who was taking me to Wiltwyck, kept trying to talk to me, but I wouldn't listen on that ninety-mile ride.

I kept thinking of my mother telling me: "You're going away, Floyd. It's going to be a nice place. You'll be able to run and play and do all the things you want to do. I'll come and visit you as much as I can."

"I don't want to go," I protested.

"Nothing we can do, son," she said. "It's for your benefit."

"But it's a prison," I said.

"It's not a prison," she said. "It's a school. There'll be other boys like you."

"I'll run away," I said.

"Son," she said, "they'll teach you to read and write. They'll teach you to get along with other people."

That was September, 1945. There were seven kids in our family by then. Frank and Billy and especially my sister Deanna seemed sorry to see me go. Sherman, Raymond and Larry were babies. What difference did it make to them? It didn't make much difference to me either, except that I couldn't think of the Wiltwyck School for Boys being anything but a jail with bars on the windows and guards with guns. "Five-to-ten, ten-to-twenty," I said to myself, like I heard the judge say to a criminal in the movies when he was sentencing him.

I couldn't conceive of anybody wanting to help me. I'd never seen open fields or hills or mountains or horses kids could ride or counselors or teachers who would care about you enough to want to help you out. I couldn't imagine, even if Wiltwyck had been described to me before we took that long drive up the Hudson and over the bridge at Poughkeepsie, that there would be three hundred and fifty acres of ground on an estate that used to belong to the Whitney family.

At first, as we started from Brooklyn, I was scared. That was normal for me. I never seemed not scared. As mile after mile passed behind us and I wouldn't talk to Mr. Cooper, he stopped trying to talk to me and I fell asleep, but as the car made a turn approaching Wiltwyck, I woke up and all the frightful thoughts came back again.

There were stone buildings, four of them, with white wood trim, and hills in the background. When I was led into the building I looked around, but there were no bars, no fences, no uniformed guards. The kids I saw were dressed in clothes that fit. What about me in my raggedy, ill-fitting things, I thought. I'll look as funny here as I did in Brooklyn.

I don't want to jump ahead of my story, but every time I think of Wiltwyck the joy bubbles up inside of me and I can't wait to say the good things about the place. I can't withhold my love and respect for the fine people there who helped to straighten me out. They taught me to read and write. They gave me a sense of belonging. I learned how to make friends

w to live with myself and others. I found freedom
e gone back there many times. Once I even trained
ck for a fight. I'll come to all that later, but first let
e what the school is like before I go into what it
ne as an individual.

The school is privately financed, but New York City and
New York State help out with funds. Generally there are
about a hundred boys being cared for. They range in age from
eight to twelve and most of them are emotionally disturbed one
way or another so that, like I was, they are unmanageable at
home or in regular schools. Some people would call it a re-
formatory. It reformed me, but I wouldn't put it in that class.

The school is situated on what used to be farm land. There
are barns, cows and chickens. There's a kind of lake in Black
Creek where kids can swim and fish. There are four dormi-
tories for the boys, a classroom building, a gymnasium, a craft
shop, an art hall and a big dining room. If a kid can't get along
in that setup, he's really in trouble.

But there is understanding at Wiltwyck. There are four
psychiatric social workers and a psychotherapist who live at
the school. If a kid comes in who has a case history of being
extra mean, a special psychologist and psychiatrist are called
in. In addition, there are counselors, specially trained, who are
assigned to look after the kids in each dormitory. When I was
at Wiltwyck there were two to handle each group of ten kids
bunking together.

The boys themselves are in charge of the school banks in
which they deposit their own money. There is a weekly al-
lowance and an opportunity to earn more through special
work. There is a canteen which the boys run themselves. Every
effort is made to keep a sense of democracy alive in the school
and alive in the boys. A student council is elected and there are
different committees, like the food committee, sports committee and job committee. Whatever problems arise among the
boys, they are encouraged to work out among themselves before reporting them to the counselors at the weekly assemblies.

You can only know how far you have come by looking backward to see where you started from. This was my beginning—at the Wiltwyck School for Boys in Esopus, New York. I don't look like much in the plaid shirt and dirty hand-me-down, oversized clothes, but I was beginning to smile, learning how to make friends. (I wish I could remember the name of the other boy. I just don't.)

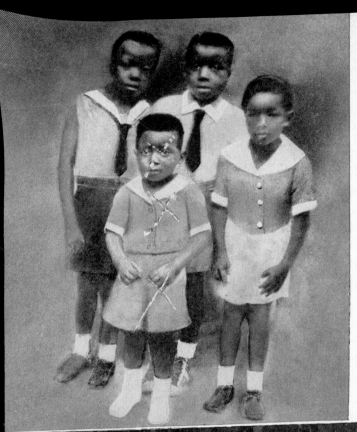

This is a picture of me at age two. Behind me, left to right, are my brother Billy, my uncle (Charles Johnson) and my brother Frank. The three X's over my face and body were added by me at the age of nine. I guess this was my way of expressing my unhappiness and the dislike I felt for myself in the days before Wiltwyck.

After two years at Wiltwyck I was sent back home, but I had to attend P.S. 614, one of the special New York City schools for problem children. My graduation in 1952 was a big event for me, and I've gone back to attend every graduation since then. Here I am meeting some of the boys.

Wide World Photo

I was still attending P.S. 614 when I became an amateur fighter trying to move up to a place on our 1952 Olympic team. There were detours, of course. One of them (below) was when I fought Ralph Guerrero, a southpaw, in an intercity tournament and was beaten by him when his style confused me.

Wide World Photos

It was a thrill to make it to Helsinki, Finland, as a member of what may have been our greatest Olympic boxing team of all time. We won five titles. I gained the heavy middleweight crown by winning four bouts. The first of these was against Omar Tabakka of France (above).

It's a long way between being an Olympic titleholder and a world's professional champion, but the road was paved for that big leap when I signed to fight Hurricane Jackson in a title elimination bout at Madison Square Garden after Rocky Marciano had retired. Left to right are Jim Norris, then president of the IBC; Lippy Breidbart, Jackson's manager; and NYS Athletic Commission Chairman Julius Helfand. My manager, Cus D'Amato, is looking on behind Helfand as I put my signature to the contract.

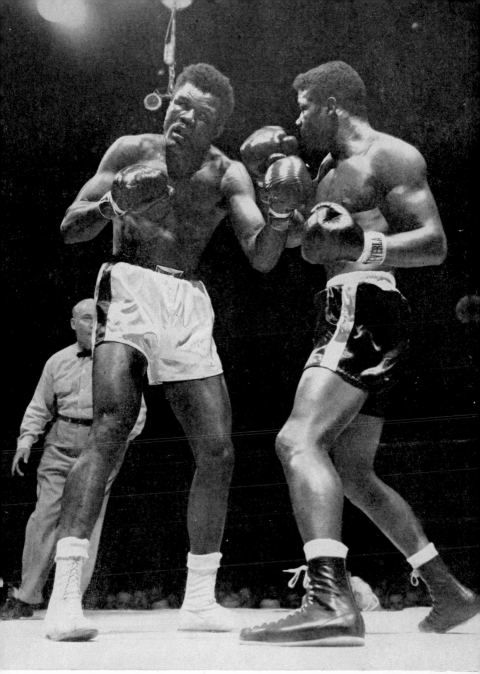

Tommy Jackson and I had trained together many times. At Greenwood Lake, New York, we had hunted together and eaten together. But when we got into the ring together at Madison Square Garden, friendship was forgotten. There was too much at stake. I beat him in a ten-round split decision. Referee Harry Kessler voted the fight to Jackson. I broke a bone in my hand in that fight, which delayed my meeting with Archie Moore for the title.

I was not yet twenty-two years old when I became the youngest man in history to win the world's heavyweight crown. This is the sequence of photos demonstrating how that was done. It all started with a left hook that caught Archie Moore cleanly on the chin. Referee Frank Sikora, counting over Archie, reached nine when Moore got back on his feet after that fifth-round knockdown. I kept after him. The next time he went down in that round, he didn't get up. I was the champion.

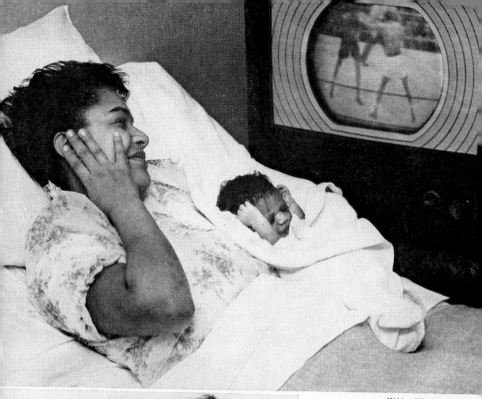

Only a few hours before I won the title, my wife Sandra gave birth to our first child, in New York City, but I didn't know that Jeannie had come until after the fight was over. Nor did I know that Sandra had been able to watch my victory on a television set that had been installed in her room.

The next day when I arrived at the hospital after driving all night from Chicago, Sandra greeted me: "The new champion and a new baby all in one day." Jeannie, who was christened Seneca, weighed in at 6 pounds, 2 ounces.

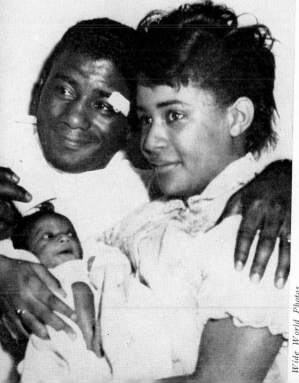

Wide World Photo.

We had so much to be grateful for. My parents (above), with my little brother Alvin, who was four then, were able to move into a new home in Mount Vernon, New York. Below, my wife, my brother Raymond on her right, my brother Larry, and my sister Carolyn help us celebrate.

Wide World Photo

Buster Watson, my close friend and co-trainer with Danny Florio, keeps me on the ball in camp. As I trained for the first defense of my title against Hurricane Jackson, there was a group of kids in Greenwood Lake, New York, whom I taught a little about boxing. Two of them, Ray Pollaro (center) and Robert LaParte, joined me in roadwork.

Wide World Photos

Twenty-three days after I made the first successful defense of my title, I went back into the ring on August 22, 1957, against Pete Rademacher, the former Olympic champion who was fighting as a pro for the first time. I knocked him out in the sixth round but was tagged by his right hand in the second and went down myself. I was more embarrassed than hurt as I took a four count.

Wide World Photos

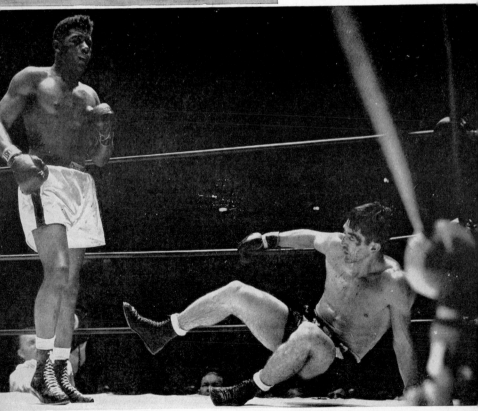

I was at my worst as the champion, no more than eleven per cent of myself, when I knocked out Roy Harris, who couldn't come out for the thirteenth, in our bout at Los Angeles. All I could see in Harris' face was bruised flesh and blood. I didn't want to hit him any more.

My knockout victory over Brian London (above) isn't something I'm proud of. He was to be a warmup for my meeting with Sweden's Ingemar Johansson a month and a half later. I put London away in the eleventh, but Ingemar put me away in three rounds, after beating me to the canvas seven times. This was the first of the knockdowns.

 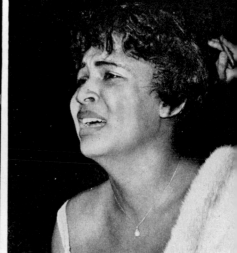

Wide World Photo

The time that elapsed between the loss of my title and my recapture of it was a black year for me. Certainly it was the same for my wife, who wanted me to quit the ring after the defeat. Most of that year I was not fit company to be with. I was in danger of reverting to emotional instability. The only thing that kept me going was the hope that I would get a rematch. There were many months when I despaired even of that.

Wide World Photos

I found myself on the night of June 20, 1960. That was the most important night of my life. I became the only man in boxing history ever to regain the world's heavyweight title. In the sequence above, I kayoed Ingemar in the fifth round and Referee Arthur Mercante counted him out. Immediately after the count, I knelt beside my unconscious opponent. I was afraid I had hurt him badly, but at the same time I wanted to assure him he would be given another chance at me.

Raymond, my eighteen-year-old brother, has become a fighter, too. I'm training him as an amateur and intend to manage him when he turns pro. But there's more to teach him than how to fight. He's got to understand what it all means.

If there is a greater meaning for me for the good fortune I've had, it has been captured in this photograph of Mrs. Franklin Delano Roosevelt and myself at the dedication of the Floyd Patterson House, a group residence of the Wiltwyck School, which gave me my start. I contributed some money to the purchase of the two brownstones, which are a kind of halfway house for youngsters on their way back to society. Mrs. Roosevelt helped to found the Wiltwyck School.

Look again at the first photo in this section, as I've done, and then look at me here, as I am today. Way back there as a bedraggled youngster, emotionally disturbed, with no talent and no outlook, could I ever imagine it would some day be possible for me to meet the President of the United States?

Maybe the big thing, at least that was one of the first things which struck me, is that there is no punishment in the sense a kid off the streets expects. Nobody gets whipped or locked up.

It was a wonderful thing when I first heard the idea explained to me by Ernst Papanek, a psychoanalyst who was the executive director when I was at Wiltwyck. Dr. Papanek is now an associate professor of education at Queens College and the executive vice president of a mental hygiene clinic.

"Punishment," he said, "teaches the child only how to punish. Scolding teaches him how to scold. By showing him that we understand, we teach him to understand. By helping him, we teach him to help. He learns cooperation by cooperating."

For a boy like me, a Negro for whom there had been a growing awareness of what a difference in color meant, the interracial activities, whites being treated the same as the colored with no preference at all, this was a tremendous awakening. All religions were represented among the boys, but none was treated better or worse than any of the others.

It hadn't been that way in Brooklyn. Deep inside myself I'd kept the bitter memory of the first time I was called a name because of the color of my skin. I didn't know what it meant then. When I saw my mother that night I had to ask her what it meant.

She sighed. I know why now. All colored mothers wait for it to come. They realize they've got to build a kind of callus for their children so that maybe the name will hurt a little less than it does as you grow older.

"You'll learn," she said, "that when one person makes another one angry, the one that's angry will want to hit back. Sometimes they do it one way, sometimes another. This time the boy called you a name. It's supposed to hurt you because your skin is dark."

"You're dark," I said.

"So I am, Floyd," she said. "The Lord made some people light and some dark. We're all God's children. We're all equal in His eyes, only some people don't think so."

I met a lot of them who didn't think that until I got to Wiltwyck. There, for the first time in my life, perhaps the only time in my life, it seemed color didn't make any difference. In fact, that's what helped to bring me out of the shell in which I had been living and what helped me to make friends finally. I had always wanted to be friends with somebody, but I never knew how. Here there was no difference. We dressed the same, did the same, ate the same.

In my dormitory my cot was between the cots occupied by a boy named Galento and a boy named Saunders. Galento was white, Saunders colored. At first I'd lay there between these two, never saying a word to them, just listening to them talk and kidding around with each other. After maybe a month I wanted badly to do what they did.

Every night, it seemed, just before the lights went out, Galento would throw his pillow at Saunders and Saunders would throw it back at Galento over my head. I wanted to get into it and eventually I did. It was fun. I started to laugh and enjoy myself. There were maybe forty to fifty Negro boys in the school at the time, thirty or so whites and the extraordinary thing to me was that they all got along. There were arguments and fights, sure, but never with a vulgar word about a boy's color, never the way it had been in Brooklyn.

Galento and I, in fact, got to be real good friends up there, but then after he left Wiltwyck and I got out of it after almost two years, we never saw each other again. Funny thing, just before my first fight with Ingemar I received a letter from him at Ehsan's where I was training. He told me he was a hunter and was about to leave for Africa or some such place. I answered him very quickly. I wanted to see him, but I guess he had left by the time my letter arrived.

I thought so much about him after that, how kind he was to me, how much he helped me out, how he'd let me go with him into the hills and the forests and teach me about snakes, frogs and such. He loved the forest. I guess it was only natural for him to become a hunter.

That was the beginning of my love of nature, and my ambition some day to own a farm. When I'm out in the woods for a walk or doing some roadwork, I often stop and pick up a snake. I collect them and put them in jars and feed them. When I was training for Pete Rademacher in Seattle I had several garter snakes I fed with an eye dropper in a mayonnaise jar. The last thing I did before leaving camp was to release them. When I trained in Miami and went for a walk, I'd look at the different kinds of trees you could see, get some of the leaves off them and send them home to my wife. At Wiltwyck, I remember, we used to go into the woods to look for redwood, from which we'd make bows and arrows.

All of it really started with Galento. At first I was afraid, but he taught me how to catch a snake and pick it up. He told me which ones were poisonous. He knew so much about the woods. It was as if that was the place where he could find happiness. And I wanted to join in it. At first he wouldn't let me go with him. We all had jobs to do—sweeping the floors, mopping the halls or washing the walls—but after our schooling was over and the work was over, we were free to wander wherever we wanted to on the grounds. I'd see Galento go off, always by himself, and he wouldn't even come back sometimes for the next meal. When he came back, he always had some kind of turtle or a chipmunk or field mouse or whatnot.

I asked him if I could go with him. The first time he chased me. The next day I followed him. He chased me again. I tried to follow him once more and he discovered me again. "I'd like to go into the hills with you," I said.

He thought a moment before saying, "Okay, but don't get in my way." After that I went with him practically every day. Among my books now I've got one entitled *Reptiles and*

27

Amphibians. That would seem a strange thing for me to read and enjoy. Yet I do read it and I do enjoy it because there is so much significance for me in that book. After I'd captured my first snake I found more interest in my classes. I once asked Dr. Papanek about the animals in the woods. He told me I could learn about them in my classroom. The schoolroom took on new meaning for me.

Then, of course, there was Miss Vivian Costen. I've waited a bit to bring her into this story, because what she did for me is a story all by itself. She was an old-maid school teacher and somehow she took a liking to me and I took to her. I'd go to her every time I had a problem. She was like a mother to me. She left the school soon after I did. She died a little less than a year before I won the title. It was a great loss to me.

Miss Costen gave me confidence in myself. She made me feel I was important. She could tell that I was impressionable and a great sufferer. She knew that I was hurt by a raised voice. She wouldn't accept my protests that I couldn't learn to read or write. She was so kind and considerate and understanding that I wanted more than anything else in the world to please her. She bought me clothes and gave me little gifts. I had to return that to her in some way, and the only way I knew—or was able to—was to be what she wanted me to be.

The big thing, I guess, was the individual attention she gave me without my realizing I was getting it. Back in Brooklyn there were thirty or thirty-five kids in a class, and the teachers had no time to work with those who didn't get everything right away. The teachers would write something on the blackboard once and that was it. You got it or you didn't. There was no going back to check if you understood. At Wiltwyck there were seven or eight of us in a classroom. At first I didn't think I'd be able to catch on, but Miss Costen would pick one boy a week to be a special monitor who stayed after class and cleaned the blackboards. She'd always have a bag of candy for him. When I got through with my work, she'd say to me:

"Floyd, I think there was a little problem you didn't get. Let me show you how it works." She'd tell me once. If I didn't seem to understand she'd tell me again, maybe three or four times. She never laughed if you didn't understand right away. She'd never seem angry. She made you want to learn.

I imagine I was a little slow, even with her patience, because in the classroom when she'd ask a question I still didn't dare raise my hand to answer. One day she asked a question of all the kids. She went around the room asking this one and that one. Everybody answered but me. I said I didn't know the answer. Then she told us the answer. Everybody in the class had been wrong, but the answer I had in my mind was correct, and I had not had nerve enough to say it out loud.

That made me furious. I just stood up and ran right out of that room and down the hall. I could hear footsteps after me, but I didn't care. It was Miss Costen. She took me by the shoulder and lifted my head to look into my eyes. There were tears of shame and anger in them.

"I knew you knew the answer, Floyd," she said. "That's why you're crying. This should prove to you that if you have an idea, speak it out."

"I was afraid I'd sound stupid and everybody would laugh," I said.

Miss Costen put her arms around me and said, "Always remember this, Floyd Patterson. You're not stupid. You're the same as any other boy your own age. From now on I want you to answer. If you're wrong, you're wrong. Nobody's always one hundred per cent right, but you'll be right more often than you're wrong."

Well, after that I sort of woke up. I began answering questions. I wasn't right more often than I was wrong. It was the other way at first, but gradually I was right fifty per cent of the time, then sixty per cent. I got to the point where I began to grasp the thing. I felt equal to the other boys. I didn't feel any more that I had to sit there like an idiot, knowing nothing, saying nothing and caring about nothing.

After a while, in fact, I won the highest award one of the boys in my class could win, at least in my own mind. Miss Costen would invite the boy who did the best work for the week to her own home for a weekend. I was able to stay there a couple of times. It was like being in a regular house, the kind I used to dream about when I'd hide away in the movies.

After one of these weekends, Miss Costen offered me a box of candy. "You've done so well in your work," she said, "I think you deserve a special award."

There wasn't anything I wanted more than candy, but a friend in my dormitory and I had made a promise to each other. We were going to split everything fifty-fifty, which was all right with me, until Miss Costen added: "Don't let the rest of the boys eat it up on you."

The way I felt about Miss Costen, that would have meant breaking a promise to her if I let my friend share the candy with me. I turned down the candy and it wasn't until much later that Miss Costen learned why I did. "You're a good, honest boy, Floyd," she said. "You stand by a promise even if it's not to your advantage."

Something else happened at Wiltwyck which was to my great advantage, although I didn't realize it then. I got into the ring and boxed with another boy for the first time with gloves on and all.

There were a lot of sports activities at the school. We played baseball and basketball. We went horseback riding. We could swim in Black Creek and fish there. Three or four times a year, though, Mr. Walter Johnson, the executive director of the school and sort of our senior counselor, put on boxing bouts among the fellows.

In later years, after I became the champion and the magazines and papers started to write me up a lot, some of the writers talked to Mr. Johnson about me. I read where he said, "As I remember, Floyd wouldn't participate in group activities." That was right, at least about the boxing. When Mr. Johnson first asked me if I'd like to be in the tournament, I told him, "I don't like boxing. I don't want to go to the gym. I don't want to fight."

"Are you afraid?" he asked.

"I'm not afraid. I just don't want to," I said.

By that time my two older brothers were doing some amateur boxing in the gym at the Carlton Y.M.C.A. in Brooklyn. My mother told me on one of her visits soon after Mr. Johnson spoke to me that he had spoken to her too about my not wanting to join in with the group.

"Maybe boxing will be good for my boy," she told him. "Maybe it will help him get the chip off his shoulder and be more like the other boys."

Well, they practically had to force me to get into the ring. First I watched a couple of bouts before I agreed to fight. I remember after that writing one of my rare letters home to my mother. "Tell brothers I'll join them in the ring some day," I wrote.

I fought three bouts at Wiltwyck and won them all. The first time I put the gloves on I boxed a boy I knew I couldn't beat. I saw him fight other boys and he was bigger than I. But the strangest thing is that when we put the gloves on he didn't seem to be even as big as I was. I don't say I knocked him around, but the important thing is he didn't knock me around. When it was over, he had the bloody nose. He was so mad afterward, too, because he couldn't do with me what he wanted to do. To this day I remember his first name. It was Randolph.

The other kids loved to watch me box, not that I was so good, but because I was so funny. And what made me feel good was that when they laughed at me in the ring, I didn't feel ashamed at all like I used to. Even then I jumped when I threw a punch sometimes. Later on the writers began to call it "the gazelle punch," but I had no name for it or anything. I figured the easiest way for me to get at a guy was to jump up at him and throw the punch at the same time. That way I was flying through the air and punching. The way I boxed I'd miss the punch and land on my head. I must have done that a dozen times, but they had to give me the decision. I landed enough punches to earn it.

Each time my mother came up to visit—and the round-trip fare was three dollars, a lot in our home—she could see me getting better and better. Not boxing, I mean, but as a boy. One day when we had a chance to sit down together and talk quietly, she asked me the question that apparently had been on her mind ever since she agreed with the judge that I had to be sent away.

"Floyd, boy," she asked, "is it a jail?"

"It isn't, Momma," I said. "It's a school. It's the best one I ever went to."

It was, too, because from that point on I never had trouble again and never lacked the desire to read better and write legibly. I wanted to learn more and be like the other kids. From the time I went into Wiltwyck, the nightmares stopped and I never walked in my sleep any more. Until then it had been almost as though I was locked in a box and there was no way out wherever I turned.

I was there for two years. I was past twelve when I was discharged and allowed to go back to live with my parents and my brothers and sisters. I wasn't a scholar by any means then. I still am not now. But I learned right from wrong at Esopus. The way was opened there for my continued education, such as it is. I could look people in the eye, and when they talked to me, I didn't want to run and hide any more.

When I was sent to Wiltwyck originally, the police, juvenile courts and Child Guidance had to consider me worth "saving." To leave Wiltwyck I had to show that I had conquered a good deal of what had bothered me and confused me. When you go back into the world again, you are recommended for further care of the Child Guidance authorities. Some of us are considered worthy of the same kind of treatment, only a little more advanced.

The next step for me then was to enter one of the "600" schools in New York City. There are fifteen of them nowadays, but when I was entered at the Cyrus W. Field School in 1947, there were only two of them. They were in the experimental stage then. They are vocational elementary schools, but the Board of Education also called them "Schools of Opportunity." One was uptown at 113 East 87th Street. The other was at 113 East 4th Street. The one uptown was P.S. 612. Mine was P.S. 614. It helped to make me a champion. More important, it helped to make me a man.

Chapter Four

Let me get ahead of my story a bit to explain how I feel about P.S. 614.

One thing after another seemed to be delaying the weighing-in ceremonies of my first fight against Ingemar Johansson. Ordinarily that wouldn't have bothered me. I'd gotten to be kind of unconcerned about things like that. After you've been a champion awhile you realize that what you do attracts attention and people, and when there are crowds around things don't run clock smooth. Still I was annoyed and impatient.

Others may have thought I was nervous about the fight because that was the morning of June 25, 1959, but it wasn't so. That also was graduation day at P.S. 614, my alma mater, and I was eager not to be late, much less to miss it.

From the time I was handed my diploma so many years before, I had attended every graduation at the school. At first I just went there to be there because of the good that had been done for me in the school. Then after I began to make a name for myself in the boxing profession, I went there because my presence meant something to the kids who were maladjusted the way I had been when I was their age.

So I fretted in the ballroom at the Hotel Commodore. The room was jammed with newspapermen, photographers, newsreel people, radio and television commentators, boxing officials and the curious just in off the street. The weigh-in for a heavy-weight title fight is like a band parading and playing down the street. It attracts crowds, and crowds mean delay.

Naturally, I had slept as late as possible that morning. I hadn't eaten anything. Usually you eat after the ceremonies are over and you've returned to your hotel. Finally, the thing was done. I hurriedly got into my clothes. My entire party was with me—my manager, trainers and detectives who are assigned to the champion as bodyguards by the police department. I virtually ran outside and got into my car with them.

"Drive downtown on Third Avenue," I told the chauffeur, "and then go east on Fourth Street."

"What's this?" my manager said.

"You haven't had any breakfast yet and you've got to lie down and rest," said one trainer.

"We'll have to take a walk after you eat," said another.

"I'm late now," I said.

"Late for what?" they asked.

"The graduation," I said. "It's graduation day at P.S. 614. They're expecting me. I wouldn't disappoint them. I've never missed one. I don't intend to miss this one just because I haven't had any breakfast."

That's how I felt—and still feel—about 614. There, as at Wiltwyck, they gave special help to boys who needed personal attention. The lost boys, put on the road back at the first place, were firmly and understandingly directed to a life of useful citizenship at the second.

When I first came to P.S. 614, Mrs. Lillian L. Rashkis, a pioneer in these corrective schools, was the supervisor. Mr. Alex Miller was the principal. On the staff were Miss Blossom Lewis, Mr. Joseph Del Barto, Miss Helen Sandiford, Miss Norma Marenstein, Miss O'Brien and so many others who worked so hard straightening out kids who needed and wanted straightening out.

Miss Sandiford, for instance, was my favorite there, just as Miss Costen had been at Wiltwyck. She'd keep me after class, not as punishment, but to be certain I understood the things they were trying to teach me. There they gave us a sense of personal responsibility and responsibility to the group. You developed a sense of pride in being recognized by the teachers.

A teacher would drop something and these kids, who thought they were tough, would hurry to pick it up. A kid who had rebelled against any kind of authority soon learned that authority had been given to *him*. He would be made a monitor of a row or a monitor of the whole class or a whole stairway or an exit at the school. At first it didn't dawn on any of us that we were handling traffic. We were, as a matter of fact, policemen in the school, like the cop outside who walked a beat or directed traffic. Imagine how it hit us when we realized that we were enforcing law and order. Not too long before that we had practically been outlaws—kids with no regard for law and order.

You've got to really appreciate what that would mean to somebody like me. I had been the receiver. Now I wanted to be the giver. They had handed me my diploma one day, after I'd finished the eighth grade, and I was able to go on to high school. Even before that, I had been singled out for an award for the consistently best sportsmanship in my class. It was presented to me by Mr. Charles Schwefel, who owned and operated the Gramercy Park Hotel near the school.

Mr. Schwefel, who was to become a guiding influence in my life, was a member of the board of volunteer sponsors at P.S. 614. When you were able to come into contact with such fine people, you knew it was your duty to keep in contact with the boys at the school.

That's why I hurried that day, despite the wishes of my people, to get to the graduation. The diplomas had already been given out by the time we arrived, but there still was time enough for me to hear some of the speeches. So many of my former teachers were still there, and I felt rather proud when I got on the line with the kids to get my milk.

Mr. Del Barto, who had become the principal, insisted I take two containers. He had a hot lunch with me in the school lunchroom. We talked a little about the fight that was coming up. I didn't even know then that the bout had been delayed one day because of the rain. The next night, of course, I was beaten by Ingemar, but a year later I reversed that defeat and I came back to P.S. 614 as the champion again. I've gone back every year to present the Floyd Patterson Trophy for sportsmanship. I learned a lot of my understanding of it there, just as I was about to learn so much of my profession soon after I got out of P.S. 614.

I attended Alexander Hamilton Vocational High School for one year after that, but my mind already was taken up with boxing. As a matter of fact, early in my days at P.S. 614, the first term, if I remember correctly, Mr. Miller interviewed me about my plans for the future.

"I want to fight," I said. "I mean I want to be a professional boxer."

Mr. Miller seemed kind of surprised, although he knew that as soon as school was out each day, I'd head for the Gramercy Park Gym on East 14th Street where my two older brothers already were in training.

"Why would you want to do that, Floyd?" he asked.

"It's the quickest way I know to start earning some money to help out my family," I said.

You see, the ambition had been born soon after I came home from Esopus. Frank and Billy already were working out under Frank Lavelle, who was employed by the United States Customs House as his regular job but trained amateur fighters on the side. At that time they used the Carlton Y.M.C.A. gymnasium, and when my brothers went there for their gym sessions, sometimes they'd let me come along with them.

There was no ring, or anything, just the big gym floor, with squares marked off on the basketball court. In one corner of the big floor there was a speed bag and all over the place fellows were sparring with each other. For a kid my age this looked like fun. Later on, Lavelle trained his fighters in a regular ring. He had worked out a deal at the Gramercy Park Gym at 116 East 14th Street, just a few blocks from my school. For years after, whenever I thought of it, I spelled it "Gramacy" in my own mind. That's how the painter who printed the name on that door a long time ago spelled it.

By the time I started to go there, the paint had long since peeled off the walls. There were two creaking flights of wooden stairs up past a couple of garbage cans. In the front door there was a square hole covered by chicken wire, and through this hole a vicious police dog would snarl at the first sound coming up the stairs. For a long time Cus D'Amato lived in the back of that gym with that dog as his only companion at night.

Inside it was like a big barn, but to me it was the most exciting place I'd ever known. There was a ring and two heavy punching bags. There was a light bag, whose rat-tat-tat sound as the boxers worked on it for hand speed always fascinated me. There was a rubbing table, some cracked mirrors on the wall with somebody always shadow boxing in front of them, some showers and a few steel lockers. The windows were always closed, the air always hot inside. It smelled of sweat and the smell seemed to cling to the dirty walls, but I learned later on how much this place helped to keep some kids from the 13th Police Precinct off the streets and out of trouble.

Some, of course, like myself, had already been in trouble. One, in particular, I was told about. He was a rough kid from Second Avenue with a thick head of black hair and a tough way of talking. He came up to the gym with some friends and just watched awhile, the way I did later. After a while he got talked into putting the gloves on. Finally he started to train. That's how Rocco Barbella, who started in the Gramercy Gym, became Rocky Graziano, the world's middleweight champion.

For me, though, there was no question of what I wanted to

do. I wanted to learn to fight. But my old-time embarrassment kept me from it for a while. It wasn't the fear of getting hurt. It was the fear of starting something new. By that time Billy had become a professional fighter. He could punch, but he went into the Army later, served in Korea and came back with a detached retina, which forced him to retire. Frank, boxing men say, had the promise of becoming great. Teddy Brenner, the present Madison Square Garden matchmaker and the matchmaker of so many of my early professional fights at the Eastern Parkway Arena, once said, "Frank had better natural boxing moves than Floyd. He looked like a pro when he was an amateur."

In 1949 Frank became the New York Golden Gloves Open champion for the 160-pound class. In the semifinal of that tournament he kayoed Ralph Jones, who later went on to become a contender for the middleweight title under the name of Tiger Jones. As a pro, though, Frank didn't get too far. He didn't seem to have a settled mind for the kind of application and concentration it had to take.

The same year that Frank won his amateur title I went up those steps to the gym alone, determined that I'd finally try my hand at fighting. I was only a little past fourteen, maybe closer to fifteen, but I was built well. My shoulders sloped, my arms were long. I thought I was strong, but I didn't know really how long that strength would stay when and if I was hit with a solid punch.

I figured I could hit, because not too long before that I'd knocked out a kid at school. I made an ashtray in the woodworking shop. He tried to take it away from me. He hit me with a right hand and I hit him with a jab the way I'd seen my brothers do it in the gym. Then I leaped at him and hit him right on the jaw with a right hand. He went right down and his head hit the concrete.

It was something else, though, getting into trunks, shoes, sox, foul protector and T-shirt that D'Amato handed me when I told him I wanted to start working out. The equipment cost me nothing. I knew the arrangement from my brothers. I could train for nothing and get instruction from Lavelle for nothing, but since Cus had the gym he'd automatically become the manager of any kid who was good enough to be turned pro.

It was almost routine for a while after the excitement of that first day. They told me to work on the heavy bag first. They showed me how my feet had to be shifted when I threw a punch. I practiced the jab and how to hold one hand up to protect myself while punching with the other. I tried to do the things I'd seen Frank do, but two weeks after I began my instruction I got into the ring with Frank and learned it isn't so easy when there's somebody hitting back at you.

After I'd begun to make a name for myself as an Olympic champion and whatnot, Lester Bromberg, the boxing writer for the World-Telegram and Sun, came to talk to Frank about me. "I'd like to say that I always knew it was in Floyd," Frank told Bromberg, "but I have to be honest about it. I can't get used to my kid brother being a name fighter. I remember him as the boy who would cry if I hit him too hard when we boxed in the gym and as the green kid who would blow up if I pressed him."

He pressed me that day, all right. He almost made me quit before I had ever really started. He threw a hard left hook to my head and I felt like a window shade had come down in front of my eyes. I staggered groggily. My head was spinning and I fell into the ropes. I reached for the ropes and held onto them. I would have fallen down if I hadn't grabbed them. I wanted to get out of that ring as fast as I could.

Right then I was in danger again of turning into a kid who was ashamed of being shown up. It wasn't the shock of the punch so much as the thought that all these years I'd figured I would follow my brothers into boxing and the first time I got into the ring with one of them I discovered that I couldn't take a punch.

In the dressing room I just sat there with my ring clothes on. I wasn't dazed any more, just hopelessly embittered at my own shortcomings, and I guess I cried. Cus followed me back into the room and stood over me telling me not to be too down-hearted. That happened to a lot of kinds trying to box for the first time.

Undoubtedly I needed that consolation, but at that moment and for the rest of that day and night, I doubted that anything could help me. At home that night I sat at the supper table not thinking of what was on my plate but of the punch. When I went to bed I couldn't sleep. When I finally did fall asleep I slept unsoundly. Once I woke up with the light seeping through the windows and I jumped up with a start. I imagined I was being punched again by Frank. It was like those old nightmares I used to have, but Frank was sleeping soundly in the bed beside me. I made up my mind right then I'd have to keep trying. I didn't want any more nightmares. I'd come too far from the old days on St. Andrews Place when my mother had to come to my bed to comfort me.

The next day I almost shivered in anticipation in the class-room. I couldn't wait to get back to the gym. At the same time I knew I was scared. I was determined to overcome that fear. In the weeks that followed I think I did. At least, I kept go-ing back to the gym every day. I worked out several months more before I had my first amateur bout, but in the meantime I was learning.

Once, after I'd gotten rid of the fear of getting hit again, I was boxing a boy who weighed about 140 pounds, which was my weight then. He was bullying me around and coming in at me in a crouch. I couldn't seem to stop him.

From outside the ring I heard them yelling at me, "Uppercut him, Floyd."

I didn't know what they meant. Between rounds I asked, "What's an uppercut?"

Everybody thought it was funny—a guy in the ring not knowing that kind of a punch. But they showed me what it was—a punch coming from way down and moving upward to keep an opponent from coming in at you low.

The next round the kid started coming at me the same way again. I let go with an uppercut. It landed on his chin, luckily, and he dropped to the canvas.

Almost six months after I first got into the ring with my brother, it was decided that I was ready for my first registered amateur bout. The Empire Athletic Association, a boxing club accredited as a member of the Metropolitan Amateur Athletic Union, was in the Gramercy Gym. All the boys who boxed under Cus and Lavelle fought in the Empire colors, but not all of them were considered ready by January, 1950. I wondered for a long time as the New York *Daily News'* annual Golden Gloves tournament approached whether they would enter my name. They did. My debut in the ring was made in the sub-novice division of the 147-pound class. I was just about fifteen.

My first opponent didn't show up at the Ridgewood Grove, an old boxing club in Queens, New York. I was the winner by default and advanced to a bout at the Downtown Athletic Club.

My first official opponent was a sailor, older than I, of course, and five pounds heavier. To me at that point anybody in the service was a grown man. I was so nervous I didn't know where I was or what I was doing. Cus was in my corner with his brother Nick and Lavelle. Every time this guy came near me I started throwing punches, not knowing where they were going or even caring. I don't think I got hit at all. At least in the excitement of it all I don't remember getting hit. Between the rounds they tried to talk some sense into my head about putting what I had learned in the gym into practice there in the ring. I didn't hear a thing they said.

The guy came at me fast in the second round. I continued to flail away. Then an astonishing thing happened. My right hand

42

landed on his jaw and down he went. The referee started to count. I was certain he'd get up. In the movies you'd see cowboys fight and they'd hit each other over the head with fists and chairs and tables and they'd keep coming back for more. It seemed to me I had just tapped this fellow on the chin, but the referee had counted him out.

I'll always remember it. His name was Edward W. Wallace and he represented the Riveredge Athletic and Social Club. My first victory was a kayo in thirty-four seconds of the second round. It made me feel real good, but it also gave me a false sense of security. A few nights later in that sub-novice tournament I was beaten. I'll remember that as much as I'll remember my first win, because I learned more lessons in defeat than I did in victory.

As the years have gone on I've been very close with all members of my family, except one—my brother Billy. It could be that the gap between us first began to take shape in my mind after that defeat. It could be, too, that deep in my mind, I knew that Billy and I had never hit it off well. I remember that when I was a kid of seven or eight—and at such loose ends—Billy would never let me go with him and Frank. They had friends. They'd go somewhere, like to Prospect Park with the other kids, and I'd want to go along.

"Where do you think you're going?" Billy would say.

"I want to go along with you," I'd answer.

"Get back home. Who wants a kid like you dragging along with us?"

I'd wait until the whole bunch of them had started walking away and I'd try to follow. I'd hide behind a garbage barrel or a tree or a stoop trying to make myself smaller than I was so Billy wouldn't see me, but he always did. Sometimes he'd just chase me. Sometimes he'd give me a whack. Sometimes he'd throw stones at me. I didn't realize it then. Maybe he was just trying to be a big guy in front of the other kids and didn't want a little kid like me dragging along and spoiling his fun. It got to be a kind of a joke with the other kids. As soon as they'd start out somewhere they'd know I'd be right behind and they knew Billy would chase me.

The morning of my second amateur fight I did what I always did. I went to Prospect Park for a little light roadwork. I was all through running and was leaving the park when Billy came along. He knew I was fighting that night against a kid named Joseph Baglio of the Police Athletic League. He knew a lot more about fighting, conditioning, and what you should do on the day of a fight, and I knew he did.

"Come on, run with me," Billy said.

"I finished my running," I answered.

"Run some more," he said. "It'll make you stronger."

Well, we ran together, four more miles. That night I had no energy at all. Baglio boxed rings around me in the third round when I needed all the energy I could summon and didn't have any. I had come out in the first round throwing punches all the time. I won the round easily. The second round was the same for a while. I still had the strength to go, but then I felt the weariness coming on me, and I couldn't do a thing to stop it.

Baglio must have known it, too. A kid from the P.A.L., although fighting in the sub-novice class as I was, could have been piling up experience in the ring since he was ten years old. If he'd ever won a P.A.L. tournament he couldn't have been in the sub-novice. But Baglio never had won. Still he had more experience than I did and used it. When I tired he came on. He whipped me badly in the third round. I'd left my fight in Prospect Park with my brother Billy. I learned a lesson, though. I was severely taught that a fighter has to pace himself.

I was fast. I had good hand speed, but I wasn't able to adjust to situations with which I was not too familiar. Besides, I was getting hit too often. My manager and trainers worried about that.

You could see it after I was eliminated from the Golden Gloves. My next fight was arranged in an A.A.U. tournament at the Jamaica Arena. It was an open class and I had to go five two-minute rounds. There were even prizes, watches, radios and small gift orders for clothes. I could have used them, only Ray Drake, my opponent for my third bout, knew too much for me. He was in and out, beating me inside and gone by the time I could counter.

I lost a second fight to Drake later on at Dexter Park, my first outdoor bout. I knocked him down three times with clean, solid punches, but in between the knockdowns he must have beaten me badly.

There was nothing else to do but go to studying defense. It's kind of a dreary thing, really. When a kid's young and wants to fight, all he thinks about is beating up the other guy. He doesn't realize the opponent has the same thought in mind. Theoretically, at least, a good offense is a good defense, but you've got to have both or else you're going to take punches you should not be taking. So a good part of my first year in the ring was occupied with learning how to avoid taking those punches that can't possibly do a fighter any good.

That's where my so-called peek-a-boo defense began to take shape. It sort of grew on me as I began to appreciate the importance of avoiding being hit. My confidence in myself was good, but I knew that if I took too many punches, it would ebb away from me.

I was like a kid going to school to study his lessons. I could repeat almost from memory the things that were being told to me in those days. "Keep your hands high. Hold your right hand near your face, alongside your chin. Touch your ear— the lobe of your right ear with the thumb of your glove as a reminder. Keep your right elbow in close to protect your liver. Once you get hit in the liver you'll know it. It's a terrible pain."

There were times when I'd even shadow box with a rolled-up newspaper tucked under my right arm. As I jabbed and moved around I had to keep that elbow close enough to my ribs to keep the paper from dropping to the floor. If it dropped, my guard was wrong. My chin had to be hidden behind my left shoulder with my head tilted so that a punch would glance off it.

There was another gimmick which helped me immeasurably. It was what we've come to call a pendulum bag. Nick D'Amato thought of it. He took a regular leather speed bag, but instead of having it blown up, he filled it with about ten pounds of sand. It was hung from a chain from the ceiling so that it was suspended just about at the height of my own face when I crouched.

I'd push the bag forward and wait until it swung back toward me. I'd try to wait until it almost touched my face. The idea was to "slip" the bag, just as a fighter slips a punch being thrown at him. As the bag comes back in its pendulum motion from behind you, you even slip it without seeing it.

It gives a fighter a wonderful exercise both for vision and the development of his reflexes. As you are moving one way and then another while the bag is swinging, you hold your hands in readiness for punching on your own. You develop balance and a controlled eagerness.

At that time I used to spar regularly with a very strong middleweight named Harold Drucker. At first I couldn't get inside him at all and he used to use me up pretty good without much chance of me getting back at him. But the longer we worked together the harder he found it to get at me and the easier I was able to get in a few licks of my own. We had some real good sparring sessions, two rounds of three minutes each. When he hit me I felt it, but he was hitting me less. I noticed how the other kids in the gym used to stop their own work to watch us when we went at it. Other fighters don't usually stop their own training to look at somebody else—unless that somebody in the ring is interesting enough to watch. So the start of

1951 was a big year for me. I had grown, and at sixteen I found myself fighting in the Golden Gloves Open 160-pound class.

It may not have been important to other people, but what was really significant to me is that the kids at P.S. 614 knew I was a fighter and I had their respect. Miss Lewis and Miss O'Brien, two of my teachers, actually accepted my invitation to come to Madison Square Garden to watch me box.

I was credited with two third-round technical knockouts when the referee stopped my first two bouts of the tournament to save my opponents from further punishment. I overwhelmed Harvey Lammers of the Salem-Crescent A.C. in two minutes and 43 seconds of the first round. I stopped Eddie Henderson of the Riveredge A. and S.C. in two minutes and 38 seconds of the second round when the ref stepped in. Richard Hill of the Police Athletic League stood in the way of the first of eleven amateur boxing titles I was to win. I won the decision over him. I was a champion.

The next step up the fistic ladder was the Eastern Championships of the Golden Gloves. Winners in competition went on to Chicago to fight the Western winner for the Intercity title. I won my second title, but more important than that I beat Ray Drake, who had beaten me twice before. Later on I fought him a fourth and fifth time, finally kayoing him in the fifth round the last time we met. It was Drake's final amateur bout.

In this same Eastern championship tournament I also set some sort of a record for myself. I finished a fight in twenty-two seconds against a boy named Charley Williams from Buffalo. The first three punches I threw at him landed. The ref figured it was enough. He ended the fight right there.

When I won a three-round decision over Johnny Gibson from Syracuse I was on my way. At least, all the way to Chicago, the first visit I'd made to any big city. Even the authorities at P.S. 614 appreciated how important this was to me. I missed some school, but my teachers allowed me to make up the work later.

When I came back to school, though, I was kind of ashamed.

I had lost to a southpaw named Ralph Guerrero. A southpaw's a left-hander. Where I fight with my left hand extended, he fights with his right hand. He troubled me in the first round, but in the second I thought I had solved how to move into him. Then in the third he confused me completely. He turned over. That is, he started to fight in right-handed fashion. That kind of problem was too much for me that early in my career.

The defeat caused me some grief, but it made me appreciate once more that no matter how high you go in life you just can't leave problems behind.

Chapter Five

My interests, you could say, were narrow—work, worry and running. My running, though, had taken on a purpose. On some Saturday mornings Frank Lavelle would pick me up and we'd go to Coney Island in the early mornings, but not to watch other people enjoying themselves going on the rides as I used to do. This time it was serious business. To develop my ankles, calves and thighs, I was made to run in the sand on the beach. It's not pleasant when you do it for miles at a stretch, but it gave me the leg power a fighter needs.

I didn't think it unusual to be up before dawn, dress in long underwear, heavy army shoes, a sweat shirt, overalls and a hood and run for five miles in Prospect Park. Very often I was accompanied by an uncle, Charley Johnson, who was in his early twenties then. It was a grind, but it was my only interest, because I saw boxing as the way out for me and my family.

While other kids my age were having the fun that kids have, going out with girls or going to dances and whatnot, I'd shadow box in front of the mirror in the bathroom at home. Or I'd practice jabbing at the string that hung down from the kitchen light. Or I'd blow up a paper bag, hang it from the string and punch at it. I'd even take a pillow, make believe it was the heavy bag, and uppercut at it. You can hit a pillow in

49

the middle and it will double over. Or you can hit it with an uppercut and it will flip back like a man being knocked out.

Eventually, though, even a kid who is so wrapped up in boxing that he knows little else has got to be with other kids his own age. I had made a friend, a fellow named Freddy Hill. Unlike myself, he was a big talker. He just rattled on and on. He was enthusiastic about everything. He'd talk and talk and talk, and I guess I needed that kind of companionship.

Freddy had a girl. I don't even remember her name, but he'd walk over to see her every now and then and I'd walk along with him. One night there was another girl there. I thought she was awful pretty. When she smiled and her white teeth showed, she looked beautiful. Her teeth were even. She seemed as shy as I was. Her name was Sandra Elizabeth Hicks. I thought she was about my age—sixteen.

Later on Sandra told me that when I was introduced to her she knew right away that I was a gentleman. How she knew that I don't know to this day. All I'd do would be to mumble or nod my head, but Sandra seemed just as shy as I was. She had trouble looking me in the eye—as much as I was having looking at her. But I kept sneaking peeks and I kept coming back.

Occasionally while Freddy rattled on, talking about this and that, I'd look at her and notice her looking at me and we'd sort of exchange smiles. By the time Freddy said goodbye to the girls that first day I'd made up my mind to see Sandra again, only I didn't know how I'd be able to do it.

If I went to see her without Freddy, I'd have to carry the conversational ball, and I didn't think I'd be able to do it. If I said something stupid and Sandra laughed at me, I'd never be able to go back to see her again. I was in a torment. I really was, but I'd never had this kind of feeling inside of me before. I wanted to be able to talk to that girl as freely and easily and confidently as Freddy could. I think I prayed then for the first time asking for help to be able to open my mouth. I don't think I ever wanted anything as much before then or since then.

50

I guess Freddy got the idea how much I wanted to be friends with Sandra because he started playing up to her. Vaguely I appreciated the position I was in. I needed Freddy as an excuse to see her and as the fellow who could keep a conversation going. At the same time I was afraid that with his gift of gab Sandra would think me dull and uninteresting. Funny thing, Freddy kept suggesting that we go over and see the girls more and more often and I'd go, but what I wanted to do most was to be able to go over alone, so we could be on the stoop alone and maybe even touch hands by accident.

I don't know how many nights I lay awake planning how I could avoid Freddy, work up enough nerve to go to see Sandra alone and carry on an interesting conversation with her. I used to twist and turn in bed carrying on such imaginary conversations. I imagined myself as witty as Freddy. I thought about how I could get some money together so that I could buy her a gift and maybe that would take the place of talk, but where could I get money? Between training and going to school, there wasn't time for much else. I had never wanted anything else. But now I wanted more.

For a while I contented myself just with walking by her house on Bainbridge Street. My grandmother, Julia Johnson, my mother's mother, that is, lived nearby on Bainbridge. I didn't used to see her much, certainly not walking over on my own, but now I started to visit Grandma at her home a lot. She seemed glad to see me. She never asked how come I'd suddenly become so interested in the old folks. Maybe she suspected. I never asked.

Maybe Sandra began to suspect, too, that I wasn't coming by her house so often just to see my grandmother as I'd tell her. More and more I'd see her just hanging around outside near her house and our conversations became longer and longer. She seemed to lose her timidity as I seemed to lose mine. The first few times she'd ask me where Freddy Hill was. After a while she didn't bother to ask. I guess she began to understand that I had ducked him deliberately just to be alone with her. She didn't seem to mind. I certainly didn't.

Little by little, Sandra brought out all the things about me. I told her about Wiltwyck and P.S. 614 and how I was getting along in boxing. She seemed truly interested. She thought fighting was dangerous, but she also thought it was exciting. It took me a long time before I worked up nerve enough to ask her if she'd like to see one of my fights. She seemed so pleased, but she said she would have to ask her mother for permission to go.

Mrs. Hicks had seen me around often enough by that time. She was an extremely nice woman, who had tried to make me feel at home and at ease. I thought she was one of the kindest women I'd ever known. She looked very much like Sandra, but when Sandra told her about my invitation to go to see me fight, her face kind of changed. She looked a little worried.

Sandra stood there looking at her mother with a funny kind of look on her face. "Say yes, Momma, please," Sandra pleaded.

"I wouldn't mind so much," Mrs. Hicks said, "but, Honey, I don't think Floyd knows so much about you."

Then Mrs. Hicks looked at me, as though she was seeing me for the first time. It was like she was examining my size. I was big for my age. My shoulders were broad. I looked strong.

"Floyd," Mrs. Hicks finally said, "you're almost a grown man. You're a gentlemanly young man and we've been pleased to have you visit Sandra, but do you have any idea how old Sandra is?"

"Momma!"

I looked at Sandra. Her face was crinkling up as though she was about to start to cry.

"No, Mrs. Hicks," I answered truthfully. "Sandra and I have never discussed that. I guess she's a little younger than me, but not too much younger."

"Well, Sandra's only . . ."

Sandra fled from the room sobbing. I could hear her pleading voice from the bedroom.

"Please, Momma, please. Don't tell him," she called. "Oh, please, Momma. Why do you have to?"

"Floyd," Mrs. Hicks said just the same, "Sandra's only thirteen years old."

It wasn't a blow to me, but I was surprised, and for the moment I wondered if Mrs. Hicks had thought I was doing something wrong wanting so much to be with Sandra. I must admit I had never considered the thought that she could be that young. I imagine her mother assumed I was eighteen or even nineteen because of the fact that I was fighting. Mrs. Hicks didn't say she didn't want me to be visiting her daughter so often, but I left there that night with the feeling that I couldn't rush things.

Well, I couldn't have rushed them anyway as much as I would have liked to. There was always the question of money. You can't take out a girl without it. There was still the question of clothes. I wasn't walking around wearing my father's hand-me-downs any more, but I wasn't a dandy either. My clothes were clean, if old, but not the dress-up kind. And then there was the question of Sandra's faith.

Her family were devout Catholics. I suppose I believed in God, but I seldom went to church. Sandra, in fact, attended the Holy Rosary Parochial School over on Chauncey Street. During the summer vacation in 1951, I managed to get a construction job. Most of my salary went to my mother for the family, but occasionally I'd get a tip, and when I got enough together, I'd visit Sandra or bring her a little gift, or we'd take a walk and I'd be able to buy her a box of candy or something.

In that way we managed to see each other often enough to keep alive the spark that had sprung up between us. However, just before Christmas that year, I reached what must have been the bluest time in my life since Wiltwyck, except for the time Ingemar took away my championship. I wanted to pay a visit to Sandra and her folks, not just wander by her block and wait for her to come downstairs. I wanted to come with gifts in my arms and a nice new suit of clothes on my back, but I didn't have a dime. I wanted to buy a present for my mother and for some of my teachers who were so kind to me. The thought that I couldn't buy anything for anybody drove me frantic. My brother Frank was in the same bad way. At his suggestion both of us went out looking for work, any kind of work that would provide a few dollars.

Luck was with us. Away out on Long Island there was some building going on and they were signing on construction gangs. Most of those hired were adults, men with families, but nobody could say that I couldn't and didn't do a man's work. I had everything all planned out. I was going to get about ninety dollars. With it there'd be a present for Sandra, for my mother, for Mrs. Hicks, who had never told me to stop seeing her daughter, and even some clothes. I didn't imagine I could afford to buy a suit, but I knew that if I shopped carefully and cheaply, I'd be able to buy a new jacket and a pair of slacks. The thought of all this made me lift more and work faster than anybody on the project. I kept telling myself all that hard work was good for my body besides.

Payday finally came around. All the men lined up and waited for their names to be called. The list of men unpaid kept getting smaller and smaller, but we never heard the paymaster yell, "Floyd Patterson," or "Frank Patterson." After a while the paymaster stopped calling any names at all. I was left there with my mouth hanging open.

I rushed up to him to tell him he'd made some mistake.

"You didn't call my name," I said.

"What is it?"

I told him. He ran his finger down a long sheet of paper with a list of names. "I didn't skip you," he said. "Your name's not here. How long have you been working? What's your pay number?"

We gave him that information and went with him to an office. He came out of the office and said: "You don't get paid today. You get paid next week. We hold back the first week's salary."

"Mister," I pleaded, "Christmas is only a few days away. I depended on this money to buy my presents."

"I understand," he said, "but there's nothing I can do. I only work here. When you were hired they explained the pay system to you."

"I guess maybe they did," I said, "but I didn't understand. Isn't there something I can do, like borrowing against what's coming to me?"

"Go on into the office and see what they say in there," he said, "but I doubt very much that you'll have any luck."

Frank and I went inside, hoping against hope. We got very little satisfaction. "While you're standing here arguing you're cheating us out of time," the clerk in the office said. "You'd better get back on the job this minute or you're out and you'll have to wait until next week for your money as well."

We went back on the job, but my heart wasn't in it. I felt as though my whole world had collapsed about me again. In my pocket I had the shopping list I had written out and it burned a hole there.

That night, weary from my labor and wearier still from my disappointment, I went home and just sat on the bed and stared at the shopping list. I couldn't bring myself to eat or go out of the house, certainly not take the walk over to Bainbridge empty-handed. What could I do but let Sandra know that I wasn't man enough to be able to put a few dollars together to buy her a gift?

I deliberately stayed away several more days. I knew she expected to see me, wanted to see me, in fact. Sandra had a phone at her house, but I thought how lucky it was for me right then that we didn't have one at ours. I felt it was the perfect excuse for not calling her, and I knew that she couldn't call me.

On Christmas Day my blue mood was worst of all. If it wasn't for the fact that I couldn't stand the smell of whiskey, much less the taste, I know I'd have gone out and gotten drunk to bury my pain. I'd seen enough people doing that in our neighborhood. I couldn't ever understand it before, but sitting alone I had an understanding of it then. I thought nothing worse could ever happen to me.

That night something worse did happen. A telegram was delivered to me from Sandra. "Please come around," it read. "I haven't heard from you in several days. Are you angry with me? I'll wait all night for you, no matter how late you come over."

I was broke, but that telegram really broke me up into pieces. I went into the bathroom, locked the door, and cried like a little baby.

Frank tried to console me, but I wouldn't listen. "What can I tell Sandra?" I said. "She bought a present for me, I know, but I can't even buy one for her."

I got some crazy ideas then. I roamed around the house looking for something I could take out and hock. I thought that if my mother had some jewelry I could borrow it, get some money on it, and then redeem it after I got paid. It was a daydream, just like so many I'd had over the years. My mother had nothing, not even a son who could bring her a gift. I couldn't even stand facing my mother then. I imagined her looking at me with hurt eyes wondering when I was going to hand her a package and say, "Merry Christmas."

"Let's get out of the house," I said to Frank. He wasn't feeling much better than I was. We went out after midnight. Inevitably my steps took me over to Bainbridge and past Sandra's house. It was 1:30 in the morning, but I looked up at the window and saw the light burning in her bedroom. She was waiting, just as she said she would, but empty-handed I didn't have the nerve to walk up her steps and ring her bell.

When Frank and I got home in the early hours of that morning I had hit on a plan. I suggested that a letter be written to

Sandra telling her that I had had to go to a training camp unexpectedly but hurriedly. Frank put it into words for me and wrote it. After it was done we went out and mailed it. A week later I finally paid Sandra the visit. This time I came the way I should have come before Christmas. I was dressed up. I had a present for Sandra and her mother and I was full of lies about where I had been for all that time and where I had gotten the money.

Not until long after we were married did I tell Sandra the full story of my shame, embarrassment and poverty. She told me what a fool I had been. I didn't appreciate then that what Sandra wanted was just to be with me. She didn't want what I could bring her.

It kept on that way for a long time, though. I'd show up when I had money enough in my pocket to take her to Coney Island or to a movie. I made sure I was always clean and dressed properly. I'd be careful about the things I said and the way I talked. I'd talk to her about her school work and her religion. I wanted so much to please her that I'd even worry about whether my breath smelled right. If I thought it didn't, I'd buy a package of Sen-Sen.

The thing I didn't want was for Sandra to get tired of me or think I was stupid or something or be ashamed of me in any way. Because of that fear I deliberately withheld from her the address where I lived. I didn't want her to know how many Pattersons there were living in such a flat. I didn't tell her much about my family. Her folks weren't rich or anything, but it seemed to me, in my strange way of viewing things, that there was nothing for her to be ashamed of in her house and there was so much for me in mine.

After a while she had to find out about me and my family. That's how she knew where to send the wire. Maybe she found out from my grandmother. I never asked her. I was so busy thinking up stories that would still keep her away from my block. I told her that my mother didn't want any girls chasing after her boys. I told her my mother and father had bad tempers. I said my manager would resent her. Anything that came to my mind, anything at all that would keep her from seeing the way we were at home. I was crazy with fear that for some reason she'd stop seeing me.

But Sandra seemed to like me in spite of everything I had been and was. She smiled so often and laughed so often. She had a good sense of humor. She was kind. I remember once we stopped at a hamburger hut and had milk and hamburgers. It took every cent I had in my pocket, but I was only too glad to be able to treat her. While we were eating, the girl behind the counter kept complaining what cheap customers came into the place. "Nobody," she said, "ever leaves a big tip."

Right there I figured I was in trouble. How could I be with my girl and not leave a tip after that? I just didn't have it in my pocket. As we stood up to go, I bowed from the waist and tipped my hat to the girl. "There's a big tip for you," I said. She looked kind of struck dumb.

Outside, Sandra broke into laughter and just couldn't stop. Her laughter infected me. I broke into a grin and then into the best laugh I ever remember having. Imagine me, the kid who never learned to laugh or have fun, almost breaking up right there on the street.

When I finally caught my breath I said to her, "What's the big joke?"

"Floyd," she said, "you're so funny. You're so clever."

I knew that somebody as sweet and decent as Sandra didn't just come that way. Her mother was a wonderful woman. So was mine, but I still didn't have what Sandra had. I thought about it a long time. Finally a conclusion came to me. I wondered if her belief in the Catholic faith didn't make her what she was. We talked about it a lot after that. I know she wouldn't have tried to push me into becoming a convert to Catholicism, but I told her I'd like to try. She advised me it would have to take a considerable amount of instruction. I was willing to take the time.

One day early in 1952 I met her outside of the Holy Rosary School after her classes for the day were over. She took me by the hand and led me back to the Parish house at 142 Chauncey Street. She rang the bell and it was answered by a tall, partly bald priest who had very blue eyes and a kind-looking face. He was Reverend Archibald McLeese.

"Father," Sandra said, "I would like you to meet a friend of mine. He wants to talk to you about taking instruction."

I was going on from there to the Gramercy Gym. I had a bag with me and all my equipment. It may seem strange that somebody who would want religion could go out and fight in the ring. I don't think so. Neither did the priest.

Just about this same time I became close with two other people who were to have a profound influence on my life. One was Mr. Schwefel, who presented me with the sportsmanship and character award I won at P.S. 614. The other was Aaron Watson, who came into my dressing room one night after a fight just to talk. He told me everybody called him Buster. He was a happy-go-lucky kind of guy with big eyes, which he rolled around. He laughed easily. He said he was an amateur boxer, too. He just wanted to talk fights and fighting.

I was kind of suspicious of him. I held off people. There wasn't anything he could get out of me, yet I didn't want people I didn't know well getting too close to me. I was close-mouthed with him. I didn't expect to see him again, but one day he showed up at my house. The way my mind worked in those days, I figured that anybody who would come to my house without being invited would have to be living in conditions worse than ours.

It wasn't that way at all. Buster lived much better than I did. He had a vic and a lot of records and he liked sitting around and listening to music when he wasn't talking fights. I began to go to his place a lot. I listened to his records and we became close friends. He'd come to my fights. I'd watch him train. It always surprised me to think of him as a fighter. He wasn't the type. After he finally decided to give it up himself, he was with me all the time. He became a kind of unpaid trainer for me for a while. When I started becoming successful as a professional, he became one of my trainers and constant companion. He still is today.

Mr. Schwefel, who was instrumental in helping to set up New York's "600" schools, was a man who had his hand in a lot of things—the hotel business, as I said before, politics, charity and activities for young people. He was chairman of the 13th Police Precinct Youth Council, an A.A.U. official and a big man in the Rotary Club.

At first I couldn't figure out why he'd be interested in a boy like me. One day he finally told me he'd been keeping tabs on my attendance and schoolwork at P.S. 614. He said he had learned I was fighting amateur and was pleased with that, as well as my school record. That day he said to me, "You've heard of Babe Ruth, haven't you? Well, the Babe was a good friend of mine until his last days. He got to be the greatest in baseball history and where did he grow up? In an industrial home in Baltimore, not very much different from Wiltwyck and certainly not as good as we have here at P.S. 614."

That was sort of an inspiration to me. I looked at this big, hearty-looking, gray-haired man who obviously had so much himself and I felt that if he thought there was enough good in me to try to help me, I certainly should think well of myself. After I turned professional and Cus became my manager, Mr. Schwefel had Cus investigated. He wanted to be certain that I wouldn't be mishandled in any way. In those early days he set up a financial arrangement for me with Cus and was the over-seer of my end of the deal. He died before I had a chance to win the title. Like Miss Costen before him, I wish Mr. Schwefel had been around when that took place. I'm certain he would have been as happy for me as I was.

But I'm getting ahead of myself again. I guess I'm a little overeager, just as I was in late 1951 when I came to Cus and talked to him about wanting to begin earning some money in the ring. "You can't turn professional now," he said.

"Don't you think I'm good enough?" I asked.

"Certainly you're good enough," he said. "There are plenty of pros your weight you can take, but you're not going to be rushed. First place, you're too young. Second place, if I'd let you turn pro, you wouldn't have a chance to make the Olympic team."

The Olympics didn't mean a thing to me then. You couldn't eat medals and you couldn't pawn them for much to buy food or clothes or a car or have a little jingling money in your pocket. My big interest still was making some money. I was going to graduate from P.S. 614 by February, 1952, and I wanted to begin bringing some money home steadily.

Not even my folks had talked to me about quitting school, but that was on my mind. Somehow, though, I got talked out of it for almost another year. I enrolled at Alexander Hamilton Vocational High School, not too far from my home, to study metal-working. I went there one year. By the time that year was over, I understood what the Olympics could mean and what a wonderful springboard it could be to a young fighter trying to get ahead in the ring.

Chapter Six

When you're rootless and aimless, you're very much like a stray dog roaming the streets. You go one way and then you go another, but you never have any real direction. You never know what you're looking for. I was that way until 1952, although I knew I was improving as a fighter. Once the talk of the Olympics began, however, there was direction. There was also more work and more fights than I ever imagined I could have in one year. I fought nineteen times before I made the team. I knocked out fourteen of these opponents, beat four on decisions and one on a default.

It started, as it did earlier, with the New York Golden Gloves tournament. By this time I knew that it wouldn't be too long before I could turn pro. I could still have fought as a 160-pounder, but I was entered in the 175-pound class. I had been growing steadily. From my bone structure it was clear that sooner or later I'd be a heavyweight, but I wasn't thinking about the heavyweight division being the richest one. I wanted to go against the heavier amateur fighters because they're slower as a class. They have more power in their punches and more strength in their bodies, but I had speed and figured it would be to my advantage to be able to move in and out on them before they could get set to take a real swipe at me.

Everything seemed to be working out the way it was planned. I had three bouts and won all three on one-round knockouts. I won the last one in forty seconds. I thought that made me an Olympian. I was way off base. I had to fight my way through five more tournaments before making the Olympic team.

A couple of weeks after the Golden Gloves tourney, I was back in the ring at Madison Square Garden for four more bouts. In the first and last I won by a first-round knockout. In between I was pressed to take three-round decisions. I recall the bouts clearly because they kept me from thinking I had the world by the tail. Before you learn what it's all about in the ring, you have an idea that you can go in with a prearranged plan. If that's the only way you can fight, then you'd better be prepared to get lumped. The fighters who get along are those who can improvise, expect the unexpected and are able to make their adjustments to it. I paid with some lumps on my face before I learned that lesson.

One time I let the man get the jump on me. He was punching fast and effectively. My legs became unsteady and my vision blurred a little bit. I wasn't unconscious, but I realized right quick that I wasn't too far from dreamland. Like most fellows, I tried to get the guy slowed down by bombing for the face. Some people call it head-hunting, but it's not smart fighting.

I needed a breather badly. There was one way I could get it. I had to work on him downstairs. In other words, as we often were advised in the early stages of training at the gym, "Hit a flurry." To put it into even blunter language, you keep a guy honest if you can "pound his belly to jelly."

I think I recalled that advice myself. Perhaps they were yelling it from my corner. I really don't know. The crowd was whooping it up. It looked like I was about to go out, and the ringside fight fans, sensing my trouble, were shouting encouragement to my opponent. "One more! One more!" they implored him.

Suddenly I planted my feet, dropped my head, and began

to beat a tattoo as fast and as hard as I could at his body. I pumped my arms like pistons into his mid-section. At least, I hoped that's where the punches would land. Many of them landed on elbows, arms and on his gloves. Some of them landed on his ribs and stomach. If he didn't give before I got arm-weary I was done. But there's another battle cry that always should be remembered in the ring. "Kill the body and the head must die." I guess that's just about what I did to this guy who was so close to having me out. My body-punching forced him to back off. I got the breather I wanted, pulled myself together, and went on to beat him.

I also won the Inter-City Golden Gloves by beating a light-heavy from Chicago named Eddie Jones, and then I faced my first real big decision. The National A.A.U. championships, the next step up the Olympic ladder, were scheduled for Boston. That meant hard, intensive training. It also meant being away from school. I was so close to my goal, school no longer interested me, but I was not the truant I used to be. I wanted to leave school, but it had to be done legally. I wanted no more trouble. I had had my fill of running out on things as a youngster.

However, it was necessary to have the promise of some kind of steady employment to get my working papers. Aside from the construction job I had had when I wanted so badly to make some money to buy Sandra a Christmas present, I had worked off and on during school holidays as a longshoreman, in the Fulton Fish Market, and as a helper for my father, who drove a garbage truck at the time. But all of these jobs were temporary. I knew nothing but boxing, so I was in kind of a trap, until Mr. Schwefel came to my help again.

He provided me with the job. He assured the school authorities that I would have steady employment in his Gramercy Park Hotel on East 20th Street. As Mr. Schwefel explained to me later, he intended to have me learn the hotel business by working around in every department of the hotel. The hotel business actually is many businesses in one. That way I could get all-around experience and get any number of jobs. I started out as a helper for the hotel's interior decorator, but I must confess that I was more interested in decorating myself in an Olympic uniform. Mr. Schwefel understood that. The Gramercy Gym was only six blocks from the hotel. After I worked part of a day, I was free to train there, before making the trip to Boston for the tournament in early April.

I won in Boston and again in Albany, New York, where the Eastern Olympic tryouts were held, but even as you advance you run into pitfalls. Boxing, I think, is especially that way. The more you learn, the more you learn you still must learn. If you get cocky, it's like sticking out your chin and asking for trouble. Shamefacedly, I admit now that I was getting pretty cocky.

Tony Anthony, who fought in the light middleweight division, once we got into the Olympic trials, was on our New York team. Maybe I'd better explain that the Olympic weights are a little different than the weight classifications we use in our normal amateur bouts. In the middleweight class, for instance, there are two divisions—one with a limit of 156 pounds, the other with a 165-pound limit. I was the "heavy" middleweight, Tony the "light" one. We became good friends and had kind of a challenging game going between us.

We were both seventeen and, I hope you understand, we were kind of braggarts, the way kids can be at that age. If he knocked out somebody, he'd come back to the dressing room and tell me in what round and how fast. "Okay, I can do better than that," I'd say. If it were I who put the crusher on first, Tony'd look at me with mock disdain and say, "What took you so long? Watch me beat it."

This game almost beat me in Kansas City. I went out for one bout determined to cut the time on Tony's record. I estimated it would not be hard, because I had seen my opponent fight a few days before that, and I knew I had better hand speed than he did. The way I had it planned, I'd come right to him with some fast combinations, finish him off with a hook, and go back to the dressing room saying, "Yah-h-h-h!" to Anthony.

I walked in all right—but directly into a straight right to my face that staggered me and sent me plunging into a haze. I grabbed and held for the rest of the round. I back-pedaled and had all I could do to last out the round. That knocked the "beat-him" game out of my head. For the next two rounds I concerned myself with the other guy rather than Tony.

My last fight for a berth on the Olympic team ended in one minute and forty-two seconds of the first round. I beat a college guy—me who had trouble getting through grammar school. My opponent was Gordon Gladson, who had won the National Collegiate championship only a short while before. But I hit him with a left hook and made the team.

Until that point the boxing critics, managers, and such who follow amateur bouts looking for prospective professionals, had me tabbed as a right-hand nut. I was using my gazelle punch a lot in those days, and most of my finishing jobs were accomplished with the right hand thrown from the leap. However, in Kansas City I scored three knockouts. It was a matter of pride to me to know that I put each of my opponents away with a left hand.

I'm told that the experts considered our 1952 Olympic boxing team the best the United States has ever sent over for the games. I'd like to believe that. It gives me a sense of pride. Before we went over to Helsinki, Finland, Pete Mello, one of our coaches from the Catholic Youth Organization in New York, predicted we'd win five individual titles. We did. Nate Brooks won the flyweight crown; Charley Adkins, the light welter; I took the heavy middle; Norval Lee, the light heavy; and Ed Sanders, the heavyweight.

Since then I've done a considerable amount of traveling, both in this country and overseas, but the first trip over, particularly as an Olympian, is something you never forget. When they handed out the official clothes and our uniforms to us, I could scarcely believe my eyes. Every competitor on our team dressed exactly alike—cap, jacket, flannel trousers—all in red, white and blue. I had to come four thousand miles from home to really begin to feel that I was like everybody else. I belonged.

There were moments, of course, when I felt that I needed some encouragement, a kind, intimate personal word. The long northern nights, when Finland had sunshine so late and the sun rose so early that it was hard to sleep, bothered me a little. There were some days when I would feel blue and lonesome. Once I felt so moody that I sat down and wrote a long letter to Father McLeese, who was giving me instruction in Catholicism. "Father, I feel in need of a friendly letter," I wrote. Almost by return air mail, that letter came to pick me up.

Another time, as we walked through the Olympic village, we passed the Russian boxing team. They were all lined up in their blue sweat shirts. An instructor stood in front of them as if it was close order drill in the Army and they were doing it by the numbers. The instructor would shout an order and all of them would jab at once and all in the same way. Then the instructor would throw a right and all of them would throw a right. After that I stopped worrying, at least about the Russians.

Besides, there was so much to do in training and so much to see. Tony Anthony and I loved to visit the amusement parks, which reminded us of Coney Island, only the rides there were higher and faster. We'd wander through the compounds where the athletes of the other nations were quartered. There was some trouble with language, of course, but we managed to make ourselves understood. Once I traded with a Russian for his sweat pants and sweat shirt monogrammed with CCCP on the shirt front.

Wandering around that way I discovered something else, too. The United States athletes ate real well. We could have all the steaks we wanted to eat and there always seemed to be more. The Finns, though, didn't get so much. I knew about hunger from my younger days, although these fellows weren't starving or anything. Their main course seemed to me to be fish, fish, fish, of one kind or another.

One day there was a platter left in front of me after the meal with several steaks on it. I got some paper, wrapped the steaks in a package, and was about to go over to the Finnish side to offer the extra meat to them when Pete Mello saw me. He must have thought I was taking the steaks to my own room for a midnight snack or something.

I felt a little silly, but I had to tell him I had no thought of eating those steaks. "There's no reason why this good meat should go to waste," I said. "I was going to take it over and give it to the Finns. No harm in that, is there?"

I didn't have much trouble in the ring once the competition got under way. As usual, my worries were exaggerated. We'd been told all about the strange Olympic rules. You can be disqualified for almost anything. Once, throwing a right hand, I went all the way around and dipped my body below my opponent's waist. The referee raised one finger at me. A second time I threw a left hook and went into a natural crouch from it. Another finger went up. A third finger and I'd have been out. Fortunately the third finger never was raised, but I did help the Stars and Stripes to be raised.

When it was all over, I had spent approximately eighteen minutes against four opponents. My first big write-up, really, came from Red Smith, the *Herald Tribune*'s syndicated columnist, who covered the Olympic games. Mr. Smith has written quite a bit about me since, but in the scrapbook of my early days there is this clipping written about me from ringside: "He has faster paws than a subway pickpocket and they cause more suffering. He confuses his opponents with his impetuous style, lunging forward to throw his first blow, sometimes missing with that opening punch. He doesn't mind if he does miss because he has six or seven other hands to follow up."

The fights were held in an arena called Messahulli. I fought a Frenchman named Omar Tabakka first. He went the distance. He seemed very strong, but I was awarded the decision. The next was a Hollander, named Leonardus Jansen. I walked into a real good hook to my chin that shook me up, but I was lucky enough to knock him out. I was so pleased I walked over to shake hands with him and his second. I even shook hands with the referee.

My third bout was against a Swede, Stig Stolin. I scored three knockdowns in the second round. Instead of ruling it a technical knockout, Stolin was disqualified for holding. I want to dwell on him for a minute, because this was the first time I'd ever come up against the Swedish style of defensive boxing. As you know, after I became the professional champion, I experienced considerable difficulty with Ingemar in my first and third bouts with him. I saw Ingemar fight for the first time in the finals of the Olympics that year. He was disqualified in a bout with Sanders, who was later killed in the ring after he had turned professional.

Anyway, Stolin and Ingemar fought very much alike. Basically, they depended upon their defense to set up the offense—which, in Johansson's case, was a straight right-hand punch following directly over the light, flicking left jab or left hook, which disconcerts you more than hurts you.

Ingemar suffered a long time for his disqualification against Sanders. His country's sports writers made it seem as though he had been afraid of Sanders. Ed was a big man, extremely strong, and it would have been no shame at all to be cautious against a fighter his size. He looked as if he could punch you apart, but Ingemar was wronged, because he fought his kind of fight, a counter-fight, on instructions from his coaches. It turned out that Sanders wanted to counter, too. Ingemar got the rap when he was disqualified for not fighting.

Now, with Stolin I really had a hard time, harder than it appeared. He came out in an upright stance. His left arm was held out before him, much as I was to see Ingemar's in a later year. Stolin held his head behind his left shoulder, and it was hard to land a solid punch on him. As I said, I was lucky to be able to accomplish that.

I was only one bout away from an Olympic gold medal as I climbed into the ring for my final fight against Vasile Tita, a Rumanian, who naturally had the Soviets cheering for him. It was over so fast it was hard to realize it. I was warned twice by the referee, a Pole named Neudning. Right off I missed with a left hook, but I moved right back in after him. I hit him with a right-hand uppercut directly on the point of the chin. His head snapped back. He went down and out. It was over in twenty seconds.

How do you describe the feeling somebody like myself can have at a time like that? I'd come up out of the cellars and the subway dungeons, and here I was standing on the platform above Tita and the boxer who finished in third place as the winning representative of the United States. The band was playing *The Star-Spangled Banner* and a gold medal was placed around my neck on a ribbon. The crowd was cheering and I had to express my gratitude in some way. I don't think I had ever bowed to the public before. I did this time.

I placed one hand on my stomach and the other on my back, the way you see children do in the movies at a dancing school, and I bent low from the waist. The hair on the back of my neck was standing up. I felt the chill of excitement up and down my spine. I don't know how long I remained in that pose. Long enough, anyway, for somebody to say, "All right now, Floyd." Then I straightened up to allow the other boxers to receive their medals.

After the Olympics I heard that Eddie Eagan, who once was an Olympic boxer himself and later became the chairman of the New York State Athletic Commission, said: "I think Patterson could take Sugar Ray Robinson right now." I don't want to say anything unkind about somebody who said a kind thing about me, but Mr. Eagan was way off base at that point. I was

70

an Olympic champion, which is a long, long way from being a professional champion.

A few days after my return to New York on August 7, 1952, I learned just how far. My plane was met by Cus D'Amato and with him was Miss Vivian Costen. There were newspapermen there, and immediately they wanted to know whether I was going to continue to fight as an amateur or turn pro. I had had forty-five bouts—won all but five, most by knockouts—and in my mind there was no question about starting out after the money. But I kept my mouth shut. My answer was that Cus answered the questions, and it was to remain that way for many years. He not only provided all the answers, but I did what I was told to do by him. He handled me extremely well until a certain point. There's no question about that.

The first thing Cus told me was that I had outgrown his Gramercy Park Gym. I was happy about that, but in a way it was like a kid leaving home for the first time. It was a big step into a bigger world. A few days later I reported to Stillman's Gym on Eighth Avenue, where the greatest fighters in the world have always trained. In such an atmosphere—professional surroundings—I would be able to get stronger and faster sparring partners whose experience in the ring would be of benefit to me.

If I had any idea that I was a hot-shot, however, Danny Florio, who had trained former heavyweight champion Jersey Joe Walcott, former featherweight champion Tony Canzoneri and many other top-notch fighters, knocked that out of my head in quick order.

"He has to learn everything," Dan said soon after D'Amato hired him to act as my co-trainer. In the years since I first met Danny, he's been with me more consistently than anybody else in the whole world. He knows me as well as any person could. Maybe it took me down a peg or two when Danny said, "His stance. He fights with his legs too far apart. He hops around all the time. He jumps like a kangaroo and throws a right. He don't keep his hands up."

71

I had to wonder right then what I had been doing for all the time I thought I had been making myself into a fighter. But the first time I climbed the dark hall and creaking stairs up to Stillman's I appreciated the difference between being an amateur and being a pro.

One is like a sprint race. You go all out because you know you don't have to go far. The other is like a distance race—you have to pace yourself and look out that your opponent doesn't have too much for you at the finish. I was only starting out in this race and I knew it.

Going to Stillman's you could see the successful and unsuccessful fighters and those in between. You could see who the big-time managers kept their eyes on all the time. You could see the guys who wanted to give it all they had and those who didn't have their hearts in the business. You could see the fighters who might have been great but were pushed ahead too fast and finally found themselves in over their heads.

Consequently, there was more to learn and more to see than the two big rings with other fighters in them all the time or the many fighters working upstairs in a kind of balcony room where there were the heavy and light bags, the mats for exercising, the mirrors on the wall for shadow boxing, and the rope-skipping areas.

Lou Stillman, who owned the gym and ran it, ruled over this whole thing. He decided when a fighter got into the ring to work three-minute rounds with another, but it was my handlers and manager who decided when I was ready to try to spar with a big-name fighter. They tell me it was the same way when Rocky Marciano was coming up. He worked out first and for a long time downtown at the C.Y.O. gym under trainer Charley Goldman and his manager, Al Weill. At that time Rocky was so clumsy, Weill did not want him to be exposed to the public view of those who knew about fighting, because their ridicule might have hurt him. Only when they thought Marciano had learned enough did they transfer his training base from the C.Y.O. to Stillman's.

It was much the same way with me, so far as being exposed to a real tough sparmate was concerned. Strangely enough, it was little Charley Goldman who brought that about. One day he asked me if I'd like to go a couple of rounds with Tommy Harrison, who was an up-and-coming pro and one of Marciano's regular sparring partners. I passed the request on to D'Amato. Surprisingly enough, he agreed to let me get in the ring with Harrison.

I really didn't expect to be able to do much with him, maybe land a jab or two. He had a really good jab of his own. Besides, he was taller and heavier than I was. He also was fast for his size. Starting out, he hit me a dozen jabs. I didn't want to get tagged with a hook coming off the jab so I bobbed and weaved, but his jab kept finding its target. I could feel those jabs, too. I hadn't been hit with anything as heavy as that before.

At the start of the second round I devised a little scheme of my own. Never before had I improvised just that way in the ring. I began to time Harrison's jab. I waited and waited for the right time. When it came, I let go with a straight right over his jab. It landed flush on his face and he staggered, even with the big training gloves we were wearing. That one punch made him respect me. My trick forced him to change his tactics and go partially defensive. Every time he threw his jab after that, he pulled it back real fast. Once he thought I was going to throw the straight right over the jab again and quickly moved out of range. This was a big moment for me.

The next big moment came on September 12, 1952, when I fought my first professional bout. My opponent was Eddie Godbold, a seasoned middleweight. It was the semifinal of the opening of the fall boxing season at the St. Nicholas Arena. I weighed in at 164½. It was all very well for the press to comment that Godbold had been hand-picked for my pro debut, but it wasn't that simple.

In the New York *Journal-American*, veteran boxing writer

Lewis Burton wrote: "By designating Godbold as the sacrificial lamb, Matchmaker Billy Brown and Manager Cus D'Amato exercised the ultimate in caution. It is a guaranteed knockout."

What's it like when the whole world is right there before you and the time finally comes to take your first big step into it? I'll tell you. I wondered if I could go six rounds. I was worried. I was nervous. I left my family's flat early that morning, but my mother stopped me in the doorway. My father had stayed home for my departure. So had my brothers and sisters.

They made me feel as though it was my first day going off to school. "You won the Olympics, Floyd," my mother said, "and you'll win this, too. You're with good people and you have a good body."

One of the people was right there. "Come on, we've got to get going," said Frank Lavelle. Frank bent down and picked up my bag. I grinned to the family, and off we went for the subway.

Along with Lavelle had come Lester Bromberg, the fight writer, who wanted to do a feature story on my first day as a pro. I turned to Les, as we stood waiting for the train to take us to New York and the weighing-in ceremonies at the offices of the New York State Athletic Commission.

"You want a chocolate bar?" I asked. I went to the candy counter at the station and bought two bars. "Chocolate gives me energy," I said.

At the commission office we were met by D'Amato. He seemed quite excited. "Did you weigh him?" he asked Lavelle.

"We haven't been to the gym," Lavelle answered. "We came straight from his house."

"Oh, yeah, yeah, yeah," Cus said. "I forgot . . . Did he eat this morning?"

"A little breakfast and . . ."

"I know. I know," Cus said, "a candy bar."

A deputy commissioner, at least I guessed he was, began to yell: "Preliminary fighters for tonight over here." I got up to go over, but somebody stopped me. The boxing commissioner, Bob Christenberry, wanted to talk to me. Reporters were with him. They asked questions and the photographers were shooting off their flash bulbs. I didn't like so much conversation. Neither did Cus. He acted anxious.

"Too much talk," he said. "It's getting him all tensed up."

He was right. I had begun to perspire. I was glad when I finally could get out of there and go off to a hotel for a nap after getting a steak for lunch. At 6:30 Frank and I had to meet Cus at the Gramercy Gym before going uptown.

"It's just another fight, Floyd," Cus said. "You'll lick him easy."

In the dressing room at St. Nick's, though, nobody seemed any more at ease than I was. I tried to lie down to rest before the bout. I've always been able to nap before a fight. To illustrate how easy it is for me to pop off to sleep, let me tell you that the night before I fought Archie Moore for the title, I slept eleven and one-half hours. I skipped breakfast, waking up just late enough to dress and get to the weigh-in. I slept three more hours in the late afternoon before going to the arena and had another nap in the dressing room just before the fight.

But this time it was impossible, despite the certain knockout predictions made by the press. I got off the table and Buster Watson came into the room and said, "Why don't you lay down?" I watched Buster and he started to pace the floor like it was him going in to fight his first pro bout. He sat, stood, sat again, got up to take off his jacket, hung it on a hook, then took it off the hook and hung it on a hanger. He got up again and put the jacket back on the hook.

"Take it easy, Buster," I said, not being able to conceal my smile, despite my own nervousness.

"It's better having it on the hook," said Buster, leaving the room, but coming right back in again in a few minutes.

When Lavelle started to bandage my hands I knew we were getting close to ring time. A man came in with gloves. Cus started to help me on with them. They looked so small compared to what I had been used to.

"These are six-ouncers," he said. "The ten-ouncers you've been fighting with pound you. These sixes stun you."

I was stunned enough with nervousness. I could hardly wait for the bout to start. There was a knock on the door. A guy stuck his head in. "Patterson . . . . . ready?" he yelled. I had been waiting for this moment all my life. I was ready. I walked out of the dressing room and through the corridor to the ring. I was wearing my white Olympic robe with the USA emblazoned across the back. It wasn't only the country—it was the whole world stretching out before me.

Chapter Seven

A day or two after I won my first professional bout in two minutes and thirty-nine seconds of the fourth round, I was back at work at the Gramercy Park Hotel. Some time during the morning I was told that Mr. Schwefel wanted to see me in his office.

He was sitting behind his desk looking as pleasant as usual, but there was a serious side to the way he started to talk to me after congratulating me on my victory over Godbold. He reached into a drawer and took out three one-hundred dollar bills. He laid them on the desk side-by-side. I looked at them almost as though I was hypnotized. The sight of those bills carried me back to the days when I used to daydream about being a millionaire with three hundred dollars in my pocket. Almost as though he could read my thoughts, Mr. Schwefel said:

"Floyd, that's what you earned the other night at the St. Nick's. It looks like a lot of money."

It certainly did to me. My salary at the hotel was forty-four dollars a week, but twenty-five dollars of it went to my mother every payday.

"That really isn't much money, Floyd," Mr. Schwefel said. "It's only a drop of water in the ocean of what you're going to make if you can continue to be as good in the ring as some of us think you can. But things can go wrong. You can be beaten, you know. So I want you to continue to work here with us between fights. It will be the safer way for you."

I was only too happy to keep working at the hotel, but the one thing I did want was that money in my pocket. For a long time afterward I'd take my share of the purses in cash and carry it around with me in my pocket. Maybe I counted it every once in a while, too. After all of those years of having nothing in my pocket, finally knowing you can put your hand in there and feel something, it does something for your confidence. It did something for my folks, too. Half of my first purse went to my mother. For several years thereafter, as a matter of fact, that was my policy. Fifty per cent of what I made went home for the folks. Our apartment began to be a place that was much more pleasant to live in.

We finally got a telephone, a TV set, a piano for my sisters and other modern appliances that made life a little bit easier for my mother. My father was making seventy-three dollars a week at the time, when he was able to get work. He was a good family man, but it's so much easier keeping a family healthy and happy when so many people don't have to live on what's left over from that kind of salary after all the deductions are made for old age benefits and whatnot.

As for myself, I started to expand a little, too. I no longer slept with my two older brothers. I began to share a bed with my kid brother Larry. I also indulged myself in clothes. I bought new things like there was no tomorrow. Suits, shoes, shirts, underwear, ties, sports jackets, slacks, everything I never had before and now was able to have. I was like a man who had been starving and then sits down to a full table to eat. He can't stop until he overeats and becomes sick.

I hope you understand how it was. All those years I had to dress like a ragpicker, and suddenly I felt like some kind of Cinderella touched by a magic wand. No longer did I have to stand outside of haberdasheries looking in through the window and feeling as though my heart would break. Now I could walk into a store, see something I'd like, and tell the clerk to wrap it up.

After beating Godbold, I fought and knocked out a veteran middleweight, Sammy Walker, and then Lester Jackson, who had given me a hard time in the amateurs. All this happened within thirty days, and in that short period of time I earned $1,100 for twenty-two minutes of actually being in the ring. I would have had to work maybe a year and a half in a grocery store or shined maybe a hundred thousand pairs of shoes for that kind of money, and things had to get better for me.

So I bought—I didn't know the meaning of the word or its significance then, but I do now—obsessively. I purchased myself right out of my parents' flat. I had no more room to put the things I owned in the sparse closet space. I moved into a flat of my own a few blocks from where my parents lived and near enough to Bainbridge so that I could be close to Sandra.

One thing more I wanted—it had been another of my dreams for years—and I finally was able to get it. I bought a Cadillac. Actually, it wasn't my first car, but my second. My first was an old Oldsmobile, just a few wheel-spins from the junk heap, that I had purchased for thirty-five dollars cash somewhat earlier. It wound up as an abandoned car on the street just six hours after it had become mine.

I had driven off in it after paying the thirty-five dollars, feeling like a rich property owner. Everything went well for a few miles, but then it stopped running. I got it going again, only to get stuck in traffic once more. After a dozen or so stops, the car just sputtered and died, never to run again. Sadly I got out of it and left it right where it expired. For all I know it might still be there on Atlantic Avenue, if the Police Department hasn't hauled it away.

The Cadillac was something different, though. It was what is known as a status symbol—the luxurious proof that a man has arrived. Some people seem to think that this is peculiar to fighters. That's not true. Everybody who has the mistaken notion that he's becoming somebody seems to feel he needs some kind of a badge to prove it. I don't care if the man's in sports or business or whatnot. It marks him as having made some kind of success—at least he thinks so.

Well, that's the way it was with me for a year or so after I had turned pro, but then I got a rude awakening. Mr. Schwefel had me in his office again. He had been taking care of my records for me. At that time I had no idea of the value of a lawyer or an accountant. I've learned since, but Mr. Schwefel had it all down on paper—what I had made, what went out for sparring partners and trainers, training expenses and my manager's share. Mr. Schwefel did all this for me out of pure friendship. He didn't want or take a penny for himself.

"Okay," he said to me, sounding more businesslike than he ever did before. "You've fulfilled an ambition. You're driving a big car. You can't drive two of them at once, so suppose we start becoming practical and realistic about your money."

The first thing he did was persuade me to open a checking account. Then he told me that from then on I wasn't going to see all of my money. Some of it had to be taken out right away for the payment of future taxes. I wasn't old enough or smart enough then to appreciate what had happened to so many fighters who made big money during their careers only to wind up badly in debt to the government for nonpayment of taxes. Joe Louis, for instance.

"None of my friends pay income tax," I argued.

"Your friends," he said, "are not making and will not make the kind of money of which you are capable. Before you get into real trouble, you'll have to start recognizing the dangers that lie ahead for you. This is for your own benefit, Floyd, not for anybody else's."

By then I knew that Mr. Schwefel was speaking the hard truth. It was March, 1953, and I had been made to realize that I had been living like an idiot with no thought to the future at all, outside the ring. Every time I fought I spent my money as fast, it seemed, as it was possible. I had had no withholding on my purses. Even the money I had given to my mother was subject to taxes and, naturally, they had not been paid originally and now had to be. When they were, the brutal fact struck me. I was broke.

It was only a temporary thing, of course, and any time I wanted any money quickly I could have gone to D'Amato, I suppose, and borrowed it. He was good to me, but I was the kind of person who didn't feel comfortable having to put myself too much into somebody else's debt.

It got so bad one night that I had nothing in my apartment to eat and no money in my pocket to go out to a restaurant. It was almost funny. There I was with a closet full of clothes, a car in the street, a TV set, record player, tape recorder and my own motion-picture projector in the apartment and not a morsel of food in the refrigerator. In the neighborhood, everybody looked at me as a rich man. I never went out any more without being neatly dressed, and my name was in the papers now and then. How could I possibly be in a position where I was hungry and so broke I couldn't buy myself a meal?

I figured I'd go to bed and try to hold out until the morning when I would go into Manhattan and get a few dollars from Cus. I tried to sleep, which ordinarily I can do without any effort, but the hunger in my stomach became a real pain. It was only a few hours since I had had something to eat, but my stomach felt as though I hadn't put anything in it in weeks.

Around midnight I couldn't stand it any more. I got out of bed, washed and dressed and drove over to Buster Watson's place on Jefferson Avenue. Like myself, he was living alone. He had taken a little apartment on the first floor. We were real close friends by that time. He was helping to train me, and at the same time he held down a job at Ebinger's baking factory. We shared our thoughts and our problems. Even then I didn't have many acquaintances, much less close friends. I felt that if you get an acquaintance, the first thing you know he starts to do things for you and the next thing you're in his debt and right after that he's looking to borrow from you.

My feeling for Buster was different. From the time I started visiting him and listening to his records, we'd become closer and closer. He still had the ambition to be a fighter, too, and we boxed a lot together. Whatever I learned I tried to show him, and many a night we sat around together talking about the strategy of a fight and the theory of it.

Buster and I did a lot of roadwork together, too. I'd get up at six, drive over to his place and pick him up, and then we'd drive to Prospect Park where we'd run. After that I'd drive him over to Ebinger's. We'd have some hot tea in a cafeteria nearby and then he'd wash, change into working clothes and report for work at nine. I'd go back to my apartment to sleep and later on, if I was able to, I'd pick him up after work.

There came a time, finally, when Buster concluded that he wasn't cut out to be a fighter. He entered the Golden Gloves in the 160-pound sub-novice class. I went along as his second for his first and only fight against a strong kid named David Staton from the Salem-Crescent A.C. Buster knocked down his opponent in the third round, but during the rest of the fight he took an awful body beating. That convinced him. After that, whenever he got into the ring, I was wearing the gloves and he was carrying the water bottle and towel.

Well, I was carrying a great hunger as I arrived at Jefferson Avenue. Buster's windows were dark. I rang the bell and when he didn't answer I went up and knocked on his door. He was in his pajamas. He had been fast asleep. I played it cute. I just said I hadn't been able to sleep and thought I would drop around for a visit despite the late hour.

Buster put on some music and we sat around for a little while listening and chatting. "Got a drink of soda here?" I asked. "I'm kind of thirsty."

Buster started to get up, but I pushed him back down. "I know the way," I said. "I'll get it myself."

I went to the kitchen and opened the refrigerator. I was certain there'd be something to eat—some chicken maybe or something left over that Buster had made himself for dinner. He worked in Ebinger's. Surely there would have been some bread or cake he'd have brought home from the bakery. There was nothing, except a jar of mayonnaise.

"Don't you have anything around here to eat?" I called to him, forgetting completely that I was playing it cool.

"Floyd," he said, "I was going to visit you tonight hoping you had something around your flat to eat, but I was ashamed to. I'm broke. I haven't had anything to eat since lunchtime. That and carfare back here took every cent I had in my pocket. This week I had to pay my rent. I had an installment to pay on the furniture, the TV set, and that sharp suit of clothes I bought a couple of weeks ago. My stomach feels like my throat's been cut."

"You think it would be all right if both of us wandered over to my mother's house?" I asked. "She might have something there left over from supper."

"Your family's probably all asleep," Buster said.

"This is an emergency," I said, "but don't let's tell Mom we're hungry. I don't want her to know I haven't been able to manage on what I've been making."

We dropped over to my mother's. Sure enough, the family was all in bed, but Mom was so glad to see me she got right up. Like most mothers, as soon as we'd barely said hello and told her we were just driving by and decided to come up and say hello, she was at the stove fixing us a little snack.

"Don't bother, Mom," I said. "We had a big meal tonight in a restaurant and couldn't take another bite."

Buster looked at me with big eyes like I was crazy.

"Well, just a little snack," he said.

"Okay, a small one," I agreed casually.

My mother's busy efforts at the stove awoke the rest of the family. Out they came into the kitchen. So we had a family feast. Only one thing was wrong. I kept wondering if my mother knew that this wasn't a social call. She looked at me with her wise eyes and saw the way I was pushing that food into me. I wasn't eating just to be polite.

I was learning a lot of other things all during this early period of my professional career. Against Godbold I again had to suffer a little to learn that a pro must pace himself. I was disappointed with myself, despite the victory. I felt I had fought amateurishly. For three rounds he let me punch myself out. Until I landed one on his chin, he had been keeping me busy in the fourth. Against Jackson, which was my first appearance in the Garden since the amateurs, I learned the value of countering a left hook with a quick right. I beat him to the punch. He went down and out for about five minutes in the third round. The ref never completed his count. I was moving up, no question about it.

On December 29, 1952, I fought my first main event. My opponent was Lalu Sabotin, who had been fighting ten-rounders and had already beaten Charley Norkus, an up-and-coming heavyweight. He was heavier than I, and I expected much more opposition from him than I received. I came out throwing punches, figuring to show him he couldn't boss me around. Pacing was important, especially with the bout scheduled for eight rounds, but it also was important to show Sabotin that even though this was only my fourth pro fight I wasn't going to allow myself to be bullied.

I bloodied his nose in the first round. That's not significant in a fight, except that sometimes it keeps a fighter from breathing properly. Blood can clog his nose and throat. My early rush took all the aggressiveness out of Sabotin, if he had any in mind. The fight was stopped in the fifth. The next day I had the unique pleasure of seeing my name in a headline in the boxing story in *The New York Times*. I no longer had to look down to the bottom of a story to search for my name in the agate type of the preliminary results. My fourth straight kayo rated a little more attention.

I don't think I'm being overly boastful when I say that. The fight crowd was watching me regularly. I was still only a middleweight, but some of the experts, at least, were saying that within a year I'd be up with the leading heavyweights. They figured I'd be adding weight to my big bone structure. Some of the veteran boxing people—for instance, Ray Arcel, who'd been a manager, handler and promoter for many years, and Teddy Brenner, the matchmaker at the Eastern Parkway Arena—were already saying I was the best young fighter of any weight in the world.

Remember, these were their words, not mine. I was just content to be doing what I was told to do. Brenner's boss was Emil Lence, who held the promoting license at Eastern Parkway. The club had a TV contract for a weekly boxing show and Cus sort of made an alliance with Lence. I'd be booked into the club, kind of becoming the house fighter who had a good neighborhood draw, and for making me available to the Eastern Parkway, Cus was given the right to select my early opponents.

Nobody can complain about such an arrangement because, as it was explained to me, advancing as a fighter is something like climbing up a fistic ladder. You must go up step-by-step. I ended up by being criticized for the way I was handled in those early days, but I can't knock any of it. A fighter has to be tested—for speed, for distance, for punching power, for developing the ability to work his way out of tough spots against opponents who have more experience. You don't take a young fighter and throw him in over his head, no matter what his potential is. He can be ruined if he's pushed too fast. It shouldn't be a case of sink or swim. You've got to learn to walk before you can run. I was learning. I couldn't ask for more.

We got our first big break shortly after my eighteenth birthday. We were booked for an appearance on a network TV show coming out of Chicago. It wasn't the kind of deal I was to get later on when, as the champion, TV meant real big money. For this one I was to get one thousand dollars, plus expenses to Chicago and back for a party of four. We needed another break even to get that.

The Wednesday Night Fights were, of course, controlled by Madison Square Garden. Usually, on national TV, the principals would be big-name fighters, but one week there was a quick knockout in the main event and the television time had to be filled by the fighters in a stand-by bout. They put on a real crowd-pleasing show. The sponsor obviously felt this was reason enough to make an experimental change in policy. It was decided to carefully select four up-and-coming youngsters to match in two six-round bouts. I was one of them. My opponent was Chester Mieszala, who was developing a good reputation in and around Chicago.

This was a big step. We arrived in Chicago a week ahead of the fight to train at the Midtown Gym. Not until we got there did we learn that Mieszala used this gym as his regular training base.

"That'll give you a chance to see what he's like. You should be able to learn something about him watching him work," D'Amato said.

"I don't want to watch him until I get into the ring with him," I said.

"There's nothing wrong with knowing something about an opponent," Cus said.

"If he wants to he can watch me," I answered. "I think that would be taking an unfair advantage. If I'm going to win, I'm going to do it in the ring by figuring him out as the fight goes on."

Lots of people, after hearing about that incident, must have thought I was crazy. A lot of them thought I was too soft then and since then. They see a fighter as somebody who would rub salt in another fellow's cuts once he has gashed him in the ring. As I said earlier, I'm not vicious. I never wanted to be. I don't now. In many of my fights, once I've had my opponent cut up

I've laid off the bloody areas of his face. Several times I virtually pleaded with a referee to stop a fight. I recall doing it in a bout against Tommy Harrison. In the first defense of my title, in fact, against Tommy (Hurricane) Jackson, whom I had known for years, had trained with and palled with at camps, I stopped punching several times to give Referee Ruby Goldstein a chance to save him from further unnecessary punishment. If that's the wrong attitude for a fighter to have toward another fighter, then I'm wrong, but there's nothing I can do about it. The feeling is ingrained in me and I can't alter it. Nor do I want to, because boxing is a sport.

I've encountered so many people in the years I've been in the ring who seem so surprised that I'm a quiet sort of person, who prefers to stay out of the limelight. Oh, I'd like to be the way Ingemar was after he beat me. I'd enjoy being able to make all kinds of public appearances, be almost "an actor." That's Ingemar's nature. Mine is different, and beneath everything else I've learned through the years is the underlying understanding that it doesn't make you any bigger, stronger or more important to take advantage of another person. He's a human being, too. Let others who are able to, or care to, indulge in sharp practices. It's not for me.

For example, in this bout with Mieszala, we were fighting in close in one of the late rounds when one of my punches knocked his mouthpiece to the canvas. Apparently he wasn't thinking. He bent over to pick it up in his boxing gloves and ram it back into his mouth. It isn't easy to grab something in a wet glove, especially a wet mouthpiece. He was fumbling for it. I could have stepped right in and belted away at him within the rules. Instead I bent over, too, and tried to help him.

The crowd must have thought it was funny, watching the two of us fumbling around when we should have been going at each other. Finally the referee, Bill Dewey, came between us. He stooped, picked up the mouthpiece, cleaned it off and held it up for Mieszala to put back into his mouth. Not too much later, I knocked him out.

The next time I got into the ring was two and a half months later and I thought I was going to be knocked out that time. Until then I never knew what it was like to be subjected to a determined body attack. If I ever doubted the truth about the head dying when you kill the body, I didn't after Dick Wagner, a hard-punching light heavyweight from Toppenish, Washington, got through with me. He gave me as bad a beating as I've had, except from Ingemar. Maybe it was worse. What Johansson did to me didn't hurt, except in my mind. What Wagner did left me unable to eat anything but soup for three days afterward. I got the decision, but he beat my belly to a pulp.

As it was explained to me afterward, this was another of those fights in the plan to determine what my ceiling of resistance was. Every fight I had to be put under pressure in a new way to get me used to another phase of fighting. Wagner was going to test my stomach. He certainly did. My instructions were to box him and train my body to go the full distance of eight rounds, which I had not gone yet.

I kept waiting for Wagner to bring up his punches, expecting he'd be figuring I'd have to lower my guard to protect my mid-section and therefore open myself to a head attack. He just never did. In the fourth round he had me in the corner and was pounding away with both hands at my body. I could feel myself weakening.

The crowd must have sensed it, too. They jumped off the benches to their feet yelling, "He's out on his feet!"

How I survived that beating, I'll never know. Youth was on my side, I guess. I finished fairly strong. I wasn't quite sure I'd get the decision. I landed quite a few blows, but Wagner's arms were going all the time, beating my belly like a drum. One judge didn't think I made it. He voted for Wagner. The other judge and referee voted for me. It was my first split decision.

We wanted Wagner right back again for a return. It was a crowd-pleasing fight for the fans, but Dick had hurt an ankle and the bout couldn't come off until the following December.

In the meantime I knocked out Gordon Wallace and then had to go eight rounds against Wes Bascom, a heavyweight who had beaten Bob Satterfield. That gave me two eight-rounders under my belt. When I got into the ring with Wagner again, Cus let me fight the way I wanted to. I took the initiative from the start. I tried to keep Wagner from forcing me into corners. I made up for everything I was unable to do in the first fight. I knocked Wagner out in the fifth. He retired after that fight. I'll always remember Dick as a game, tough fighter.

When he quit boxing, he took a job as a railroad switchman on the West Coast. He raised a nice family and was living quietly, but had an accident on his job in 1959. I heard about it and dropped him a note. Unthinkingly, I invited him to my next fight. I should have known that a man with four children doesn't just hop a plane or train and come ahead. When I realized that, I sent him a couple of ringside tickets and a check for the fare and hotel expenses. I wasn't being a big-shot. I was just trying to show my admiration for an old opponent. Right now, thinking back on it, I can still feel the cramps in my stomach from the way Wagner whacked away at it.

There was another reason to mark off Dick as a milestone in my life because, until I fought him, I had been living a lie. In the immediate aftermath of the Wagner fight the lie was discovered.

The reporters pressed Cus about me moving up from the eight-round class into the ten-round class. According to what they knew about me, I should have become eligible under New York State boxing law to fight ten-rounders. They assumed that I would be twenty years old on January 4, 1954, roughly three weeks after the Wagner fight.

"All I can tell you," Cus answered, "is that I know he hasn't had enough experience to go ten yet."

"Well, he's going to be twenty," the reporters insisted.

"I don't know if he is or not," Cus said, and he was telling the truth. When I came to him in late 1949 I told him I was fifteen. Actually I was fourteen. I was afraid he wouldn't let me train if he really knew how young I was.

"What are you guys trying to do?" he demanded of the reporters. "Make him take fights he's not ready for?"

I don't imagine the reporters wanted that at all. But one of them checked the United States Olympic records and found a passport application giving my date of birth as January 4, 1935. I was still three weeks short of my nineteenth birthday. The boxing commission suspended me after that until I could prove my age. I got a sworn statement from the authorities in Cleveland County, North Carolina, which verified I was nineteen. That meant I couldn't fight ten-rounders, even if I and my manager wanted to, for another year.

It didn't matter really, because soon after that I began reading talk about me fighting Joey Maxim, the former light heavyweight champion of the world. I didn't take too much stock in the talk. All I could remember was sitting with D'Amato the night that Maxim fought Archie Moore the second time. The first time Moore had beaten Joey for the title. Archie defended it successfully the next time they met, and as they announced the decision on TV, I turned to Cus inquiringly.

"You didn't turn him down, too?" I asked, meaning Maxim.

"I turned him down," Cus said. "When I get ready, you'll get him, not a fight or a minute before."

That was on June 24, 1953. I had had only seven professional fights and I was impatiently feeling my oats.

Chapter Eight

Impatience is a characteristic of youth, and I was still young. I was, in fact, a rookie, as newcomers in baseball are known. I wanted to be moving faster than I was. That's how kids trip and get skinned knees. But there were plenty of reasons for thinking I was on my way.

For one thing, the New York Boxing Writers voted for me as their "Ring Rookie of the Year" for 1953. At their annual dinner in January, 1954, I found myself sitting on the dais at the Hotel Astor. When the time came for me to be presented with the three-foot high trophy, emblematic of the honor that was bestowed on me, I could barely mutter my thanks to the writers and the hundreds of others present at the affair.

There was another reason. Joe Louis, the former heavyweight champion of the world, made the presentation to me, and you've got to understand how it was for somebody like me to stand beside Louis as he handed me the trophy and the photographers took pictures.

As a fighter, Louis' reputation and record were on a par with the best. As a Negro fighter, his importance was emphasized for me and every other person of my race. A Louis, Jackie Robinson, Dr. Ralph Bunche—these people hold a very special significance for Negroes that goes beyond the normal respect which must be paid to those who achieve distinction. They were all champions in their fields, but more than champions. They were men of history in the social progress of my people's fight for the dignity of equality.

To demonstrate more fully how I feel about them, let me try to describe two other meetings I had with Louis later on, after I had become the world's heavyweight champion. The first was a casual sort of thing. We happened to meet at another dinner. I addressed Joe as "Champ," when greeting him. He returned my greeting. "How's it going, Champ?" he said.

"Am I really the champ?" I asked myself. "Or is Joe still the champ?" I felt at that moment that he still was the champ and I wasn't. I felt that he would always be the champ, no matter what I did.

The next time Joe and I met, he came to see me. Cus' feud with the International Boxing Club was pretty hot. He was fighting Jim Norris, his millions and his monopoly, and I was my manager's big gun. It put me in a funny spot because, at the time, Joe was listed as an officer of the I.B.C. and on its payroll. As much as I respected Joe, I had the greater responsibility of loyalty to Cus and his cause. When Joe made a suggestion that I see some of the I.B.C. bigwigs about a match they had in mind, I couldn't say no to Joe, but I couldn't say yes, either. All I could tell him was that D'Amato arranged my fights. I gave him Cus' phone number. I knew what Cus' answer would be.

Joe realized the helplessness of his position as much as he understood the touchiness of mine. "Thanks, Champ," he said, "but I just had to try to talk to you about it."

Well, just after I turned nineteen, the I.B.C. put out some feelers about my boxing Maxim. He was thirty-two years old and had been in 107 fights. I'd had about a dozen as a pro.

Until this time, too, I'd been fighting strictly as a middle-weight or at weights close enough to it. I could make 160 without hurting myself, but we'd let the word out that I really was a light heavyweight, which is the 175-pound class. The managers of most of the fellows I'd been fighting against always thought that coming on as a middleweight had to leave me weak.

All this while, though, I'd been put on a diet designed to pick up my weight. It was a change from what I'd been used to. I was a pork chop and sweet potato eater. I hadn't eaten much steak as a kid—who could afford it?—but now Cus insisted that I go on a high protein diet. Much as I disliked steak, I ate what I was told. My body became stronger, and each time I stepped on a scale there was something more to see. I had become a full-fledged light heavyweight, and none of Cus' schemes was going to hide it any longer.

Instead of accepting a match with Maxim, he continued to put it off. He booked me, instead, for three main events at the Eastern Parkway and one in Washington, D.C.—all eight-rounders, naturally. Only one didn't go the distance. I kayoed Sam Brown in two rounds, but had myself a much harder time in all three in Brooklyn against Yvon Durelle, Alvin Williams and Jesse Turner. I just couldn't do against them the things I had practiced in the gym.

Durelle, especially, gave me trouble. He was hitting me with uppercuts and bobbing and weaving away from my punches more than I liked. He was the most complicated fighter I'd ever fought up to then.

There was something to be gained, though, even when I was so dissatisfied with myself. The three decisions provided me with twenty-four more rounds of hard fighting against guys I couldn't push over. One other thing happened. Teddy Brenner beat the I.B.C. to the punch. He got Maxim to sign with the Eastern Parkway for ten thousand dollars for an eight-rounder against me. Cus decided the time was ripe for me to go against a man who had been a champion and had the experience that would act as a steppingstone for me. Besides, Brenner offered me a purse of five thousand dollars—the most I had ever made.

Before he signed for the match, though, Cus had a most serious talk with me. "I turned him down six months ago because I didn't think you were ready," he said. "Now I think you are."

"I am," I said simply.

Maybe he thought I was taking Maxim lightly. "I don't care what you hear about him," Cus said. "I'm telling you he's still good. He was a champion."

"Do you think I can beat him?" I asked.

"He won't be easy," Cus said, "but I think you can beat him."

When I was six years old, Maxim was starting his professional career. In his time, he had fought Jersey Joe Walcott, Ezzard Charles, Gus Lesnevich, Sugar Ray Robinson and Archie Moore. I had no illusions. I knew he would be tough, but I also knew that he didn't hit hard.

As if to emphasize the importance of the fight for me, Cus told me I'd go to a regular training camp for two weeks before the fight. That was easier planned than accomplished, though.

Somehow we couldn't seem to make the proper arrangements no matter where we tried. Somebody would cancel out on a deal or else something would be lacking that we felt was necessary. We kept searching, however, and one day while driving around upstate New York looking for a place, I discovered we were very near to the Wiltwyck School. I suggested we drop in and see some of my old friends.

Miss Costen wasn't there any longer. She had retired, but Dr. Papanek and some of the others were. Mr. Johnson, in fact, made the suggestion that turned out to be the solution to our problem. "Why don't you train here?" he said. "We've got the gym, all the rest of the equipment, and there certainly are enough country roads on which you can do roadwork. There's only one thing lacking. We just don't have the dormitory space to put up you and your sparring partners and trainers."

"I know some people who have a farm not too far from

here," I said. "They're distant relations of Sandra's—Lucian and Belle Taylor. I've met them with Sandra. They're over near Poughkeepsie."

We made a hurried drive over to the Taylors. They said they'd be able to accommodate the whole party. For the next two weeks we had a regular caravan of cars. We'd leave the Taylor place about dawn, drive forty miles to Wiltwyck, put in a full day of training, and drive the forty miles back for a night's sleep. It was my first taste of training in the country. I've trained in the country ever since. For peace of mind, quiet surroundings for concentration, and the proper climate for rest—everything a fighter can want—it can't be beaten.

However, I was beaten for the first time as a pro by Maxim. He was the first fighter who never hurt me at all in the whole bout, but as time has gone by I've developed more and more respect for the way he handled me. Still and all, I didn't think then that I had lost the fight, despite the fact that I didn't utter any protest about the decision, which the judges gave to Maxim unanimously.

In the dressing room after the fight, the writers asked: "Don't you think you beat him?"

"The officials gave it to him," I said, trying to hide how much I was downcast by the defeat. "They could see it better than I could. I was too busy fighting."

I learned later why they had asked the question. In a ringside poll taken among the twelve writers, eleven of them said I had won. Unfortunately, it was the state-appointed officials, Referee Ruby Goldstein and Judges Joe Eppey and Arthur Susskind, who counted. Goldstein scored it 4–3–1, in favor of Maxim. Eppey had it 5–3, and Susskind, 7–1. The writer for the *Daily News*, however, had it 6–2 in my favor. The *Times* scored the fight 5–3, for me. The *Mirror, Journal-American* and *World-Telegram and Sun* went for me. Al Buck, veteran boxing writer of the *New York Post*, wrote: "What's another upset at the 'House of Upsets'? It happens often at the Eastern

Parkway Arena; only last night the loser looked like the winner until the three officials voted solidly for Joey Maxim . . . My tally showed Patterson the winner, 5–3."

Despite the unofficial vote of the writers, what happened in the "House of Upsets" upset me terribly. When they gave Maxim the decision, I kept saying to myself over and over again, "You lost. You lost."

Maybe I shouldn't have taken it so hard. Describing me, Maxim said: "He can belt good. He had my tail dragging after the fourth."

Cus tried to make me take the defeat lightly when he told the reporters, "The decision doesn't mean a thing. I'm not disappointed. I wanted to see how he'd go against a seasoned campaigner who knew all the tricks, and I think he went very well."

"Let's get him back again," I asked Cus later. "Make it for ten. I promise you it will be a much better fight the next time."

For some reason, I was so ashamed I hid in my apartment for four or five days. I just didn't want to face people. Finally, I had to come out. To my surprise, all of my friends in Brooklyn gathered around me and told me they also thought that I had won. What was extraordinary was that they seemed sincere. It made me feel a lot better.

I must admit, from that point, I began to believe that some day I could become a champion, too. Maxim showed me nothing in the ring I couldn't learn to handle. And he had been a champion.

That, of course, was before I started to study the film of our fight. I must have run it a hundred times before I started to realize what he had done to me in those eight rounds. He was just pulling me in and tying me up. My idea was to get at him fast, so I just leaped in. If I had given myself punching room, he never could have gotten away with as much as he did. But I had to respect him more and more each time I looked at the pictures.

He'd throw a dinky jab. He'd carry his head the wrong way. He was looking around all the time and it appeared to me that I could knock his head right off his shoulders, but he'd push me off balance and I couldn't hit him solid. He'd lay all over me and I'd be struggling while he'd be resting. Once I had my left glove a foot from his belly and never hit him. Cus never got me the return with Maxim either.

Instead, in my next fight, I underwent the experience of my first knockdown. I was going against a little-known fighter named Jacques Royer-Crecy. He had made something of a reputation for himself by winning as a 5–1 underdog from Tiger Jones. Maybe I figured that was a fluke. I was nonchalant about him—undoubtedly too much so. I was coming off the ropes late in the first round when I ran smack into a left hook and went down on one knee.

I didn't remember going down, but there I was looking up at the referee. I wasn't stunned or anything, just shocked. I had to take an automatic eight-count anyway. The round was very close to its end, I knew. It was just a strange experience. I had never been punched off my feet before. At the six-count I started to rise, when the bell rang.

Back in my corner I could see the resin dust on my knee. "I got knocked down," I said to Dan Florio as soon as he removed my mouthpiece. Frank Lavelle was sponging my face. Neither one said anything, but Cus said, "You slipped; that wasn't a knockdown."

He said the same thing later in the dressing room when the reporters came in for the post-mortem after I'd stopped Royer-Crecy in the seventh. "He was off balance and he slipped," Cus told the newspapermen.

I grinned at that. "No," I said. "He knocked me down. I know he hit me because I don't remember going down. If I had slipped, I'd remember it."

I remember one thing else, starting with the second round.

97

It was the determination that had welled up in me. I felt I had to wipe out that knockdown on the ref's and judges' scorecards real quickly. That was my first taste of how my mind and body react to being hit hard enough to stun me, stagger me, or put me off my feet. I don't retreat naturally. I go forward instead. Maybe that feeling stayed with me through the next two weeks before I met Tommy Harrison.

He was the first important fighter I had sparred against at Stillman's after I turned pro. It's curious how, at the same time, you can have a special feeling for somebody and yet feel that this is the man you must surmount with as much authority as you can. I ran at him almost literally and began to throw combinations from the opening bell. He went down under the first good flurry. He got up, and I went after him again in a hurry. I had him helpless. I stopped punching and looked toward Referee Mark Conn. I didn't want to hit Harrison any more. Conn wrapped his arms around Tommy and stopped the fight. I was grateful.

It only took eighty-nine seconds. When I got back to my dressing room, I received a message from Eddie Walker, who had been acting as Harrison's manager. He thanked me for not hitting Tommy any more than was necessary. Why ruin a man?

Aside from feeling good over Walker's action, I felt great about the attention I was attracting. It seemed to me that nothing could slow me up, but at that point there didn't seem to be any big fights for me to make—at least not in public. Between August 2nd, when I fought Harrison, and October 11th, when I went in against Esau Ferdinand, I practically became a mystery fighter. I hid away at the old Madame Bey's training camp in Summit, New Jersey. It was called Ehsan's by then. Ehsan Karadag is a Turkish man with something of an air of mystery around him, and the same thing surrounded the way I trained for the next year or so. We weren't getting the opponents we wanted, so Cus hit on a novel plan to keep my progress going.

He hired real tough, experienced light heavyweights and heavyweights as my sparring partners. Some of them were training at Ehsan's. Others were brought up just to box with me. We'd fight real wars, but what I didn't know was that guys like Julio Mederos and others were getting paid as much as one hundred dollars a round to get into the ring with me, and they were coming in with specific instructions to try to knock me out.

"This is all out," Cus would tell them. "No pulling punches. Not just sparring. Go in there and bang away. See if you can knock out my fighter."

"You're kidding," they said to him at first.

"I'm telling you what your instructions are," he answered. "Do what I say or you won't get paid."

Then he'd come to me. "This fellow's going to try to put you out. He's not just sparring. Let's see you put him out."

We were wearing headgear and heavy gloves, but during that time I knocked down twenty-two of the twenty-five men who sparred with me. One guy went two rounds. None of the others went more than one. Two of the fighters, who were part of these little wars one way or another, were men I had to overcome later on in my career and who were instrumental in winning me a title shot. One was Tommy (Hurricane) Jackson, who sparred with me for money. He was one who didn't go down. Another was Jimmy Slade, who was a spectator to all this and was apparently impressed. I'll have more to say about my bouts with them later, because sooner or later a fighter experiences everything in the ring.

That fact was impressed upon me most emphatically when I met Esau Ferdinand, a light heavyweight from Richmond, California, whose claim to fame was that he had never been knocked off his feet in more than fifty fights. I had no particular feeling about him one way or the other. I just didn't know anything about him really, but he introduced himself to me quickly enough.

In the first round I walked right into a left hook that landed squarely on my eye. It blinded me and I had to move in close to him. That suited Ferdinand fine. I wasn't very good at fighting in clinches, and inside he was able to bull me around. That was bad enough, but as he was belting me in close, he kept saying things to me, trying to get me angry.

I kept getting madder and madder, but there wasn't much I could do about it, as hard as I tried, because he had just too much for me inside. He kept needling me. "Why don't you punch me, why don't you punch me?" he'd grunt at me.

Somehow I managed to get the decision over him after eight rounds, but the next morning, as battered and bruised as I was, I went into the gym to learn how to fight inside. I had been fighting on my toes. To get power into punches you've got to plant your feet and get leverage. I certainly wasn't doing that while Ferdinand was goading me and belting me.

Early the following year I fought Ferdinand again, in Oakland, California. I fought him his way—inside—although all through the bout D'Amato kept instructing me to box him. "I want to beat him *his* way," I said. This time Ferdinand didn't say a word to me, but I remembered everything he did say in our first fight.

In the tenth round—maybe for the only time in my whole career—I talked to my opponent during a fight. I said, "Why don't you punch me?" He never answered. I knocked him out.

The first win over Ferdinand more or less forced the hand of Madison Square Garden to put me on in a main event. I hadn't fought there in two years. The date they offered was October 22nd and a little explanation goes with it.

In prize fighting, the manager of the world's heavyweight champion not only has the most valuable property in the sport, but he swings the most weight. Rocky Marciano was the heavyweight champion at the time. His manager was Al Weill, who at one time also had been the Garden's matchmaker. A man in that position can dictate policy not only about championship bouts but about others, if he has other fighters. Weill had several of them. One was Willie Troy and Weill had the date for him.

Actually, therefore, when the date was offered to me, I was being given the opportunity to face Troy. However, ten days before the fight, Troy hurt his shoulder in a warmup bout at St. Louis. Weill substituted Joe Gannon, one of the sparring partners Marciano used for speed. I had just as much speed. I had him on the apron of the ring after eight rounds, as I won the decision. A little less than a month later I was supposed to meet Troy again, but again he wasn't available, and this time Jimmy Slade was proposed as my opponent. To the surprise of the boxing fraternity, we accepted Jimmy. We got $7,500 for the fight besides.

Now I've got to explain about Slade. There was a good deal of comment about this bout before it was fought, and as much afterward. Unlike me, Jimmy had not been brought up through the amateurs. Compared to the way my path was smoothed by guidance, care and maybe even caution, it was sink or swim for Jimmy. He had already been fighting as a pro for six years, but by the time we met he had only thirty-four fights. In 1951 he could get only four. The next year only three. To make any kind of living at all out of the business, he had to fight heavyweights, some as much as forty pounds heavier than him and a foot taller.

For example, he went against Ted Lowry; Earl Walls, who won the Canadian heavyweight championship; Don Cockell, who later fought Marciano; 238-pound Charley Lester; James J. Parker; Dan Bucceroni and Hurricane Jackson, who, at that point, was the hottest prospect in the heavyweight division. Slade beat him. Two weeks before he fought me, Jimmy had been beaten by Bob Baker, to whom he had to give away thirty-two pounds. Jimmy was a light heavyweight, but actually was ranked fourth among the heavyweights.

Jimmy and I had become friendly during the days at Ehsan's when sparring partners were being paid to try to knock me out. He never was one of them, but he was older than I was, and I took to him. We spent many an hour playing cards and talking about fights and one thing and another. He had a funny style of fighting and in the boxing business was recognized as a "spoiler." By that, I mean, his style could throw another fighter off and make it hard for the other man to fight his own kind of fight.

They tell me that when Cus finally accepted Slade from the names that Billy Brown, the I.B.C. matchmaker, offered, there was real surprise at the Garden. But they didn't know what Cus knew. Jimmy had watched me at my best at Ehsan's. Cus apparently had seen the expression on Slade's face. He remembered it and thought that Jimmy had to figure I might be too much for him and would go into the ring concerned.

I don't know about that. All I do know is that before Cus gave the I.B.C. the final okay, he asked me how I felt about fighting a friend. "Let me tell you now so that you'll understand," I answered. "Slade's been my friend, but when I get into the ring, I don't even know who I'm fighting."

Jimmy must have felt the same way. He was quoted in the papers as saying, "In this business, who's got friends?"

We certainly didn't fight as friends, although the crowd in the Garden that night responded to the fight by singing "Let Me Call You Sweetheart." I didn't understand it then. I don't understand it now, but who can gauge the mood of the boxing fan?

I knocked Slade down twice in the first. He went down again in the second, third and eighth. It was a one-sided fight, sure, but I guess I just got off too fast for Jimmy. His nose bled through most of the fight, his lips were cut and swollen, and one of his eyes was puffed.

Still and all, Commissioner Christenberry, perhaps swayed

102

by the fans' dissatisfaction with Slade's showing, announced he was holding up Jimmy's purse while he examined the films of the fight. "He never was hit," Christenberry said, about Jimmy's eighth-round knockdown. I knew differently. So did Christenberry after he satisfied himself by taking another look at the right hand with which I had put Slade down the last time.

I fought Jimmy once again more than a year later, in Los Angeles, and stopped him in seven. That wasn't the worst of it for Slade. As soon as the bout ended and Jimmy came back to his corner, his manager, Al Joyner, began to whack him in the face with hard, stinging slaps. What a terrible thing to have done!

I was Jimmy's friend, and if you can't understand how one fighter can have affection and sympathy for another and still fight him as hard and as fiercely as he can, it can't be helped. We're a strange breed, we men who make our living with our fists.

This is how much I cared for Slade. After I had beaten him the first time, I went to a phone booth and tried to reach him at his home. His mother answered and told me Jimmy hadn't come home yet. She asked me to call him again. I called twice more—the next day and the day following—but each time Jimmy was out and his mother took the call. I told her I wanted to be certain Jimmy wasn't angry with me. She said she was sure he wasn't.

"I had to fight him, Mrs. Slade," I said, "and I had to try to beat him."

"He tried to beat you," she said.

There couldn't be any doubt about that, but the fight mob began to explain away my victory over Jimmy by saying that Bob Baker had softened him up for me two weeks before. It was like a challenge to me. Most kids who aren't twenty yet take challenges seriously. For the first time in my career, I went to Cus with a definite suggestion for a match, almost an order.

"Get me Baker," I said. "I want to see if I can beat him."

"When you're ready to fight heavyweights, you'll fight them, all of them, not somebody like Baker," Cus answered.

"I just want to prove I can do it," I said.

"All you have to prove is that you can do what I tell you. When you do, you'll be the next champion. Do you believe that?"

Cus had cut me down. "I believe that," I said.

Chapter Nine

As much as I dislike thinking it, or even discussing it, my manager has been a suspicious man. Undoubtedly he had some reason to be, but over the years Cus allowed his suspicions about the I.B.C. and his fight against its president, Jim Norris, to warp his thinking. Without question, it also warped my career.

Early in my professional days Cus talked about "tough guys" trying to move in on me to take me away from him. He denied later on that he had ever said such things to the newspapermen, but they had written, quoting Cus, that the only way I was ever going to get the good fights was for Cus to let those "well-connected" people have a percentage of me. Once Cus was even called before the New York State Athletic Commission and asked about these charges. He said he had never told anybody any such things.

Maybe he did. Maybe he didn't. Maybe the I.B.C., Jim Norris or Al Weill never were part of a plan to control me, slow me up or sidetrack me. Frankly, after a while, I got completely fed up with what went on in the boxing offices and what had to be argued and done before I could get a bout to make money. In 1954 the purses from my bouts came to about twenty thousand dollars. All I know is that after taxes, expenses, managerial cut and such, I barely wound up with ten thousand dollars.

For a while there, it looked like Cus was doing more of the fighting than I did. He had predicted at the start of 1955—embarrassing me no little—that I would knock out everybody I faced. I did, but I fought only nine times that year and most of the time away from New York, which, after all, is my home and where I wanted to fight.

The old year ended with Cus saying our immediate aim was the light-heavyweight championship, which Archie Moore held. I knew it was just talk, though. I was about to turn twenty and D'Amato still felt I wasn't old enough or experienced enough to go against a veteran like Moore. The I.B.C. had offered him Harold Johnson, Moore's leading challenger, but Cus had turned them down, as they had known he would.

Instead, the I.B.C. insisted I go through with the contract against Willie Troy, Al Weill's fighter, which had never been fulfilled. Earlier, we had wanted that match against Troy very badly, but once I'd gotten by Slade, Troy didn't serve as any steppingstone upward. If anything, he was an annoying roadblock which just had to be removed. At least, Cus thought that way when he agreed to a January 7th date and, in a way, his suspicions were confirmed.

"Make it for ten rounds," I advised Cus.

"That's just the point," he said. "All along they kept saying they couldn't use you because you weren't old enough to go ten. Now that you can go ten, they insist on staying with the old terms—an eight-rounder and at the old weight, 165."

I was growing fast then. My natural weight was about 175, give or take a pound, but I told Cus not to worry. I'd make the contract terms.

Four days before the bout we had to report to the commission offices for a prefight physical. That, of course, included getting on the scale. I thought Cus would die when he saw me weigh in at 174. "We won't fight," he said. "We'll take a suspension for coming in overweight."

"We'll fight," I said.

"We can't," Cus answered. "Only four days to take off nine pounds. They can't give us too much of a suspension—maybe ninety days. What difference will it make? They're not giving us the right fights anyway."

"Look," I said. "You take care of the business end. I'll take care of the training and fighting. I know how to train myself by now. I'll make the weight."

"You'll be too weak."

"I'll be strong enough."

The following Friday when I stepped on the scale for the official weighing-in, the bar stopped moving at just a bit under 165. Troy actually weighed in a pound over, which was permissible under the contract.

I thought D'Amato looked worse than I felt. He was surprised and scared that I'd made the weight. I really don't think he believed I could. I felt as hungry and as thirsty as a man can be. Between the original weigh-in and the official scaling, I had not eaten a morsel of food. For almost all of that time I hadn't done more than wet my lips to keep them from becoming parched. I had literally starved myself and dried myself out. The night before the fight I couldn't stand the thirst any longer. I went into the bathroom and surreptitiously gulped a few handfuls of water. To make it worse, I had mistakenly turned on the hot water tap and what went down my parched throat was warm water. I thought I was going to be sick. I kept thinking nothing can come up. There isn't anything in there.

I was weak, no question about it. But I also went into the ring that night as a $3\frac{1}{2}$–1 favorite, and I had come too far to let my condition or Troy's record of thirty out of thirty-two, with twenty-three knockouts, stop my progress. I punished him so badly in the fifth round, he was unable to come out for the sixth. I couldn't wait to get out of that ring to a restaurant and a good meal. Buster and I joked about it afterward as we ate. We recalled that day at his apartment when there was nothing to eat and we had to go to my mother's. "Money or no money," I said, "it's better with something on your plate."

Buster rolled his big eyes and laughed. But it wasn't funny when one of the write-ups on the fight discounted my performance with the comment: "It was a light heavyweight beating a middleweight."

Whatever it was, I still had to fight. Once a fighter reaches a peak, he's got to keep going, otherwise he'll slip back. I knew that then. I knew it after I won the title, but as the champion, other considerations enter the picture. I certainly wasn't in any ninety per cent bracket back then. If the Garden didn't want me for whatever reason they had, Teddy Brenner at the Eastern Parkway did. In fact, the way he spelled out his problem, he had to have me.

This little fight club on the edge of the Brownsville section of Brooklyn could exist only because of its television contract. Without the TV fees, it would have to go under. It was an incubator in which preliminary fighters and those who had not yet gotten a big name could get the experience every fighter needs. When there are no small fight clubs, there are few small fighters and, consequently, few big ones.

I got my experience at the Eastern Parkway, and when Brenner told us that Emil Lence, the promoter, was in danger of losing his contract with the American Broadcasting Company if he couldn't get a name on his card and would have to fold up, I was all for helping him out. I'm not being immodest. I had become a big name. He had the arena; I had the drawing power.

Brenner suggested a match with Don Grant, a light heavyweight from Los Angeles who had built up a knockout reputation on the West Coast. He had fast hands and, the word was around, was a sleeper. That means somebody most people don't know too much about, but who has a lot of talent that's under cover.

He wasn't a sleeper to Dan Florio, my trainer. Dan had been out to L.A. with some other fighter and had seen Grant box. Florio advised Cus against taking the fight. In one conversation when he was arguing against it, Danny said something about Grant being "a second Floyd."

"There can't be two Pattersons in one generation," said Cus.

That made me laugh. "Take the match, Cus," I said, "so we can give Teddy a hand. But I want to tell you something. In my house there are eleven Pattersons."

I guess I was getting kind of frisky. It's possible Grant could have taken me if he had boxed me. He was fast. Instead, he tried to fight me inside and didn't know how. He wound up resting with his back against the ring post, as the ref counted him out in the fifth.

That was my last appearance at the Eastern Parkway. That was also the last time Frank Lavelle, who had worked with my brothers as fighters and had been a trainer for me from the very beginning, was in my corner. He walked out on me after that fight.

There have been stories told off and on that he was moved out when I began to move up into big-money bouts. There were other stories that he was fired because he was a Customs House employee during the day and could only train me at night. There was another that Pete Mello, who was the Olympic boxing coach, had warned Frank as far back as the time I qualified for the team in Kansas City that he should protect himself.

According to the way I heard it, Mello advised Frank to get a contract with me before Cus beat him to it. Frank is supposed to have said he trusted Cus and that I would stand up for him. Well, here is my own version of how Frank and I happened to fall apart. There is no other. Lavelle walked out on me.

While I was training for Grant at Ehsan's, I'd get awfully

lonely. Sandra and I were going steady by then—as steady, that is, as a fighter away most of the time in training can be going with a girl. We'd talk over the phone, and one Sunday we made plans for her to pay me a visit at camp. We went out on a picnic after my work for the day was over. As we parted, we made another date for the following Sunday.

"Sandra will be up to camp next week for a visit," I told Frank.

"No," he said, which surprised me. "She can't come here. I won't allow it."

"What are you talking about, Frank?" I said. "Seeing her does me good. It relaxes me. I'll finish work and pick her up at the station. We'll have dinner, see a movie, and I'll put her back on the train just like we did today."

"Didn't you hear what I said?" Lavelle answered. "I said she can't come again. This is too big a fight. Grant's too good, and I think you're taking him too lightly. You'll get beat if you don't concentrate on what you're supposed to be doing."

"The plans are made," I said. "I want her to come, and she wants to come. I won't be breaking training. For God's sake, what are we doing but holding hands and talking?"

"I said no. Now, listen to me," Frank threatened. "If she comes up here next Sunday, I'm leaving you. I won't train you any more."

I didn't believe Frank meant it. Sandra arrived on schedule and by seven that Sunday night I was back at Ehsan's all ready to say to Frank, "See, what was the point in worrying?"

He never gave me a chance to say it. "I'll finish training you for this fight, but it's the last one for me. Grant is going to knock you out because you're underestimating him."

Well, I won from Grant and I lost Lavelle. He came back to the dressing room with me after "our" victory, and then, without even saying a word, he washed up and got back into his street clothes.

"Well, kid, I'll be seeing you," he finally said.

"What do you mean, Frank?" I said, because I still didn't

110

believe him. Here I was nearing the top and the big money in which he would share. I couldn't see him walking away from that—much less walking away from a fighter whom he had been with from the beginning.

"I told you I'd train you for this fight and that would be it. Good luck."

He walked out and I haven't seen him since. At the beginning we set aside ten per cent of the purse for the trainers' fee. At first that didn't amount to much, but it kept getting bigger. When Florio was brought in after I started to train at Stillman's, Danny and Frank divided the trainers' percentage. Frank continued to be paid his share for the next six fights, but after that I told Cus not to pay him any more. He walked out on me. I didn't walk out on him. He didn't deserve to be paid any longer.

It bothered me losing Frank. It was like a team being broken up, but what annoyed me most about him was that he didn't realize how much I needed Sandra and wanted to see her. I was serious about her then. Even Mrs. Hicks knew that. As a matter of fact, as I kept seeing Sandra and the newspapermen occasionally wrote about this high school girl who was my girl, Mrs. Hicks didn't want Sandra's name associated with mine unless I had serious intentions. It was understood that we would be married, and I was looking forward to the day when this could take place. Sandra understood how much boxing meant to me and how much it would mean to our future. She understood the long periods of time we would have to be separated from each other, not just between Brooklyn and New Jersey or some other camp not too far away, but greater distances across the country and out of it when fights took me there.

For the rest of that year, as a matter of fact, six of my next seven fights were fought out of town. I was in Oakland, California, for Ferdinand, New Brunswick for Yvon Durelle,

Moncton for Alvin Williams, San Francisco for Dave Whit-
lock and Los Angeles for Calvin Brad and the second fight with
Slade.

Although I kept winning and ran up a streak of eleven
straight kayoes by the following April, it was a terrible time
for me. D'Amato knew it. He could see me getting edgy about
being away from home and from Sandra so much. Maybe he
was just trying to take my mind off my romantic troubles. Or
maybe he was getting edgy and impatient himself for the
biggest prize of all in boxing.

In any event, for the very first time, he started to talk seriously to me about Marciano. Rocky was thirty-two then and
had been the champion for more than two years. We could
not have known then that a year later he would fight his last
fight and retire, leaving the title vacant.

"Do you think you can beat him?" Cus asked.

"Right now?" I asked.

"Very soon you'll grow into a legitimate heavyweight," Cus
said. "We've got to start thinking seriously about him."

I had been thinking about him for a long time. I had been
watching his fights on TV. In the ring he looked sloppy and
awkward sometimes, but that was deceptive because he was
terribly strong, could punch and take a punch. He had fought
forty-seven times in his career and won them all. He'd knocked
out forty-one opponents. That record couldn't be overlooked.
Yes, I thought about Rocky a lot.

"Cus," I said, "I wouldn't be afraid if that's what you mean."

"I don't mean that," he said, almost disturbed. "In your heart
do you think you could beat him?"

"I've never gone more than ten rounds," I said. "I only went
that once."

I didn't see any point in carrying on such a conversation any
further. I respected Marciano. Jersey Joe Walcott had made
him miss for twelve rounds and then Rocky took his title away
in the thirteenth. Ezzard Charles seemed to be making him look

112

bad, but Rocky busted up his face something horrible to take a decision and then knocked him out the second time. Besides, we were having trouble enough as it was getting our fights.

The only one in New York the rest of that year was against Archie McBride, a heavyweight who had beaten Hurricane Jackson twice. He was my first full-fledged heavyweight opponent, but I didn't see him in the terms of Marciano. McBride kept the fight close for the first five rounds. During the rest period, my corner told me that the officials had to have it very close. I started to reach McBride in the sixth. In between rounds I told my handlers, "I think I may be able to get to him now." I finished him off in the seventh. I weighed 170.

Coming back to New York for the McBride fight, however, only made me realize how much I missed seeing Sandra and how difficult and depressing it was for me to be out of reach of her for almost a whole year.

As I look back on it now, I can see where the enforced absences sort of prepared her for what was to come later after we were married and when I spent so much time in training camps, even during the periods when I was not fighting or preparing myself for a specific bout.

I guess it's the same no matter what business a fellow is in. When he's courting a girl, he makes every effort to be with the girl as much as possible. Once they're married, he more or less goes back to tending to his job. Sometimes that job keeps him on the road for long periods of time and the wife becomes disgusted and feels neglected. I've been lucky that way. Sandra knew how much I would have to be away, even before we were married. Afterward, she understood that we might have to give up three, four or five years of our lives together to be able to spend twenty, thirty or forty years together later on. During the periods when I've locked myself away in a camp, she hasn't felt neglected. She's understood it was necessary. In that way I've been able to concentrate on my work with an easier heart.

But back in late 1955, both of us were younger and the separations were longer and harder, or so they seemed. I ran up telephone bills that must have raised the price of A.T.&T. stock a few points. I was forever putting in long distance calls from California or some distant point to Sandra and talking for an hour or two at a time. I wanted to hear everything she had done, where she had gone, and who she had seen. For my part, I would tell her about my next opponent, or my last one, what I felt I was learning in the ring, but mostly I would tell her how much I missed her, because I was lonely and homesick. I knew how close I was to the top, but I also knew how far away I was from the people I loved and the places with which I was familiar.

It's funny how the mind works, but here I was traveling around and seeing things I couldn't possibly have been able to see if I wasn't boxing, yet I found myself not very much interested in seeing anything.

I felt badly that I had to be on the road. It seemed to me that I had proved myself sufficiently to be given the right to fight in my own home town. Feeling that way, I didn't care to go sight-seeing in a beautiful city like San Francisco, which every tourist does. I didn't feel like a tourist. I felt more like an exile.

Sandra would tell me over the phone that I shouldn't feel that way and lock myself in a hotel room when I wasn't in the gym. "Some day," she said, "maybe we'll be able to visit all those cities together, and I'll want you to be like my guide, showing me all the things of interest. If you don't see them now, you won't be able to tell me about them when we get there together."

That made some sense to me, and I finally began going about the different cities and seeing some things. I used to be a great movie-goer, still am, in fact, when I'm not in training. And so, when I spent so much time in Los Angeles for my last two fights of 1955, I allowed myself to be talked into a tour of some of the movie studios.

Frank Sinatra was filming *The Man with the Golden Arm*, at the time, and I met him on location. Kim Novak played a starring role in the picture. I met her, too, and when I told Sandra about these meetings, she was so thrilled I figured I'd better meet a few more celebrities, if I could, and make her happy. Just before I fought Jimmy Slade the second time, which was my final fight of the year, I could sense kind of a commotion in my dressing room and just outside my door at the Olympic Auditorium. I had been dozing on the rubbing table as I usually do before a fight, but this time I opened my eyes to see what was going on.

"Nobody," I heard Cus saying to Dan Florio. "He's asleep. I'm not going to wake him until it's time."

"But it's Billy Eckstine, the singer," Dan said. "I think Floyd would like to meet him and say hello."

"Then let him come back after the fight, not before," D'Amato said.

I sat up on the table and said, "Where's Billy Eckstine?"

"Outside the door," Dan said. "He wants to come in and say hello."

"I'd like to say hello to him. I've been listening to his records for years. He's some singer."

Cus protested that meeting Eckstine would only break my concentration on the fight, but I insisted.

Billy came into the dressing room and I was thrilled. I figured to myself, "Wait 'til I tell Sandra about this. She won't believe it."

"You're going all the way, Floyd," Eckstine told me. "There's nobody can lay a glove on you. Right to the top."

"It's real nice of you to come into the dressing room to wish me luck and give me encouragement," I said. "I just hope I can be as successful in my profession as you've been in yours."

115

Before he left, I asked Billy for his autograph. I wanted it as a present for Sandra the next time we saw each other. He asked me for mine, but my hands had already been taped. Billy laughed and said, "Those hands are for punching, not for writing."

Well, the next time I saw Sandra I not only was able to give her a lot of autographs I had collected from celebrities during the year but I was able to supply my own autograph to our marriage certificate.

By the time I came off that year-long trip around the country and into Canada, Sandra and I felt we didn't want to wait any longer to be married. I could finally afford it. During the year, I had fought nine times, over a distance of fifty-one rounds. The money came to nothing compared to what I was to make as time went on, but it was nothing to sneeze at. My gross purses averaged out to one thousand dollars a round for the year.

"Let's get married right away," I said to Sandra as soon as I got back.

"We'll have to ask Momma," she said.

I got my parents' blessing for our marriage. Sandra got hers. We didn't waste too much time. We drove to Connecticut for the civil ceremony. Mrs. Hicks, Buster and George Warfield, another old friend, stood up for us on February 11, 1956. After I had completed my instruction in the Catholic faith and was baptized into the Church, we were married a second time in a religious ceremony the following July 13th.

As I kissed my bride after we had been declared man and wife, I looked down at her pretty face and just couldn't believe so much good luck had come to me. It seemed to me that everything good that had happened to me had come in the last four years or so, since I had met this shy little girl when she was only thirteen. She had grown and I had grown with her. She

116

taught me that you had to share what was inside yourself. She had led me to the Church and given me a goal to work hard **for**. She had given me a real purpose for living.

"I'll be a good husband to you," I vowed.

"I know you will," Sandra said, "and you'll be a good champion, too."

Chapter Ten

Except for the fact that it began when both of us were so young, my courtship of my wife wasn't much different than anybody else's romance, but it does seem something different and special to me. We were married not too long before I fought Hurricane Jackson in what really was an elimination to meet Archie Moore for the title, after Rocky Marciano made his retirement official on April 12, 1956. Our first child, Seneca, whom we call Jeannie, was born the night I won the title from Moore. Trina, our second daughter, was born three months before Ingemar knocked me out, and Floyd, Jr., my first boy, came into this world shortly after I regained the title by knocking out Johansson.

My wife was in an advanced state of pregnancy the night that I considered the most important in my life. I insisted that I didn't want her to come to the Polo Grounds that night, but she schemed to do it anyway. Not until after I'd become the champion again, did I learn in my dressing room that she had come anyway to watch me win back my crown. She told me my fights were her fights. If I had to take any blows or embarrassment, she wanted to bear the burden and the pain as much as I.

Fortunately, the excitement of that night didn't do her any harm. I was very much distressed to learn that she had endangered herself, but I understand why she would want to. I am a part of Sandra. She is a part of me. All I have to do is look on the inside of my left forearm to remind me of our devotion to each other.

There, in a blue tattoo, are the words "SANDRA—1954."

I had them put on my arm one day in a tiny tattoo parlor off the boardwalk at Coney Island. I have many wonderful memories of that seashore amusement area in Brooklyn. For many years, when Sandra and I would go on dates, we'd head for Coney Island like homing pigeons. We'd go on the rides together, have hamburgers at the boardwalk stands, play some of the games in the little booths along "The Bowery," and I'd prove to her how strong I was in one of the concession stands that is supposed to test your strength.

You probably know the game, maybe have played it yourself. It's the one where you get three tries for a dime at swinging a big wooden hammer at a gadget that propels a piece of wood straight up along a wire. The harder you'd hit it, of course, the higher it would go up the wire, and if it went all the way, it would hit a bell at the top and make the bell ring.

If you could make the wooden spool go up only a quarter of the way, the man running the game would say something like, "He's a ribbon clerk." Half the way up, say, he'd remark, "Now, there's a white collar worker." All the way, you'd win a prize and the pleasure of hearing the man say, "He's a boiler-maker."

I used to ring the bell regularly in those days, but the funny thing is that after I won the championship, Sandra and I took a drive to Coney one night and walked along the boardwalk again. We came to the same game and I said to her, "I'd sure like to try that again."

"Why don't you?" she said.

"Well," I said, "suppose I miss? It wouldn't look good for the champion not to be as strong as a boilermaker."

In those early days, we'd go for a ride out into the country after I got my first car, or we'd drive up to Harlem on a date

119

and take in a show at the Apollo theater. I had plenty of occasions to realize what a wonderful person Sandra was. She was interested in me and me alone. She would never do anything that would be embarrassing for us, and one night I had to tell her the story of a date I'd had with a girl before I ever met Sandra.

I had taken this girl to the Apollo. If I remember correctly, a singing group named the Orioles was on the bill. They were pretty good and worked hard. When they'd finished one of their numbers, they ran out on the stage for a big bow. One of the singers in the group took out his handkerchief, wiped the sweat off his face with it, and then threw it into the audience as a sort of gesture of gratitude to the people who were applauding them.

A lot of girls in the orchestra ran for the handkerchief and started scrambling for it as though it was some big prize or something. My date was one of the girls in the scramble. I don't know if she ever got it or what she thought when she got back to her seat. There was another empty one beside it. It was the one I had been sitting in. As soon as my date scrambled for that handkerchief, I left. I knew that any girl who was so interested in somebody else's sweaty handkerchief couldn't be going out with me because she was so interested in me.

Sandra became my life and, I suppose, I became hers. She had graduated from the Holy Rosary School and was attending Bishop McDonnell Memorial High School on Eastern Parkway and Classon Avenue in Brooklyn. When I wasn't training or was in the city, I'd drive there every day to wait for her and drive her home after school was out.

We'd have lunch together sometimes and at other times drive into New York for a movie or to have something to eat. We must have become the champion movie-goers of all time. On a Saturday we'd see as many as four movies, going to a double feature early, having a bite to eat, and then going to a second double feature. One Saturday we made three double features. I was almost blind. Many times we'd come back to her mother's house to eat, and Mrs. Hicks would always be sure to have sweet potatoes on the table. She knew how much I loved them. There's a birthmark on the top of my left wrist that's even shaped like a sweet potato.

Once Sandra suggested we do something a little different on a date. She said she wanted to go roller skating. I'd never been on skates. I suggested we go horseback riding instead. I learned to ride at Wiltwyck, but Sandra had never been on a horse. So we compromised and went roller skating.

That's just the way I felt about my girl. Anything she wanted to do was all right with me. All the while she was going to school she'd be helping me with my catechism, teaching me in a nice way that certain words I used were not proper English, suggesting the title of a book I might want to read, and telling me the meaning of words I didn't understand.

Without my knowing it, just being with Sandra was bringing me out of myself and making it easier for me to be with other people. I began to see that there were people around who were genuinely interested in other people for what they could do for them and not what they could get out of them.

At first, when I began going steady with Sandra, I was a real sad sack. My face was always somber and serious. I never tried to make a joke. I couldn't see anything to joke about. But her own sense of humor was a contagious thing. It finally got me to the point where I'd try to think of something humorous to say.

When I first started going away to training camps, for instance, it was all so new that I'd try to describe to Sandra what it was like—just men around and nothing but work and very little with which to amuse yourself, except playing cards or watching television.

"Floyd, aren't there any girls around the camp?" she asked me during one telephone call.

I was about to tell her that nobody was around except other

fighters and those interested in the fighters when it suddenly dawned on me that maybe she was a little jealous. "Yes," I said, "there's one girl who has been around here."

"What's she like?" Sandra asked.

"All I can tell you about her," I said, "is that she's got short hair. It's so short that anybody talking to her, even over the telephone, can tell what she has on her mind."

After a while Sheldon Hicks, Sandra's brother, made a trip or two to camp, and I suggested to him that maybe he ought to bring Sandra along after that to see for herself what a training camp was like.

Of course, there was also Connie, who provided us with so many laughs. Or maybe I'd better explain about Connie first. Connie wasn't a girl. Not even a boy. Connie was a little monkey, who was the first pet I'd ever owned. When I got Connie, I started to understand what they meant when they said, "More fun than a barrel of monkeys."

There were some pet shops along the street near the gym on Eighth Avenue. Every time I'd go to Stillman's, I'd stop a minute to watch the animals romping around in the window. My favorite was a cage of monkeys. They seemed to be performing for the benefit of the passers-by. One monkey especially took my fancy. One day as I walked by with Cus I stopped to watch him playing in the cage. Cus could see how amused I was. The next thing I knew my manager presented me with the monkey as a present. I couldn't take the little thing home. I was still living in my own flat at the time. So I took the monkey to Sandra's house instead. Together we named him Connie, and he became our pet. The name, of course, was for Cus, whose real name is Constantine.

Although Mrs. Hicks worked, she didn't mind having Connie in a cage in her home. She'd feed him when she got back from work, and when Sandra and I were there, we really spoiled the little thing. We took him out of the cage so often he quickly learned how to open it himself. Very soon, Mrs.

Hicks would come home and find that he was running around the apartment.

Connie got so that he would run up and down the curtains, ripping them in the process, naturally. He learned to take the telephone receiver off its cradle and hold it to his ear. He'd be turning the television set on and off, putting lipstick on himself, and generally being a complete circus.

I'd want to see Sandra (I'd always tell her I was coming to see Connie) so much that a few times I even left my training camp without getting permission. One time it could have proved extremely serious. I was driving along in Brooklyn toward Bainbridge Street when a cab came behind me and just couldn't pass on the crowded street. The driver began to honk his horn at me, but as much as I wanted to pull over and let him pass, I couldn't. There were too many cars parked.

Finally, I had to stop for a red light. This cab driver was so impatient, he pulled to my left and then tried to cut in front of me at the corner. I could see he was mad as he went by, but it didn't bother me any until I felt his car jolt mine and knock the taillight off my car.

I guess I got a little mad then, too, but I wasn't looking for any trouble. I just reached into the glove compartment of my car for my ownership and driver's license and was starting to get out to swap numbers with him, when this big hand came in through the window and grabbed me by the collar.

The next thing I knew the other arm came in and this guy had a small knife in his hand. I started to struggle then and got gashed on the hand for my trouble. I pushed my door open and fought my way out of the car. I wanted no part of fighting a man with a knife, but I had to defend myself, and I did the only thing I knew how to do. I lashed out at him with both fists and two punches were enough. The knife dropped from his hand and he started to sag to the gutter.

I grabbed him around the body and pulled him over to the

sidewalk. I was going to call the police, but the thought struck me then that I was out of camp without permission, and Cus and my handlers would have to learn about it if I made it a police matter.

So I just got into my car and continued on my way to Sandra's, leaving this guy lying on the sidewalk in the shade of a tree. Sandra stopped the flow of blood from my cut and dressed the wound. But I can say this—I've never left a camp since then without letting somebody know where I was going. Nor have I hit anybody outside the ring since then. That one time it was just unavoidable.

I think of this isolated incident now because once during the time we were going together, Sandra prevailed upon me to let her drive my car. It began one afternoon when I was driving her home from high school. She was fifteen but looked a lot older, and she certainly thought and talked a lot older. We were driving along Eastern Parkway when suddenly she said to me, "Floyd, let me drive."

"You don't know anything about driving," I said.

"I've been watching you and I know everything that you do to get the car started and how to stop it. All I need is a little practice."

"You aren't allowed to drive," I said. "You're not even sixteen."

"How'll I ever learn if I don't practice now?" she said.

"When you're old enough to get a learner's permit," I said, "I'll teach you."

"But," she argued, "if I start practicing now, I'll be a much better driver by the time I'm old enough for a permit."

It seemed logical enough for me. I did a man's work long before I was a man, and Sandra was dating me at an age when other girls are still playing with dolls. "Well," I said, "all right. But I won't let you drive along these streets. We've got to find some place where there's no traffic and no people."

"I know just the place," Sandra said, and I realized how long she had been preparing to coax me into letting her take the wheel. "There's a new housing development going up on Brevoort. The houses have all been knocked down for blocks around and the debris has been cleared. It should be safe enough there."

It was safe enough for a while, or until another driver happened to come through the area. Somehow Sandra happened to get the car close enough to cause a collision. If I needed any proof of how much I loved her, even in the early days of our courtship, that automobile accident was it. My car was my most precious possession. It was almost a symbol to me of my progress in the fighting profession. I used to polish it regularly and keep the chrome sparkling. I didn't go in for all the fancy gadgets a lot of young people put on their cars, but mine was so spotless you had to see it when I drove it down the street.

A dent in that car was almost like a dent in me. But here Sandra smacked it up, and I was more concerned about her than I was about the car. I didn't blame her. I blamed myself for having yielded to her coaxing. I didn't try to hide the fact from the other driver that I had done something unwise and illegal. I practically threw myself on his mercy. I told him Sandra was my girl friend, but she was only fifteen. I told him I'd pay any damage to his car. But after he examined his car, the man said there wasn't enough to worry about. Then he got into his car and drove away.

Until he did, Sandra was really scared. "Imagine," she said, "what would have happened if it had been a police car or he had reported it to the police."

"Miss Hicks," I said, "from now on I think you'd better let me handle all the arguments in this family."

"Family?" she said, getting kind of cute with her smile.

"Well," I said, embarrassed, "we will be sooner or later."

We couldn't make especially lavish plans for our honeymoon when we married, because we always had to worry about when my next fight was coming up. I was so close to the big fights, by then, it was only a matter of months. I had two more tune-up fights—a two-round kayo of Johnny Walls in New Britain, Connecticut, and a three-round kayo of Alvin Williams in Kansas City—before beating Hurricane Jackson in a twelve-rounder at Madison Square Garden on June 8, 1956.

So when Sandra and I started off for Niagara Falls, we both knew there could be an interruption in our plans if we tried to extend our honeymoon. We drove north and made our first stop at Schenectady, New York. It was the first time Sandra had been away from home, and the hotel and room service fascinated her. We planned to move on the following morning, but when Sandra said she wanted to stay another day, I was only too happy to give in.

I called Cus later on that day to learn what was going on, and he told me that he was in the midst of negotiations for a fight. I assumed it would be against Jackson, and I knew that after him there was only one place to go. At that moment we were supposed to be starting for Buffalo, but the talk with Cus took my mind off the trip. So long as I was with Sandra I was happy enough. She sensed my change in mood once I'd hung up the phone.

"Do you still want to drive up to Buffalo?" she asked.

"It's up to you," I said. "One place is as good as another with me."

"Let's forget about Buffalo," she said. "Why don't we just stay on here as long as we can?"

"We'll have room service all the time," I said, knowing how much it delighted Sandra.

"I think I'd like that," she said.

It wasn't quite a week, when Sandra sensed I was getting restless because I'd gone so long without putting in any time at the gym.

"When do you want to start back?" she asked.

"Well," I said, "Cus hasn't told me to come back, but I have the feeling he'd like me to start working out again."

126

"We might as well then," she said. "We've got to think of the next fight."

We drove back home then, but my mind wasn't completely on business, as much as I would have liked it to be. Fortunately, considerable negotiating had to go on before the Jackson match was cleared. In the meantime, there was something else that had to be done—a promise that had to be fulfilled.

I had made a vow to Sandra way back when I was still having trouble finding two coins to rub together. I said then that some day I was going to buy a house for my mother and family and get them out of the Bedford-Stuyvesant area. I told Sandra that after I'd done that, I would also buy a house for her mother, and then when that was accomplished, I would buy a third house for us. Somehow I've managed to do all this.

The first house was in Mount Vernon, New York, where my mother and father still live with Larry, Alvin, Caroline, Jerome and Anthony, my brothers and sister who are too young to marry and start building their own families. It has a nice piece of ground on a corner plot in a pleasant neighborhood. There are ten rooms in the shingled, white frame building. It is the kind of house I saw in pictures back in the days when I couldn't read, but still understood the difference between our flat and the kind of homes I'd see in magazines.

There were windows in every room, not just one at each end, the way it had been in the succession of hovels in which my family lived for all the previous years of my life. There was light and air and plenty of closet space. There was a laundry room in which my mother could wash the kids' things and a big stove on which she could cook properly. There was no worry about having to move because we couldn't meet the rent or about the nastiness of the rent collector at the door.

Many years later, when I saw the movie *A Raisin in the Sun*, about a Negro family moving out of a slum area into a home of their own, where there was grass growing in the back yard and a tree on the lawn, I confess that I cried without shame—

because my family's experience was their experience and theirs was ours.

Sandra and I joined my family in that first house. When I was able to buy a two-story, seven-room frame house in St. Albans, Long Island, for Mrs. Hicks, we moved in with my wife's family for a while until I bought my own house in Rockville Centre.

It grieves me and it pleases me to recall how my mother reacted when I told her to go ahead and buy furniture for all ten rooms and not worry a bit about the cost. She'd spent so long having to pinch one penny after another that she wasn't quite up to spending so much money in one lump sum. When I saw the kind of curtains and drapes she had picked out, I was so touched. She had bought the cheapest, trying to save money for me. She was "making do" again and that wasn't what I wanted at all for her and the kids. I wanted them to have what they'd always wanted but couldn't afford.

I kept thinking how she had never had a new dress, and how she always tried to explain it away by saying she didn't need a new one. She was always at work or at home, because of caring for the kids. She never went out to a restaurant for dinner. In fact, she was never able to go out without having to take the kids along, so why did she need new and pretty things?

I was determined that kind of thinking and buying was going to end once and for all. "We're not going to hang those drapes and curtains or use the furniture you want to buy," I said. "We're going to get more expensive and prettier stuff. I'm going downtown to the store with you and see what you choose."

At the store she'd choose a sofa or a chair and I'd choose one. She would be shocked when she looked at the price tag on the one I'd selected. It was the same with the carpeting and other things that went into the furnishing of a house. Maybe I let my enthusiasm run away with me. I spent more than I intended to spend originally. In fact, I spent more than I had at the time. However, my future seemed secure enough for me.

The way I figured it was that if I couldn't afford to buy the best for my mother on what I could do in the ring, then maybe I wasn't as good in the ring as I was beginning to believe. Anyway, I made Mom get the best. It all worked out very well.

After we'd established ourselves in the new neighborhood, my mother joined the church there, developed new interests, and made new friends. It was wonderful watching her and the kids looking their best and unafraid and not being ashamed to bring friends to the house, as I used to be. The kids went to school dressed like all the other kids, and not being ashamed, it's extraordinary how well they were able to learn. The younger ones will go to college and be able to make something of themselves—whatever they want to be. Raymond, my nineteen-year-old brother, already knows. He wants to be a fighter. In fact, I'm training him and will manage him. I keep thinking what a nice thing it would be if he became the world's heavyweight champion, too, some day. It's never happened before—two brothers holding the title.

It was in January, 1956, when we let the world know that our ambition was that same title and nothing less. I turned twenty-one that month. On my birthday, in fact, I was in a car driving upstate when I suddenly remembered that Mr. Schwefel had told me he was throwing a party for me that day. I didn't realize the significance of the party. All I thought of when the memory hit me was that I was supposed to be the guest of honor at an intimate get-together of a few friends. And here I was just remembering about it and almost certain to be late.

I drove a little faster than the law allows back to the Gramercy Park Hotel where the party was being held. I was a little breathless hurrying up to the private dining room, and when I walked through the door my breath was really taken away from me. Instead of a little gathering, which I had assumed it would be, this was a full blowout. There were more than fifty people present, and right away I recognized Hulan Jack, who was the president of the Borough of Manhattan, and John Cashmore, the president of the Borough of Brooklyn.

"What are *they* doing here?" I said to myself.

I found out soon enough when I sat down in the empty chair that was between Mr. Schwefel's and Cus'. Mr. Schwefel got up and made a speech about me and my ears must have burned with the kind things he said. Among them was: "If I have anything to do with it, there is going to be another heavyweight champion from New York pretty soon."

Then Cus got on his feet and reminded the newspapermen present that this party celebrated my twenty-first birthday, but it celebrated more.

"Floyd Patterson," he said, "is twenty-one today, and the rules allow him to fight fifteen rounds, if necessary. From now on we are ready and willing to meet anybody."

"You mean Marciano, too?" a reporter asked.

"Anybody means anybody," D'Amato said. "I am entering him in the heavyweight sweepstakes and challenging everybody—including Marciano, the champion. We're after his title."

We didn't know then that Rocky was never meant to fight again. After knocking out Archie Moore in September, 1955, he actually went into retirement. He didn't announce it until April. By that time, I was well on my way toward getting into the ring with Hurricane Jackson, who once had been a friend and sparring partner and was the I.B.C.'s hope to keep the title in their hands—or at least to regain control of it.

Chapter Eleven

I could see in Hurricane Jackson so much of what I used to be. He was disturbed, lonely, unhappy. When he was a kid, he was so much bigger than the other kids in the Rockaway Beach neighborhood where he grew up. In classes he was embarrassed by his size and made silent by his inability to answer questions properly. He couldn't read or write. The other kids would plague him, chase him, throw rocks and sticks at him. He ran away from the other kids, and later he became a fighter just to prove to them and to himself that he had never been scared.

All this I learned later, after we had fought the first of our two fights. But from the moment I met Tommy I felt sorry for him, even though he was four years older than me, heavier, and rated higher as a fighter. That was in my early days as a pro when I trained at Stillman's, and later when I started to train at the Long Pond Inn in Greenwood Lake. Tommy needed a friend, as all of us do. I became that friend.

Jackson followed me around everywhere, and he wanted to do everything I would do. We used to go down to the dumps to shoot rats or out in the woods to hunt for animals and Jackson would tag along. "When you going to eat?" he would ask me. "What you going to eat? I want to eat the same thing you do. I want to do what you do."

Tommy needed somebody, and I let him go along with me. I couldn't see anything wrong in being kind to somebody who wanted kindness and needed it so badly. Every man requires somebody he can lean on now and then. I've had several people helpful in that way in my life.

There was a time at Greenwood Lake when Cus paid Tommy to be my sparring partner. There was another time, though, when we were both working up there and there weren't any sparring partners around. Jackson and I got into the ring to spar a few rounds, and before we knew it there was more like a war going on.

It happens often with no malice intended. One guy lands a good punch and the other guy comes back with a hard one. I hit Tommy with a couple of good hooks and then landed a right hand over his eye and cut him. He went back at me hard and completed the round, but he was so angry he jumped out of the ring and started to run across the gym. He didn't notice a cable that kept the ring ropes tight and was attached to a hook in the floor. He tripped over it, went down on his face, and sprained his ankle. The bout he was training for had to be postponed.

That, however, was a long time before Tommy began to make a name for himself, but he kept moving up in the ratings until he was listed as Number Two in the heavyweight ranks. He beat Ezzard Charles, the former champion; he also beat Bob Baker, one of the contenders, and Rex Layne. When he walloped Dan Bucceroni, there was no question that he rated consideration for Marciano's title after Rocky announced his retirement.

I was moving up, too, so it was inevitable—at least after all the backstage maneuvering was completed—that Tommy should have been matched with me to decide which of us would go against Archie Moore for the crown. Maneuvering a fighter into contention is not a simple thing. It is more than fighting and winning and being matched with the man a step above you in the ratings. There is always the question of purses and manipulating for a more advantageous position and not being finessed by the promoter, who may want to control the contender to whom he gives the big opportunities. It shouldn't be that way, but it is. The heavyweight title is many things, one of which is a valuable piece of property. You work hard to get it. If you're fortunate enough to get it, you must work harder still to protect it.

We were a long time maneuvering for the chance to meet Jackson. The I.B.C. indicated its willingness to promote the fight. My manager was eager to make it, too. However, there was one great difficulty—money. The Garden first offered us the regular TV fee of four thousand dollars for a Jackson match. Cus was disdainful—as he should have been. He demanded fifty thousand dollars because he considered such a fight an elimination match for the title and worthy of an outdoor setting. I thought at first that Cus was being ridiculous and was going to argue us right out of the chance to get into the ring with Jackson.

However, when Marciano announced his retirement, the I.B.C. was forced into the position of negotiating with us on a realistic basis. Jim Norris, himself, called Cus and after weeks of haggling back and forth, the bout was arranged for twelve rounds for June 8th at Madison Square Garden. Not only would this be the next-to-the-last step before a title bout, but we were given a fifty thousand dollar purse, although the fight was a part of the weekly Friday night television series. It wasn't accomplished easily, though. Nor was the decision I won from Jackson.

To demonstrate how much I wanted this fight, let me disclose now for the first time that I fought Jackson with a right hand that was badly hurt and may have been broken. Most people seem to think that I broke a metacarpal bone above the last knuckle next to the pinky some time around the sixth round. All I know is that I hurt it painfully while sparring two weeks before the fight in my training camp at Kutsher's Country Club in Monticello, New York. I didn't say anything about it then to anybody, including my handlers. Actually, I didn't know it was broken. I didn't have the hand properly examined by a doctor. I only knew it hurt, but I remained silent because I didn't want to miss the opportunity of fighting the biggest fight of my career to that point. Had I mentioned it, the fight might have been postponed. I didn't tell anybody about it, as a matter of fact, until almost an hour after I'd won the decision.

The newspapermen had been asking me questions after the bout, and all the time I'd listened to Cus trying to explain away the fact that Jackson had gone the distance with me. "He tried to out-hurricane Hurricane," Cus said, "but he finished stronger than Jackson, and that proves he not only can go twelve rounds but he also can go fifteen."

The back of my hand was badly swollen and the knuckle merely seemed to be misplaced, but Dan Florio took a look at the hand after I winced while shaking hands with somebody, and right off he knew there was more to it than that.

Just at that point, Dr. Alexander Schiff of the boxing commission came into the dressing room, took one look at the hand and declared, "That bone is broken." X rays subsequently proved the doctor's diagnosis was right.

"It had bothered me," I said, "but I didn't realize it was broken."

"There's the real reason he wasn't able to knock out Jackson," Cus said.

Immediately, Jim Norris, who had said he was ready to stage the title bout between Moore and me for September at the Yankee Stadium, had to put the bout off. Eventually it was reset for November 30th in Chicago. In the meantime, I had a lot of training, studying and re-evaluating to do.

My victory over Jackson was a split decision. Referee Harry Kessler voted Tommy the winner, while Judges Bert Grant and Harold Barnes scored it for me. Jackson was a hard man to fight, as I knew he would be. He was so unorthodox, you never knew what he would do next. He slapped a lot and laid over me a lot. He would go into a crouch out of which his next move should have been a hook to the body, but the one punch he didn't throw was the punch he should have thrown. He had 15½ pounds on me. I weighed 179 for the fight, and he was so strong that after trying to put him away for the first six rounds and not being able to, I had to coast through the seventh, eighth and ninth to regain my own strength.

Before the fight, I had read that I had to knock him out by the fifth or sixth or lose the fight. I proved that wasn't so. However, when I came back to my corner between the eighth and ninth rounds, I could see the worry in D'Amato's face.

"I'm not going to wear out," I said. "Don't worry, I won't get tired."

I didn't, and despite my own disappointment at being unable to win by a knockout, I knew that I had passed the biggest test of my career. Soon afterward, some of the writers discounted my victory by pointing to Nino Valdes' knockout of Jackson earlier. They said this was proof I couldn't punch. They hadn't begun to say I couldn't take a punch. For all of his fury, Jackson wasn't a hard enough puncher to arouse that charge.

More and more I began to hear and read about what Moore was going to do with me. It seemed to me some of the writers just couldn't wait to see me get manhandled by Archie. I couldn't wait either, but my thought was that not even Archie, as experienced as he was, was going to keep me from the title.

Four years earlier Moore had won the light heavyweight crown from Joey Maxim. That same year I won the Olympic middleweight title. I was maybe one year old when Moore began to fight as a professional. By the time we met he had had almost two hundred fights. I had had thirty-one. It was a strange feeling to be sitting beside him in a room at the Bismarck Hotel in Chicago in September, 1956, to sign for our match for Marciano's vacated crown. All of boxing's bigwigs were there for the ceremonies—including the press, photographers, radio and television people.

At an interview right after the signing, Archie was asked by one of the press to predict the outcome of the bout. "Oh," he said, "I'll probably knock the boy out."

"And," said the interviewer to me, holding the microphone next to my face, "how do you feel about Archie's prediction, Floyd?"

"If Moore can knock me out," I answered, "more power to him."

It was the only answer I could make, but Archie must have thought I was trying to needle him. I was amazed at what he did next. He got up from the chair in which he was sitting and started to threaten, rant and rave about what he was going to do to me. Maybe this was all part of his psychological warfare. I don't know, but he started to tee off on me.

I was really astonished. More than that, I was angered. I've never tried to ridicule an opponent and never will, but Moore was embarrassing me at a time when it was completely unfair and unnecessary. I went into a quick burn. My temperature and temper must have jumped before he was through. I had all I could do to keep from swinging at him right then.

"Excuse me," I said to Cus and turned from the table at which we were sitting and started to walk away.

"Where are you going?" Cus asked.

"I'll be right back," I said.

I hurried away from all of them, down into the lobby of the hotel and out into the street. I needed a breath of fresh air to cool off. I walked a few blocks until I found a drugstore with a phone booth and put in a call to Sandra in Mount Vernon. I just poured my heart out to her for ten minutes or more—just letting all the steam escape from me. When I felt I had cooled off, I went back to the hotel and completed the interview.

Moore must have thought he had scored against me, because through much of the training period, which started six weeks before the bout, every time I listened to a sports program in which he was being interviewed and every time I'd pick up a boxing story, Archie was saying what he was going to do to me. After a while I began to wonder if Archie was doing all that talking to impress me or to impress himself.

It wasn't necessary for me to remind everybody that Rocky had kayoed Archie in the ninth round when they fought for the title. On the morning of the fight we were interviewed on a split screen on the Garroway "Today" show. Moore, of course, was at his training base at the Midtown Gym in downtown Chicago. I was at my training base at Sportsman's Park, a racetrack on the outskirts of the city. The film had been made the previous day.

I was asked how I thought I could match my meager four years of experience against Archie's twenty. "It's possible," I said, "that I've learned in the short time what it took him so much longer to learn."

Maybe it was foolhardy of me to have been so outspoken, but Archie had annoyed me, and besides, I had learned something about Moore's style of fighting by carefully studying the films of his knockout by Marciano.

This was part of our regular preparation for a fight. You can learn a considerable amount about an opponent by carefully studying the motion pictures. I had been watching Marciano-Moore over and over again, and invariably I tensed at one point in the film. "Do you see something?" Florio asked me after watching my reaction at just the same point each time I examined the fight film.

"Run it again," I said. "I think I see something."

It was run again, and when the lights came on, I said to Danny, "I know I can't throw a right-hand lead because he throws it right back at you. Every time Marciano used a right hand, Moore countered with his right out of that protective shell he uses for a defense."

Florio and D'Amato had both noticed this in their own examination of the movies. They could have told it to me and maybe it would have stayed with me, but making the observation on my own, it had to be more lasting.

Buster Watson had quit his job finally for this fight and permanently joined up as my assistant trainer. Also in camp were Grey Gavin, Dusty Rhodes and Clarence Floyd as sparring partners. Later on we also added Esau Ferdinand as a sparring partner.

I don't think I've ever been in a stranger kind of camp for six weeks. As I said, we had set up the camp at Sportsman's Park. I did my roadwork on the racetrack. I boxed in a ring set up in the penthouse of the grandstand. Buster and I slept in a room about twelve by twelve in the jockeys' quarters. As a break from the training grind, I'd ride a palomino pony around the track. I didn't sit still much. The racetrack wasn't exactly meant to be a retreat for a fighter and his party. It wasn't warm enough, and the November weather in Chicago seemed to be conspiring against us.

We had been promised the installation of adequate heating facilities, but the best that was done for us was tiny heaters in the sleeping quarters. Frankly, I don't know how D'Amato managed to keep warm or to sleep, for that matter. He was so frightened that somebody was going to try to do us in, that after I would go to sleep each night, he'd place a cot bed across the entrance to the room in which Buster and I slept. That would be D'Amato's station and sleeping quarters for the night. Half the time he wouldn't even bother to undress. He'd just get on the cot still in his clothes. He was on guard.

One day a reporter asked Cus if he wasn't overdramatizing things. "I know I sound crazy guarding him like that," Cus answered, "but you hear all these stories and you never know."

The real concern, of course, was Moore, and our plan was to force him and wear him down just as Marciano had done. Moore was favored in the odds, at first by as much as three to one, but as fight time approached the odds were backed down to seven to five. I was impressive in training. This was the opportunity for which I had been waiting, and I fought against my sparring partners the way it was planned for me to fight against Archie. I kept the pressure on them as I planned to keep it on him. We knew Moore's style of countering out of his shell and we knew the danger of it, but the plan was for me not to be there when Archie countered.

Consequently, in training I put a lot of pressure on my sparring partners. Ferdinand came out of one sparring session with a cut eye. He was supposed to fight in a preliminary bout on the card. The gashed eye naturally knocked him out of the fight and the five hundred dollars he was supposed to get as his purse for it.

It was so close to Christmas and Esau was the father of five children. I had fought him twice on my way up and had been mad enough at him once to want to beat him up as badly as I could, but at this time his children were on my mind. My wife was about to have our first child. I suggested to Cus that we make up the five hundred dollars Esau was losing by not fighting. After all, I had knocked him out of his bout. He got the extra money from us for being a good sparring partner. I understand that later on he became an ordained minister of the gospel.

Driving in a station wagon to the Chicago Stadium on November 30th, I guess I must have seemed the calmest one in our big party. I had slept well the night before, slept again after weighing in at noon at 182¼ to Moore's 187¾, and dozed later on in the dressing room before the fight.

If I seemed calm, however, I wasn't. I had confidence in myself, but what disturbed me more than anything was that following this weigh-in I tried to talk to Sandra over the phone and my call went unanswered. That meant only one thing for me. Our baby was coming sooner than expected and Sandra had already left for the hospital.

We were finally able to confirm through a phone call that

she had gone into labor. That made me more nervous still. If I couldn't talk to my wife, I wanted to talk to my mother or Sandra's or somebody in our families who could assure me that she was all right.

After a while we managed to contact Sandra's brother, Sheldon. He had driven her to the Queens Memorial Hospital. "The doctor told me she's fine, but nothing's happened yet," Sheldon said. "I'll call you as soon as I learn anything new."

It was shortly before fight time and Sheldon still hadn't called back, when we reached my mother by phone. "The hospital called here a few minutes ago," she said, "and told me to call back in a half hour."

I learned later that a telegram was sent to me as soon as Sandra came out of the anesthesia and learned that we had a six-pound, two-ounce daughter and that all was well. Somehow I never got the wire. I didn't learn until after I had knocked out Moore in the fifth round and headed back for my dressing room that my wife was well and I was the father of a new baby girl. Actually Seneca was born at 6:15 P.M., almost four hours before I got into the ring.

Everybody wanted to keep me as calm as possible and not burden me with extra worries. Sandra, however, decided I should be told the good news. At 8:20, she had the wire sent. Just before the fight went on the air over television, she had herself dressed in a new bed jacket and propped herself up in bed to watch the fight.

When I came out of the ring to the dressing room, a reporter congratulated me on my victory and fatherhood. When I seemed unbelieving, he showed me a picture of Sandra and Seneca taken in the hospital and wirephotoed across the country. I guess I was in kind of a daze. So much happening to a man in one day was almost too much.

So much of the fight was still a blur to me. I didn't remember, for instance, being hit a good right hand to the head in the first round. All I could remember was going after him with a flurry of punches and driving him back. In the second I had him on the ropes, and in my overanxiety, I missed a possible chance to finish it then. In the third I was still in command. I recalled the fourth because Moore got in a punch at my head that hurt.

In the fifth I was so eager I slipped to my knees. Moore charged me as I came up. I caught him with a long left hook to the jaw. He took a count of nine. The next time he went down he didn't get up in time. Referee Frank Sikora had counted him out.

It's funny, the strange reaction I experienced knowing I was the champion. I was elated. At the same time I was sorry for Moore. I put myself in his place and realized how badly he felt. If it had been me knocked out instead, I'd have felt horrible.

There was the usual excitement in the ring, of course, with my handlers trying to pick me up on their shoulders, and there was a victory party afterward at a Chicago restaurant, but the guest of honor had business elsewhere.

All I wanted to do was get back to my wife's bedside and see my child. An hour and a half after I got out of the dressing room I was in a car with two of my friends driving back to New York. I stopped first to send a bouquet of flowers to Sandra. We stopped once more at a roadside restaurant to get something to eat. Right away I could see the people in the place looking at my picture in the papers and looking at me. They recognized me, so I said to the fellows with me, "Grab your sandwich and let's go." I could see it was going to become embarrassing.

I had made $114,257 for the title fight. It was riches beyond my wildest dreams, but insignificant compared to what was to come. A lot more was to come besides the money, because I had no idea at all what to expect as the world's heavyweight champion. I was not yet twenty-two, and at that age you can stand at the top of the world, not understanding too much of what goes on around you.

For almost six and one-half years of my life I had been working toward this goal, and now having reached it, I anticipated nothing but complete happiness, acceptance and, I must admit, some adulation. I was the youngest ever to win the world's heavyweight title, and maybe at that age I wasn't quite as prepared for what went on outside the ring as I was for what I had to tackle inside of it.

When I greeted Sandra at the hospital the next day and she tried to get out of bed to hug and kiss me, I told her she shouldn't be up on her feet. "The new champ and a new baby in one day," she answered. "I can do anything."

I agreed with her then. It certainly seemed as though nothing could stand in my way. I had my share of happiness to that point. I didn't know then that along with everything else I had to take my share of disappointments and pain.

Chapter Twelve

Shortly after I became the world's heavyweight champion, the mayor of Mount Vernon, New York, who had once been a fighter himself, arranged for a torchlight parade in my honor. Not many people are given the privilege to sit in an open car that rides up a main street while thousands cheer you. I appreciated the distinction, but at the same time I felt very strange. I was extremely self-conscious, as though I was under some kind of microscope and had to perform for the viewers. They were good people who were celebrating my triumph, but I felt embarrassed waving back at them. It seemed to me that parades were for presidents and kings.

Later on, I had occasion to go by boat to England. As part of my wardrobe, I bought a tuxedo. We were traveling first class and for dinner the passengers were expected to wear dinner jackets. I wanted to do what was expected, but I just couldn't bring myself to get all dolled up in the monkey suit just to sit down and eat. Rather than do that, I ate all my meals in my stateroom. I felt that black ties were for people who were born into that kind of living.

The point I'm making is simply this: I wanted to be myself and not somebody else. I didn't want to change my attitude toward life and living just because I had become the titleholder.

I wanted to act in the same way I would if I were just another American Negro. In other words, I wanted to be accepted for what I had always been and not for what I had become.

Segregation and discrimination were not anything new to me. I had lived with them all my life, and like a good many Negroes, I was powerless to do anything about them until I gained a distinctive position. By the same token, however, I didn't think I should get any better or any worse treatment just because I was Floyd Patterson. I knew that in certain sections of the country I would be called what people of my race have always been called. I knew that in others I'd be greeted eagerly in front of my face but looked down upon behind my back.

I did not, however, anticipate what did happen when I went on a five-city exhibition tour in April, 1957. I was to fight exhibitions with Julio Mederos in Kansas City, Minneapolis and Joplin, and with Alvin Williams in Wichita and Fort Smith. This wasn't deep South. If it were, I might have understood it, even if I didn't like it. This was more Midwest, so far as we were concerned, except, of course, for Arkansas.

Anything that would happen in the South wouldn't have surprised me. I had had a fairly bitter taste of it in March, 1954, when I drove to Washington for my fight with Sam Brown. Dan Florio had gone ahead by train. D'Amato was in my car with me. It was a pleasant enough trip until we got to Baltimore, when I decided I wanted something to eat. I drove along looking for likely places, when I also noticed that I needed some gas.

The first gas station also had a lunchroom connected with it. I pulled up in front of the pump, told the attendant to fill it up, and then walked into the lunchroom, while Cus, who didn't want to eat at the time, waited in the car. There was an open stool at the counter. I sat on it and waited to be served.

"Please make up two hamburgers, medium," I told the counter girl when she came over to me.

I thought she was going to say something when she hesitated, but she didn't. She went into the kitchen at the back of the lunchroom. After a while she came back to me carrying a paper bag.

"That'll be forty cents," she said.

I reached into my pocket for the change, but while my hand was still in my pocket, I said, "You must have misunderstood me, ma'am. I didn't want the hamburgers to go. I want to eat them here. And I'll have a Coke with them, please."

Then the expression changed on her face. She held the bag like it was something that was bothering her. She kept glancing to the back of the lunchroom and I followed her eyes. A policeman apparently had come in through the kitchen and was standing there glaring at me, with his arms folded across his chest.

"I'm sorry," the counter girl said, "but you can't . . . we don't . . . well, you'll have to eat them outside. The Coke's outside, too, in the machine near the gas pumps."

My hand never came out of my pocket with the forty cents. I was stunned. I kept looking from the girl to the policeman, and I could feel the heat rising in my body. I wasn't trying to force myself on anybody, but I didn't want anybody to impose anything on me. It just hadn't entered my mind that the lunchroom could be segregated. It struck me how stupid the whole thing was. She was ready to accept my money, but I wasn't considered good enough to sit on the stool and eat the food which the money bought.

Just at that point, D'Amato came hurrying into the restaurant.

"Is anything wrong, Floyd?" he asked.

"Nothing's wrong," I said. "I just lost my appetite."

The girl was still holding the bag in her hand. I got off the stool, turned, and walked out of the place. So far as I was concerned, she could eat the hamburgers herself or sell them to the next customer who was more acceptable. I wasn't going to pay for them, even if I had ordered them. We got into the car and drove off. Cus told me then that there had been a police car parked in the gas station, and when I went into the lunchroom,

145

one of the policemen had gotten out of the car and entered the restaurant through the back.

"I went in through the front, Cus," I said, "and I came out through the front. I'm not going through back doors. I don't want to be where I'm not wanted, but when is this stupidity going to stop?"

It certainly didn't stop in Kansas City. We arrived there on April 13, 1957. My two sparring partners, Dan and Buster, and I decided to take a walk and look around the town after checking in at the hotel. The streets were fairly crowded. It was a Saturday afternoon. At one street crossing, we were stepping off the curb when a car trying to beat a light almost ran down Florio. He had to jump out of the way swiftly to avoid being hit by the auto. "Why don't you look where you're going?" Buster shouted at the driver.

The car pulled up to a screeching stop and the driver stuck his head out of the window. "What did you say?" he snarled.

Another man standing near us on the sidewalk took up the cry. "Yeah," he said. "What did you say?"

Neither Buster nor I made any attempt to answer. We just looked at each other. We understood. It was as though a message had passed between us. We were in one of *those* towns. Danny, too, sensed the situation. He was the only white man in our party, but it wouldn't have helped if he had argued. "Nothing," Danny said. "He didn't say anything at all. Forget it."

The man on the sidewalk and the one in the car seemed satisfied, but they moved away muttering to themselves. "Come on, fellows," Danny said quietly to us. "Let's get out of here. They're only looking for trouble."

I suppose we could have walked along the streets then looking for trouble ourselves, but what would have been the point? We decided to have lunch instead. We went into one restaurant after another and it was always the same. The look, the coldness, the embarrassment of being made to stand around while they pretended we weren't there and other customers were seated.

"Let's get back to the hotel," I finally said. I knew I was getting angrier and angrier.

"We'll pick up something and have a bite in the room," Danny said.

We bought some milk, cheese and crackers and went back to the hotel. If I hadn't been committed to the exhibition, I would have told everybody to pack and I'd have gotten out of that town right away. We stayed put in the room until it was time to go to the arena. At least the promoter had sense enough to have made arrangements for us to eat after the exhibition.

Certainly I didn't feel any better about it all when I learned that Jersey Joe Walcott, the former world's heavyweight champion, was in the same hotel for the weekend. He had come to town to referee a wrestling match. Danny had trained Walcott, just as he was training me, and he had told me so much about Jersey Joe's moves in the ring that I felt I knew him very well. As much as Kansas City distressed me, I couldn't see leaving it without paying a call on Joe. We went down to his room and knocked on the door. "It's Danny, Danny Florio," my trainer called after the knock had brought a query from inside about "Who's there?"

The next thing, we heard the chain coming off the door and the inside latch being opened and there was Jersey Joe standing barefooted in a T-shirt and shorts welcoming us into his room. He gave Danny a big bear hug and congratulated me on having won the title.

"It's a big thing to be the champ," he said to me. "It opens up an awful lot of doors to you."

Here we had just come from having restaurant doors slammed in our faces, and it seemed a curious remark to be making. It was especially strange when I noticed a bag of cookies and a bottle of milk on the sidetable next to the bed on which Walcott obviously had been sitting when our knock interrupted him. There were cookie crumbs on the bed and a glass half filled with milk beside it. This was his dinner.

Joe could see the way I was looking at the cookies and milk. He offered us some. "We've just had a bite," I said, "just the way you're having it."

"Ain't it something?" Joe said. "The former world's heavy-weight champion and the present champ, but in this town it's all the same. The oldest champ and the youngest, but both have to eat in their rooms.

"This is a nice town," he added. "Not too bad if you walk with your eyes just looking ahead and don't listen to what folks are saying. That's why I stay in the room here. Less chance of being misunderstood."

If you keep walking around with the bitterness in you, sooner or later it's got to turn into a pain that makes you want to strike out at the injustice. I would never want to do that. If I can't go some place legally, I don't want to go there at all. If I can't fight back legally, I don't want to do it viciously. At the same time, you can't overlook it and pretend it doesn't exist. After a while we took to calling our segregated meals in our room "picnics." It was kind of a bitter joke that made it all easier to swallow. Sometimes, though, you felt as though your stomach was going to turn over while you were swallowing, and maybe it would if a little light didn't penetrate the darkness.

It happened that way at Fort Smith, our last stop on the exhibition tour, which was a long and boring train ride from Wichita, Kansas. Our spirits weren't lifted any by the "reception committee," which greeted the arrival of our train. About fifty people were there as we stepped down—all frozen-faced and kind of spread out on the station platform so that they formed a half circle which blocked our path. Nobody said anything, but you got the feeling that they were saying to themselves, "So you're here and we're not too happy about it. Do you want to make something out of it?"

148

Of course, we had expected the promoter to be on hand to meet us on our arrival, but he was nowhere to be seen. So we just stood there with our luggage beside us looking at those people in silence, and they continued to stare—or maybe glare—at us. We had to go into town or else go back into the train, but we did nothing until a black-suited figure emerged from the crowd and approached us with his hand out.

"I'm Father Delaney," he said. "I want to welcome you to town and show you around."

Father Samuel J. Delaney was the pastor of St. John the Baptist Catholic Church in Fort Smith, which is part of the Little Rock Diocese. I don't know if he was a fight fan, but he certainly turned out to be a friend. He suggested we all go into town in his car, and on the way he suggested with the proper understanding of a ticklish situation that perhaps we would be more comfortable at his rectory than in a segregated hotel.

We accepted his invitation gladly and couldn't have been happier after we got there. The rooms were plain, of course, but there was an atmosphere of cordiality that we badly needed at that moment. Father Delaney typified that atmosphere. He was a short man in his early fifties, with a pleasant voice, but a realistic approach to the problem he was facing. As kindly as he could, he explained the racial situation in Fort Smith and the difficulties he was experiencing attempting to achieve integration in his church.

"I've been working on this for the eight years I've been here," he said. "We're making progress, but it's very slow."

Later on, Father Delaney told us how he also had been working so long to get some integration in the schools. He had suggested an approach to his bishop when he first arrived in Fort Smith. He wanted to take colored graduates from the eighth grade and enter them in St. Scholastica Academy, a girls' school run by the Benedictine Sisters. The Bishop agreed to the plan, which was started first with two Negro Catholic girls.

The following year Father Delaney received Bishop Fletcher's permission to enter some non-Catholic Negro girls in

St. Scholastica. The children were possible converts to Catholicism and were eager to begin their studies. "We succeeded in that," Father Delaney said, "and it certainly seems possible to succeed anywhere. My church, though, is a different proposition."

The priest then told us about the difficulties he was having trying to integrate his church. St. John the Baptist was located in a Negro area. During the hot summer months, attendance fell off. With the drop in attendance came a natural drop in contributions. Any campaign of education required money. Father Delaney just didn't have it available.

Believe it or not, despite all this, I didn't realize that I was putting on my exhibition in a segregated arena until I was in the ring boxing Alvin Williams. The crowd around ringside was well dressed and all white. They were mannerly, if subdued, for a fight crowd. However, during the course of the four rounds there was loud cheering from a section of seats a good distance away from ringside which I couldn't see because of the bright ring lights overhead. Only when I left the ring afterward could I see that the only Negroes in the audience were seated all together in that section from which the cheering had come.

I must confess I had never thought much before about being a Negro who unwittingly contributed to the oppression of my own people by fighting in an arena where segregation was practiced. I vowed right then and there that it would never happen again. If Negroes couldn't buy a ticket to sit anywhere that anybody else could, then I wasn't going to fight in any such place.

Almost as though it were an omen, a messenger came into the dressing room while I was forming this resolution in my own mind. He handed me an invitation to have dinner in a big restaurant in town. I was being invited by the owner.

"Can everybody in my party go?" I asked.

"I'll have to find out," said the man who had brought the invitation.

He returned to the dressing room in a few moments. "If you insist upon everybody coming," he said, "it's all right, but they'll have to go in through the back door. You, of course, can come through the front."

"If all of us can't go through the front door," I answered, "then none of us is going in through the back."

Gosh, I was angry. My stomach actually was heaving. I had all I could do to get any food into me at all when Father Delaney invited my whole party to have dinner at a "white" restaurant in the outskirts of the city. He had made the arrangements with the owner, whom he knew. Following the dinner I told Cus I wanted to leave that city on the first train. It didn't arrive in Fort Smith until nearly dawn. We went back to Father Delaney's rectory and talked some more about what had happened.

On the train I talked it all over with Cus. Father Delaney had been so decent to us and was trying to teach decency in Fort Smith. He needed money to further his ideas. I thought the least we could do for him was to help him get it. After returning to New York, we sent him a check for three thousand dollars, which he put to good use in his church. He bought two five-ton air conditioning units, to help combat the loss of church attendance in hot weather, and had some money left over to fix up his school a bit as well. We learned later that to some degree St. John the Baptist Church was achieving integration. Why should it be any other way? In the Lord's eyes there is no color. There are only human beings who believe.

I've gone into this touchy question so deeply here because I believe that, as the champion, I have an obligation to those who may look up to me. I don't pride myself upon being better than others whose skin is the same color as mine. I've just been luckier. But for every bit of the luck I've had, I've also taken on responsibilities that go beyond me and my immediate family and the way in which I've earned my living.

I didn't believe I could carry much weight in this fight until I became the champion. After I did, I began to see that it was possible to do some good through my position. I have never gone into the ring against a white opponent thinking it was a fight between the races. Against Roy Harris of Cut and Shoot, Texas, the thought crossed my mind before the fight. I heard tell how they were raising Confederate flags around his home and that "Roy was going to whup me." I knew my people were cheering for me more in that fight than in any other I had had before. I wanted to win very badly, but once inside the ring, Harris was just another opponent to me—not a white one, certainly not a Southern white one. I could have chopped him up after a while, but my feeling was that one man should never ruin another.

There is a point, though, where you must take a stand, and I've taken it. When my wife was refused a second appointment at a massage parlor in Rockville Centre, I sued under the anti-discrimination laws. Most people seem to think it was a beauty parlor against which I took legal action. It was not.

Before I signed for the third fight with Ingemar to take place in Miami Beach, I insisted upon a stipulation in the contract that there could be no segregation of Negroes in the sale of tickets. It would have cost the promoters a ten-thousand-dollar penalty if I had been the least bit dissatisfied with the seating arrangements.

I made them post the check with me in advance. The day after the fight, when I had concluded to my own satisfaction that no segregation whatever had been practiced, I returned the check and in its place contributed ten thousand dollars of my own money to the National Association for the Advancement of Colored People, of which I am a life member.

Some of you readers may think I am supersensitive about this subject. I think I'm merely being realistic, as anybody in my position should be. I am just part of the social history of our time and our country, and I can't lag behind it—or run too far ahead of it. Just because I've got mine is no reason to close my eyes to what still must be done.

Sure, as Floyd Patterson I can do more than other Negroes, but let me tell you what happened when I was training in Indianapolis to fight Brian London. Then put yourself in my place and in my skin and decide in your own conscience how you would feel.

My trainer, Danny, found it necessary to take our speed bag into town to a shoemaker to have the leather thong repaired. I went with him, but while the job was being done I went into a little candy store next door for a drink. The woman behind the counter looked at me inquiringly. "I'll have a Coke, please," I said.

"We got none," she said.

"A Pepsi will do," I said.

"We got none," she repeated.

There was another customer in the store drinking from a bottle that looked very much like a Coke to me. "I'll have what he's drinking," I said.

"Don't you know we don't serve *you people* in here?" she said.

Without saying another word, I left the store and went back into the shoemaker's shop where Danny was about to be handed the repaired speed bag. "Fine neighborhood we're in," I told Danny. "I went for a drink next door and was told very bluntly that they don't serve Negroes."

The shoemaker couldn't help hearing what I said. He was aghast. "Maybe," he said, "that stupid woman won't serve you, but in my shop it's a privilege."

He must have spread the story among the other shopkeepers on the street. One of them sent me a lawn mower for my home. Another sent my wife a sewing machine. Others sent notes saying how sorry they were that I had been insulted.

They must have told the candy-store woman what they

thought of her, too. "Well, how was I to know he was the heavyweight champion of the world?" she said.

Great answer, wasn't it? So long as I'm the champion I'll get the courtesy that other people normally should get, but don't. Once I lose my title, according to this woman, I'm supposed to go back to being a second-class citizen.

I don't go for that, and I'll fight against it at any cost. My deep conviction on this subject is unalterable. For the Miami Beach fight against Ingemar, for instance, the original training plans called for us to set up a camp at Homestead, Florida, a completely segregated town. The white members of my party were to sleep in one house and eat where they wanted to. The colored members were to live in another house, eat alone, and would have to find a colored barber to have their hair cut. I learned about these arrangements before I left New York. If that's the way it had to be, I would have cancelled the fight.

Fortunately, Bill Fugazy, whose Feature Sports, Inc., promoted the fight, appreciated how serious I was. He made hurried new arrangements. He rented a beautiful house for me and my entire party at 2815 Pinetree Drive, Miami Beach. A ring with full gym equipment was set up in a ballroom at the swank Deauville Hotel, where, unfortunately, I could not have the privacy I need to prepare properly for an opponent as good as Johansson was. I need seclusion. Fighting is a serious business, and preparing for a fight is just as serious. But Miami Beach is a vacation spot, and I couldn't be hiding myself away in the hotel gym holding secret training when some of the guests wanted to see me work.

I'm not using that as an excuse for getting knocked down by Ingemar a couple of times in that fight. I'm merely using it as an illustration of how far I will go to combat segregation. One night recently I mentioned this to a friend of mine.

He said, "You took an awful chance of getting beaten by training where you couldn't prepare for the fight the best way you were able to. You must have the courage of your convictions."

I have my convictions, but in this fight for the dignity of man I don't profess to have courage. Those kids down in Mississippi who were staging the lunchroom sitdowns, they had courage, more than any fighter has ever shown in the ring or ever will show. I read a story about them at the time. They came into this lunchroom and rested their hands on the counter over the menus. The man behind the counter ran into the kitchen and came out wielding a meat cleaver.

"Get your hands off there and get out or I'll chop your fingers off," he ranted.

Those kids were afraid, but they kept their fingers right where they were. That's courage.

Chapter Thirteen

I want to backtrack just a little bit here because it will demonstrate that life does not become simpler once a man achieves the goal toward which he has been striving. It takes years to make a good fighter. It takes more years to make a champion. It takes a lifetime to make a man who can truthfully say he has solved even half the riddle of living.

A couple of weeks after I knocked out Moore, I had re-established myself in training at the Long Pond Inn in Greenwood Lake, New York. At that time we didn't know what we were training for, who my next opponent would be, or when my first title defense would be held.

The government was pounding away in an antitrust action against the I.B.C. on one side, and Cus was pounding away on the other. Eventually the cat was let out of the bag when it was announced that Emil Lence, who had promoted so many of my early fights at the Eastern Parkway Arena, would promote my first defense against Hurricane Jackson on July 29, 1957, at the Polo Grounds. The significant thing here, of course, was that not since 1949 had anybody other than the I.B.C. put on a heavyweight title fight. For many years before that, Mike Jacobs' 20th-Century Sporting Club held the monopoly on such bouts.

This was the start of a new era in boxing, but the full extent of the novelty was not even known at the time Lence announced he had signed Jackson to meet me. Almost at the same time, but kept secret for a while, was the fact that it had also been arranged for me to meet Pete Rademacher, the former Olympic heavyweight champion, who never before had fought as a professional until we got into the ring. I was guaranteed $250,000 to fight an amateur. As much as that could damage my prestige, it certainly couldn't hurt my bank account.

So there I was at Greenwood Lake many months before my first bout as the champion when I was visited by Bill Heinz, a writer who had done many stories about me and with whom I had become extremely friendly. Heinz arrived about one o'clock one afternoon and sent word up to me that he wanted to sit around and chat. I told him I'd be down in about a half hour, but it wasn't until about 4:30 that I finally did meet Bill in the gym.

What happened was this: I had come downstairs to keep my date with Bill, but as I was about to come into the dining room at the Long Pond Inn, I saw that the room, which usually is quiet and deserted, had filled up with a bunch of teen-agers who had been skating on the lake. I turned around and went back upstairs to my room until the kids had left.

"You're the world's heavyweight champion now," Bill said to me when we sat down to talk. "Doesn't that give you the sense of security to walk through a room of teen-agers?"

"No," I answered truthfully. "I still don't like to be stared at."

Consider that for a moment and perhaps you'll understand me better. I wanted more than anything else in the world to be recognized and accepted as a good champion, a worthy successor to Marciano, Louis, Tunney and Dempsey, but the boxing world wasn't really accepting me as such. I knew that I had to prove myself against future opponents, but though I wore the crown, I was being derided in the papers. Because I didn't knock out Jackson the first time, I was accused of being a

157

champion without a punch. When I did knock out Moore, I was accused of having beaten an old man way over the hill who had been ruined by Marciano. A lot of people didn't think me worthy of the title because of my age, because I wasn't big enough or vicious enough. It becomes kind of a mental obstacle when you compare such judgments with what you thought the title eventually would mean while you were moving toward it.

And so, training for Jackson, I was both bothered and angered by some of the things that he was being quoted as saying. For instance, a writer who had visited Jackson's camp at Columbia, New Jersey, came directly to my camp and repeated to me a question he had asked Jackson. "What would the title mean to you if you won it?"

Jackson answered: "The championship's nothing. I wouldn't feel better winning or losing."

This answer discounted everything I was hoping for. Jackson was the Number One contender, but I couldn't help thinking, "If I beat him again, the writers will find something else to make a victory mean nothing." I was torn between my sympathy for Jackson, who needed help, and the intensity of my own ambition to prove that I was not an impostor on the heavyweight throne. It was a strange time for me because I knew that Tommy's management should guide him in the things he said and did. At the same time, I was more determined than ever to score a knockout against him. I knew I had never fought anybody so durable. From our first fight, I had learned you could stick nails in him and not hurt him.

It was a one-sided fight until Referee Ruby Goldstein stepped in and stopped the bout at 1:52 of the tenth round to save Tommy from further unnecessary punishment. I had hoped the referee would stop the fight sooner. Tommy was not defending himself much. I had knocked him down in the first, again in the second, and again in the ninth. He didn't win a single round on any of the official cards.

His left eye was swollen, his mouth was chopped up, his nose dripped blood, but he kept mumbling to me, "You're a bum."

Before I knocked him down in the ninth round and he took a count of four, he gasped at me, "You're nothing." Five, six seconds later I hooked him with a right hand and that time I thought he'd stay down. He looked dazed, but he got up.

In the dressing room later, I was asked if I became discouraged when Jackson was able to get to his feet the last time. "Why should I be discouraged?" I said. "It was him who was down, not me."

I was discouraged, though, the following morning when I read the reactions to my victory in the sports sections. I was a poor representative as a champion, it was written. I couldn't knock out a man who had no defense. What most writers glossed over in their reports was that Jackson had to be taken to the hospital the day after the fight. I was unmarked, except in my spirit.

Twenty-three days later I was back in the ring against Pete Rademacher, the former Army lieutenant who had won the Olympic and National A.A.U. heavyweight titles. He had a record of seventy-nine fights, none of them more than three rounds, but all of them as an amateur. And here he was in his first fight as a pro going against the professional champion.

It was a mistake. I knew it long before I climbed the steps into the ring at the stadium in Seattle, Washington. But the mistake was not participating in this unprecedented bout, as Julius Helfand, then boxing commissioner in New York, the National Boxing Association, and critics all over the country were shouting. Fighting an amateur for a $250,000 guarantee is never a mistake for a man who makes his living fighting.

I'll say this now without shame: Line up a dozen amateurs and guarantee me a quarter of a million dollars for fighting each one, and I'll take them on in one fight after another. My net purse against Jackson was only $46,910.11. My expenses for nine and a half months of training in 1957 came to

$119,890.78. The Rademacher bout was a matter of necessity to show a profit for the year.

No, the mistake was meeting Rademacher so soon after I had worked myself up to a physical and emotional peak for Jackson. I knew he was an amateur. I knew he had never fought more than three rounds, and we were to go fifteen, if necessary. All of it was just too much for me to continue to generate enthusiasm inside myself for combat against an opponent who had so little chance of beating me.

I realize now that, feeling that way, I was virtually going into the ring unprepared. I was to learn a more serious lesson three years later when, without realizing it, I lost interest against Johansson. More than anything else, that was the reason for being knocked out by the Swede, and this is no alibi. It will never happen again, if I can help it. No matter whom I fight from this point on I will always keep in mind that no matter who your opponent is, you must keep your interest at a maximum to keep the danger at a minimum. There is always a chance of losing the title against a good fighter, but a poor fighter wants to beat you just as much.

The fight on August 22, 1957, was a weird one, perhaps the strangest in the history of boxing. It wasn't something cooked up on the spur of the moment, certainly not from Rademacher's point of view. Ever since he won the Olympic title in 1956 he had the wild idea in mind that he could start at the top in boxing. He talked it over with a lot of people. Most of them thought it was crazy. All, that is, except Joe Gannon, who went the distance with me in 1954. Gannon was a boxing inspector in Washington, D.C., when Rademacher told him about his dream. Gannon broached the idea to Cus. At first Cus thought it was preposterous, but it's funny how a quarter of a million dollars makes the impossible look possible.

The guarantee was put up by a group called "Youth Unlimited," of which Rademacher was a vice president. Pete Jennings, a wealthy sportsman, was the guiding hand behind the group. Actually, Rademacher fought for a salary, and for what it could mean to him if he put up a good showing against me. Jack Hurley, an old-time fight promoter and manager from the Northwest, was brought in as promoter. The fight was arranged for Seattle because Rademacher had attended college in Washington and lived in Grandview out there. He was something of a local hero. Years ago it was not unusual to match a local hero against a big-time touring fighter.

It took us two and a half days to make the trip by train across the country. I don't favor flying. I exercised as best I could in my bedroom aboard the train, and sometimes during the trip I shadow boxed and skipped rope in the baggage car. I stretched my legs on station platforms when the train made an extended stop, but most of the time during the trip I slept or did some sight-seeing sitting in the train's observation dome.

In my mind, of course, was the appreciation that I didn't have to extend myself early in the bout. It was simple logic to expect that Rademacher couldn't be in condition to go too far in the fight, and my plan was to let him wear himself out early, after which I could bring the fight to him and knock him out. The experts, of course, were predicting that this lopsided match couldn't go more than the first punch or the first round—two at the most.

Actually, I knocked him down six times before he went down for a seventh in the sixth round and was counted out. But let me set the record clear for anybody who still believes that I merely slipped when I went down in the second round. Tommy Loughran, the former light heavyweight champion, who refereed the bout, didn't count, but the timekeeper reached four before I got to my feet.

As I say, I was careless. I shouldn't have been, not after Rademacher's rush at me in the first round. I got hit with a right hand in the second and I did go down. It wasn't a slip, but I was more embarrassed than hurt by the knockdown. They tell me I grinned on the canvas. I didn't know that. All I knew was that an amateur had knocked me down and I had better start putting a stop to the foolishness. I did start in the third round when I put him down for his first nine count. It was only a matter of time then before I would finish it. I will say this for Rademacher. He didn't disgrace himself that night. I don't think I did either.

If I had a bitter taste in my mouth after the Rademacher bout, it resulted from a far different reason. It was a rebuff that hurt me terribly at the time. Gradually the pain wore off, but even recalling the injustice of it now makes me uncomfortable. It all started happily when I began to train for the first defense of my title. A couple of little kids, nine or ten years old, who lived in Greenwood Lake would stop at the Long Pond Inn where I was boxing. They came around for several days and seemed so interested in what I was doing that I started to talk to them. Their enthusiasm was so great that one day I asked them if they'd like to fool around in the ring after I was done.

"Gee, could we?" they said.

"Why not? I'll show you how to do things," I said.

I'd never seen such enthusiasm in such little kids. I got my own speed bag and showed them how to punch it. I began to show them how to hold up their hands and move around and then the next thing I knew the two boys had brought one other and then two more. In a few days more we had seven in all, six white boys and one Negro.

We became such good friends that I looked forward every day to seeing the kids. Some of them I even gave nicknames, which I used whenever I addressed them. Robert LaParte, I called "Atlas." Tony Chila was "Shorty." Ray Pollaro was "Geronimo" and his twin brother Russell was "Satan." Another I named "No. 1 Son." Other kids were "Something Wrong," Albert and Philip. As time went on I kept track of their school marks. I gave a trophy to the best boy, not just for boxing, but for how he behaved. I visited their homes, had dinner with them and their parents, and the kids and I would take long walks and just talk.

I made it a point with the boys to emphasize that just because I was teaching them to box, that was no reason for them to pick on other kids at school. One day the bigger lesson I was trying to teach them got its big test. We were walking along the road to Warwick, New York, when another boy we didn't know came along the road and grabbed a stick that one of my boys was carrying and threatened them with it. I looked to see if my kids would make a fist or try to hit him, but my kids didn't. I felt good about that, although I knew my kids could handle themselves.

You see, I didn't care if they became fighters or anything like that. When they came to me, they couldn't hold up their hands, but after about six or seven months these kids were able to move around the ring throwing combinations, jabbing and hooking and hitting the light and heavy bag. The important thing was they were taking instruction from me and looking up to me, and it was a good feeling inside me that I could help these kids think right and do right.

By that time I had them all togged out in miniature boxing trunks and even mouthpieces. People began coming in to see them, and after a while I let them put on exhibitions after my training chores were over for the day. The kids obviously were enjoying themselves so much that some of them talked their parents into buying them regular boxing shoes. Unfortunately, not all of the parents could afford that. I knew it wouldn't be right for some kids to have to work in sneakers while the rest had real boxing shoes. I would have bought shoes for the rest, but I figured they might think I was giving them charity and shaming them because their folks didn't have the money.

I hit upon an idea then. I'd take out ten per cent of every dollar fee that people paid to watch me train and would set it aside for an equipment fund for them. I had to do something special for these kids by then, because they had surprised me one day by presenting me with a gift—two, in fact.

They had made a dart board on which they had a photo of Hurricane Jackson's face. Very solemnly they presented me with this gift plus two paper plates, on each of which they had drawn a boxing glove in crayon. On one glove was the letter "F" and on the other the letter "P."

I thanked the boys for their gifts very sincerely and then reached up on a shelf and took down a cigar box into which I had placed the money for our equipment fund. "Whatever we take in in training at the gate," I said, "you fellows get ten per cent. This is the share so far."

"Gee, Champ," one of the kids said, "that makes us real fighters, doesn't it?"

"Yes," I said. "That makes all of us the same now."

I don't believe I had ever gotten any more deep-down pleasure than from watching those kids develop. One of them, for instance—the last one to join the group—had come to me by himself and asked to be allowed in. I had taught him first all by himself before letting him join the others. His mother later told me how badly the boy had been doing in school and how difficult it had been for him to get along with other kids. Our project, his mother said, seemed to have straightened him out.

Something like this into which I was putting so much time and effort couldn't go unnoticed by the press, of course. The reporters who came up to see me train would stay over to watch the kids and finally stories about it began to get into the papers. TV editors asked if I would appear with the kids on shows. One night I took them to New York when I was on Ed Sullivan's show, and they sat in the audience. Martin Agronsky interviewed the children on his program. A magazine did a picture story on the boys. I brought the boys to Stillman's Gym for pictures. The photographer gave me sixty dollars. "Give it to the kids," he said. It went into the kitty, and before long we even had a Christmas Fund to distribute among the boys.

164

There were periods during that time when I had to go back to New York and stay out of training for a while, but I'd make the fifty-mile drive to Greenwood Lake just so the boys wouldn't miss their lessons. On one of the trips back I brought the kids leather jackets for Christmas. I didn't go back into serious training after the Rademacher fight until the end of January. I had an exhibition tour, that would take me to Houston, Philadelphia and London, all planned.

I almost resented the thought that I'd have to be away from my boys so long. You can imagine my sense of anticipation then when I came back to work and my anxiety when the kids stopped coming around regularly. Before, they would never let anything interfere with our classes. After my return, any little thing seemed enough for them to beg off.

It hadn't fully dawned on me that the kids had lost their interest or somebody had made them lose it. What woke me up was the request from a magazine for some pictures of the boys and an interview with them. Without checking the kids first, I okayed a definite date and time and sent word to the boys.

The magazine people showed up, but none of the boys did. I imagined they were just delayed. An hour and a half later, with the magazine people getting impatient, I decided I'd drive to the boys' houses and pick them up. "The photographers are waiting," I told them. "Don't you want to come over to the gym?"

"I don't want them taking pictures of me any more," one of them said.

Another said he'd lost interest in boxing. A third said he had something else to do. I prevailed upon them to come to the gym anyway because I had made the commitment and the magazine people had come all that way with their equipment. They came reluctantly. Afterward, when I asked them if they didn't want to work out that day, I could tell it wouldn't matter if any of them said yes. Their hearts didn't seem to be in it any more.

Truthfully, the only reason I had come back to Greenwood Lake was because of my boys. When I sensed they weren't my boys any longer, I just had to leave the Long Pond Inn in a hurry, even though at that point I didn't understand why things had changed so between us. I thought about it and thought about it. I was walking around the deck aboard the *Saxonia* en route to England some weeks later when the terrible truth hit me. These kids hadn't turned against me by themselves. They had been made to turn against me by older folks, who couldn't believe that the heavyweight champion of the world could take an unselfish interest in children.

All this was confirmed to me later on when I trained briefly at Greenwood Lake again in the spring of 1958. The kids had been advised by the townspeople that I was exploiting them by having stories written about them in the newspapers and magazines. They persuaded the children that I had made a profit by having them on television and had bolstered the gate for the Jackson fight by taking advantage of the publicity I received from the children's exhibitions. The children and I had become such good friends that the gossip which was poured into their ears had to be as strong as poison to wean them away from me.

To this day I don't understand how any adult could have poisoned a kid's mind like that. I loved those children, and through them I was planning how I would work with my own son some day when I had one. The one time after this episode when I tried Greenwood Lake again it was not pleasant. I don't think I'll ever train there again. It would be too painful. I passed through there once in 1960. I dropped in to see some of the boys. They were bigger then and apparently they never understood why I had left so suddenly. One of them asked, "Why don't you train here any more, Floyd?"

I couldn't possibly tell him. How can you tell a thirteen-year-old that you meant so well and your intentions were twisted and turned out of shape until they became like a knife in your stomach. There is enough pain in this world. Why hurt the boy just because his thoughtless elders had mistakenly done something that had hurt me so much?

Chapter Fourteen

There are two things a fighter wants. Early in his career the immediate aim is money. This, of course, is the primary goal. Kids who become professionals don't come from homes where all they have to do is ask for something and they get it. If a parent can afford to give a child good food, adequate clothing, toys and the proper education, that child isn't likely to try to make a living punching and being punched. You don't bleed for glory. You hope that at the end of the painful, dedicated, lonely road in boxing there will be the pot of gold.

Not too many are lucky enough to reach the championship level. I have been among the luckiest because the title I hold is the most profitable, especially in these days of network and closed-circuit television. There is an obstacle, though, and in a way the obstacle cancels out the advantage somewhat. That obstacle is taxes. I'd like to fight four or five times a year, but I can't. After a couple of fights I virtually would be fighting for nothing. It wouldn't make sense or be financially sound. It comes down to a matter of mathematics, not desire.

In the year in which I fought Jackson and Rademacher, my accountants and lawyer told me I was in the ninety per cent bracket. In any other business, when a man reaches that stage, he might decide to lie around, relax and enjoy himself. A fighter can't indulge himself in that luxury. For one thing, if he allows himself to lay out of training too long, he loses his condition and it becomes that much harder and takes that much longer to get back into shape.

For another thing, if a fighter has any pride—and all champions do—he is bitten by ambition that is almost as sharp as the tax bite. He wants to be hailed as a good champion if not a great one. He wants people to speak of him as they spoke of Dempsey and Louis. He wants—if you'll forgive the use of the word—glory.

So a fellow like myself is caught on the horns of a dilemma. Fight for nothing or don't fight and become regarded as a champ who's keeping his title on ice. I'm not kidding myself. That's the way I was regarded for almost a year between the Rademacher fight and the one against Roy Harris in Los Angeles on August 18, 1958. I went on a short exhibition tour, but for much of the year I kept myself isolated in training camps. Being away from everybody and everything didn't protect me from learning what people in boxing were saying about me. I was being called "the unknown champion."

In the back of my mind there was a dream. I was hoping that Rocky Marciano could be enticed out of retirement to fight me. That was the one bout I wanted. I spoke about it to Emil Lence, who promoted my first title defense. He was all for it. He made a guaranteed offer of one million dollars to Marciano to come back for this one fight, but it was no more than a delusion. Rocky had had it in the ring. He had lost interest in fighting. He was smart. He made his money and got out.

We couldn't get him, and it disappointed me because I wanted Marciano as an opponent, not to prove myself to the public, but to prove myself to myself. Rocky had his own reasons for not wanting to torture himself to get back into fighting trim, as he told Frank Sinatra and Irving B. Kahn, the head of TelePrompTer Corporation. Sinatra wanted to promote a fight between Rocky and me just for the kicks. He told Rocky he could have the profits of the promotion. Kahn was in touch with Rocky five or six times with a proposition that seemed irresistible. It was a tax deal that would have guaranteed Marciano something like $750,000 in cash and stock in Kahn's company; this would have enabled him to take advantage of the capital gains law. Rocky wanted no part of it.

That was the start of my association with Kahn and Tele-PrompTer, which specialized in setting up closed circuit telecasts. Bill Rosensohn, who worked for Kahn at one time, subsequently set up shop as a Los Angeles promoter. He had never promoted a fight before, but after an agreement was reached for my next fight with Roy Harris of Cut and Shoot, Texas, Rosensohn was designated to promote the bout.

TelePrompTer guaranteed a sizeable sum to get the closed-circuit rights. In addition, I was to get fifty per cent of the gate for the bout at Wrigley Field that originally was set for August 4, but had to be rescheduled for August 18, 1958. We were still having trouble trying to get suitable opponents who were not pledged to the I.B.C. By guaranteeing Harris $100,-000 we were able to get him.

This fight, though, was not without the usual recriminations. Harris was little known in the East, which was less a rap at him than it was at the so-called boxing experts. He had never fought on national TV, and the way boxing has been in recent years that immediately put him into the class of a stranger. Naturally enough the charge was made that Harris had been hand-picked.

However, he was the Texas State heavyweight champion and ranked behind Zora Folley and Eddie Machen in the N.B.A. ratings. He had beaten Bob Baker, Willie Pastrano and Willi Besmanoff and had gone unbeaten in twenty-two pro fights, all of which were fought in and around Houston, where his manager, Lou Viscusi, ran a fight club. What was amusing, of course, was that, while the press was knocking him as a logical contender and opponent for me, practically all of the prefight

169

publicity was about Harris. I was virtually forgotten in the write-ups, which was all right by me.

Harris was a natural for the promotional build-up. Before he became a fighter, he used to wrestle alligators in the swamps around his home, which was in a woods and forest area called the Big Thicket. His family lived in a kind of log cabin and their background was so colorful that for a time I wondered if some publicity man had made it all up out of his own imagination. Roy himself was a college graduate and a teacher, but his father was an old bare-knuckled fighter, who weighed 230 pounds. When I read about the rest of the family, I thought I was reading about Li'l Abner and Dogpatch in the comics. There were Uncle Cleve, Cousins Hominy, Coon and Armadillo, and Wildman Woodman, who were kinfolk one way or the other. There were dogs of all kinds around Harris' home and chickens and hogs roaming around, and in the middle of it all was a big wooden shed in which the family had built a ring in which Roy trained. Roy himself had been named after Roy Tipton, who was once a member of Machine Gun Kelly's gang and hid out in the woods around Cut and Shoot when the law was after him.

I never saw all of this myself. I just read about it and about how some of the people down his way were trying to make this a fight between the North and the South. I certainly needed some incentive like this to spur me on, because when I finally went into training at Kutsher's Country Club in Monticello, New York, I discovered to my dismay that I wasn't myself. Something seemed to have happened to my reflexes. I couldn't put my combinations together or pinpoint punches. I was as conscientious in my preparations as I had ever been, but somehow something was lacking. I felt better after the bout was finally signed than I did before it was signed, but my concentration was not sharp enough to satisfy me. The fight was still some time away and I consoled myself that after we moved our base to Oceanside, California, about ninety miles from Los Angeles, I'd reach the peak I wanted to reach.

Too many things weren't right. There was rust on me and a sense of boredom I didn't quite understand. I felt slow to myself, and so we removed some of the padding in the ring in the community center where I worked out in California. I played a lot of cards and watched a lot of television. I would have preferred to walk in the woods, but this was a camp at a beach resort. Cus went out and bought me a couple of air rifles and I amused myself doing some shooting. Then came a two-week postponement of the fight that further upset my schedule. All in all, I went into the ring not very satisfied with myself, and I came out of it nearly disgusted with myself.

I believe I said earlier that I'm my own most severe critic. Maybe I should have been satisfied that I knocked out Harris in twelve rounds, but the time it took me to find myself in that ring was as hard on me as it was on my opponent when I finally got to him. People may think I'm putting it on when I judge myself harshly. That's not so. I am a perfectionist, although I'm aware that nobody ever achieves perfection. I've actually been fighting in the ring for almost half of my life, and every day there is something new to learn, so that I know that every time you get close to perfection, perfection moves away from you. Only two of my championship fights have pleased me completely—when I knocked out Moore to win the title and when I won it back from Ingemar. I would not change anything I did, any move I made in those two fights, but if I were perfect, certainly I could have knocked out my opponents sooner.

My system is to put a percentage value on every one of the fights. I've never been one hundred per cent of what I could be. Against Harris I was the worst I have ever been as the champion. I would say I was able to give only about eleven per cent of myself that night. For a long time I just couldn't seem to get myself together. I'd bob and I'd weave and Harris would be open for all kinds of punches, and instead of punching I'd pull back. I knew I could beat him and that I'd take him sometime, but actually I was discouraged. Even when I did throw a punch, I didn't throw it naturally and instinctively. I had to think before letting a punch go, and that's no way to fight.

My footwork, for the most part, is designed for coming in. In the second round, going away from Harris in order to get myself thinking properly, I was off balance and was hit with a right uppercut, which Harris followed with a left hand that was more of a push than a punch. I tripped and went down. Mushy Callahan ruled it a four-count knockdown. In my own mind it was not a knockdown, but maybe that helped to wake me up.

In any event, it took me about seven rounds in all to start getting something of myself back again. I knocked Harris down with a right hand for an eight-count in the seventh. In the eighth he went down twice for seven and three counts, once from a left and then from a right. He had begun to bleed badly by then. In the twelfth, a right put him down in what was almost a delayed reaction. A second or two seemed to pass after the punch before his knees gave way. He started up, but collapsed once more to the canvas. He took a count of nine on one knee, and the ref could have stopped it then, because Roy had gone down without being hit.

The fight was stopped with Harris on his stool in the corner between rounds. I was happy it was over. Harris was chopped up so badly it would have hurt me to hit him any more, and it might have ruined him. One punch I hit him rocked his head so sharply that the blood on his face was whisked off by the movement. Bill Gore, who trained Harris and worked his corner for the fight, could see the futility of Roy going on. He signaled the referee that the fight was over, although Roy wanted to go on. But his father, who also was in the corner, said: "It ain't no use, boy."

As much as I look back on the fight with misgivings, I know that two things were proved by it. First, it proved that closed circuit was a very profitable medium for heavyweight championships. It was a relatively new undertaking, but Tele-PrompTer had 196, 762 spectators in the theaters watching the fight over their facilities. Add that to the 21,680 who paid to see it at Wrigley Field. More important, I learned that for me to fight effectively I couldn't lay out a whole year. The inactivity robbed me of my sharpness. I was determined that, taxes or not, Cus' real or imagined difficulties with what remained of the I.B.C., his open or undercover enemies, I just had to fight more to regain the peak that I had somehow lost after becoming the champion.

As I saw it, the way for me to redeem myself and receive unqualified recognition as a good champion was to start at the top with the Number One contender and work my way down through the list of those ranked among the first ten. At the time, the three outstanding contenders were Eddie Machen, Zora Folley and Willie Pastrano. Pastrano, however, had been offered the opportunity to meet me after I won the title, but had turned down the bout. Machen and Folley went over to Europe for what they must have thought would be easy fights and quick money and walked into an ambush. It changed the whole heavyweight picture and altered the course of boxing history for more years than any of us know even now.

Machen was knocked out in one round by Johansson on September 14, at Göteborg, Sweden. Pastrano was knocked out by Brian London, the British heavyweight champion, in the fifth round on September 30. Two weeks later Folley lost a ten-round decision to Henry Cooper in London. In January, 1959, Cooper also outpointed London for the British Empire title. Cooper had already agreed to meet me sometime in the spring of 1959. We had guaranteed him $75,000 for a match, but following his win over London, he put the squeeze on us for twice that much. Naturally, we wouldn't give in.

What generally was unknown long before this was that Bill Rosensohn, eager to continue as a promoter following the Harris fight, had gone to Göteborg for Johansson's kayo of

173

Machen and succeeded in signing Ingemar to an option. Johansson agreed to fight for Rosensohn as promoter if Bill could sign me to a contract for a fight with Ingemar within forty days. Rosensohn had to pay Johansson $10,000 if he couldn't get me to agree to a bout within that time. If I agreed, it would cost Bill nothing, and in the event Johansson was able to beat me, he would also have Ingemar under promotional contract for the return bout.

Eventually, and after considerable backstage maneuvering, which I will describe later at greater length, Cus agreed to Johansson as a challenger for my title. Johansson and his advisor, Edwin Ahlquist, made several trips to this country to work out the details of the bout. On January 29, we formally signed the agreement, although at the time the date and site of the fight were not set. Nor could I possibly anticipate the many things that would happen in the months to follow as a result of putting my name on that contract.

One part of the agreement should be mentioned here. That was the right I reserved for myself to engage in one tune-up bout before meeting Ingemar. In order to preserve Johansson's attractiveness as the Number One contender, which he had become, he could not fight again until we met.

The reason for that is that we were about to close with Brian London. Cus had substituted him as an opponent after Cooper had demanded twice as much money as he had agreed to accept for a bout against me. That seemed to settle our problems for my work for the rest of the year. I couldn't possibly have known that my problems were just beginning.

In line with D'Amato's plans to have independent promoters stage my bouts, he accepted a proposition by Cecil Rhodes, Jr. to put on the fight with London. Rhodes seemed to be everything that you could want in boxing. He was a lawyer, a business executive, a Harvard man and, seemingly, well connected with Gillette, the razor blade company which sponsored boxing bouts, and with N.B.C.

After Cus had installed him as the promoter, Rhodes held a press conference at Madison Square Garden Club, where he announced that I would defend my title against London on May 1 at Las Vegas and that the bout would be telecast over N.B.C. Tom Gallery, the sports director of N.B.C., was also at the meeting, and he added that Gillette and N.B.C. would combine their forces with Rhodes to telecast other bouts of mine after the London and Johansson fights, but Rhodes later said that there had only been an agreement to discuss further bouts.

The funny thing about these announcements was that Cus wasn't at the meeting at which they were made. I was already in training at Ehsan's and, unsuspectingly, I was greatly heartened by them. "Now I can be a fighting champion," I told myself, but the next thing I knew was that four days later Rhodes announced from Indianapolis that the fight would take place there and not in Las Vegas. It didn't concern me especially where I would fight, just so long as I did. However, a few days were to pass when there was another shift of the winds. Rhodes was out as the promoter and Rosensohn was persuaded to go to Indianapolis to assist Al Farb, who was put in as the nominal promoter of the bout.

At least, I had an inkling that something like that was about to happen. I had met Rhodes once. Cus had come up with him to my camp early in April to sign four sets of agreements drawn up for the fight. Cus advised me he had read them carefully and it was all right for me to put my signature to them.

A week later Cus came up to camp early one morning. Instead of coming in to greet me himself, however, he sent in a friend of ours, Angelo Bruno, who had driven him up. "Floyd," Angelo said, "you'd better go out to the car to talk to Cus."

"Why doesn't he come in?" I asked.

"He wants to see you out there. I think you'd better go out to him. He's very upset."

I'd seen Cus upset before. Usually there was no real reason to worry. He had a habit of making things more serious than they really were. Still, I went out. He really looked disturbed, sitting in the back of the car. I got in with him, and he told me that the papers were not what he had thought they were, so that I would be getting less to engage in the London fight and subsequent ones. It was quite a mess. However, we had to go through with the London fight, but for a while we had no television guarantee and no time to really whip up a promotion in Indianapolis. London still was back home in England waiting for word to come over and, in fact, would have to violate a ruling by the British Board of Boxing Control to fight me. They had turned down his application with the explanation, such as it was, that a bout between us would not be "in the best interests of British boxing."

London defied their ruling. On our side, we managed to get Rhodes out of the picture and, in the end, came up with a television contract for the fight. It went on over N.B.C. after all, but until it did there had to be considerably more of the backstage maneuvering that cast a shadow over the bout.

For one thing, London was met at Idlewild by a representative of my manager and spirited away from newspapermen who wanted to talk to him at the airport. It seemed fishy, but the reason for London not lending himself to a prefight ballyhoo was that he might have revealed how much the promotion of the bout was in jeopardy if he had talked at all.

I must confess that if I were on the outside looking in, I would have wondered about the bout myself. During the time he was hidden in New York before leaving for Indianapolis after all the details were straightened out, London trained at Cus' Gramercy Park gym. A *New York Times* reporter saw him there one day. He even boxed against sparring partners I had been using. But he had to keep in shape, and if he had worked at Stillman's, say, the entire promotion might have gone up in smoke if Brian had uttered a careless word.

To train him, Cus also arranged for London to have Nick Baffi, an American trainer friendly to Cus. Naturally, this, too, created suspicion, but Nick worked hard with Brian for two weeks and London admitted he learned more from Baffi than he had been taught at home. Brian came into the ring against me in better condition than he had been against Henry Cooper, according to those who saw both fights.

The fact that the fight was able to come off at all was a near-miracle. It was one of the things which encouraged me. I was discouraged, of course, that London didn't give me much opposition, but heartened by my appreciation that I was so much better against him than I had been against Harris. It made me feel that I was right in my view that to keep a competitive edge I must fight at least a couple of times a year.

I missed punches a lot in the fight and didn't put him down until the tenth round, when my body attack forced him to lower his guard. A right hand sent him to the canvas for the first time in his career. The bell rang at the count of five. The next round I finished him off.

On the basis of what I was able to do against London, I figured I would be fifty per cent better against Johansson, whom I was to meet on June 25 at the Yankee Stadium. Johansson had watched me in action against London from a working-press seat at ringside. All I knew about him was what could be seen on the film clips of his knockout against Machen. Ingemar now had seen me against an opponent in the flesh and, from what I gathered he said after the fight, he wasn't quite sure that he had seen all of me.

"I don't know after this how good Patterson really is," Ingemar was quoted as saying, "because he was not pressed. If somebody push him harder, we know more."

Well, while I wasn't exactly ecstatic, I was content with

myself. I had wanted a tune-up and I had got it. Now, ahead of me, was an international match of the biggest proportions. I saw Ingemar as the kind of fighter who finally would be my steppingstone to complete acceptance as a champion by the boxing press.

It wasn't too long after I went back into serious training, however, that I began to see Johansson derided in the stories about him. I finally said to one writer: "Suppose I knocked him out in the first round, what would you say about Johansson?"

"I'd say he was a bum," the writer said.

"And suppose he beat me, what would you say?"

"I'd say you were a bum," he answered.

"Tell me," I asked him, "how can I win? If I win, I lose, the way you figure it."

Chapter Fifteen

Between the time I fought Roy Harris and the night of June 26, 1959, when I walked up the steps of the Yankee Stadium ring to put my title on the line against Ingemar, I boxed more than five hundred rounds in training. This is something that was measured and timed, and it shows how much I wanted to be in the best shape against the one opponent I figured would finally give me the stature I wanted.

My body was in tremendous condition, but there was something that couldn't be measured—the condition of my mind. A fighter's mental attitude is something few people know about. And sometimes even the fighter cannot judge accurately whether his mood is a winning one beforehand.

During the course of my training at Ehsan's in Summit, New Jersey, I tried to get myself feeling meaner and meaner. I worked over my sparring partners mercilessly. They represented everything I wanted to accomplish against Johansson, and some of them, poor fellows, took more beatings than were necessary in the weeks leading up to the fight.

Everything about me was geared to the same mood, in contrast to what it was like at Johansson's camp. Ingemar was set up in a $100,000 private home near Grossinger's in the Catskills. He had a private chef to cook his meals. He trained in the ski lodge of that world-famous resort hotel. He spent his evenings in the Terrace Room listening to the comedians and seeing the shows and dancing. He played some golf and went horseback riding and swimming. He had his girl friend, mother and father, sister and brother and his brother's fiancee living with him at his training quarters. It was he who lived like the king while preparing to become one.

Me? I lived like a fighter in training for a heavyweight-championship fight. The single room in which I slept was only a couple of nails above a squatter's shack. For amusement I'd play some cards with Buster, who slept in an iron bed next to mine in my room. Sweaty work clothes hung from nails hammered into the wall. At night we covered ourselves with old, rough khaki army blankets. For entertainment we'd turn on the television or listen to a record player. We'd go for walks along the country roads and do roadwork in the hills.

I didn't see my wife and children for weeks. More weeks would go by without talking to her over the phone. She knew and I knew that this is how it had to be. You don't build yourself up mentally and emotionally for a fight by being kind to yourself or those you love. It is a hard business. There is no easy way to succeed in it.

What I was trying to do, of course, was develop an attitude of respect for Johansson. He was undefeated in twenty-one fights and had knocked out thirteen of his opponents. He was the European heavyweight champion, whose right-hand punch was supposed to be the kind of weapon that could put away any opponent he hit with it. Any fighter with any sense prepares for this kind of a bout by taking a realistic view of the danger he faces. Machen lasted less than a round with Ingemar. I tried to keep that in my mind.

There was one thing, however, I could not eliminate from my consciousness, no matter how hard I tried. That was my one view of Ingemar as a fighter in the flesh. That had come in the Olympic games of 1952 when I won as a middleweight and

Ingemar had been disqualified against Eddie Sanders, a huge man who really was scary to look at.

Ingemar was a counter-fighter and so was Sanders. Each waited for the other to lead in the ring, but the referee decided Johansson wasn't doing any fighting at all and threw him out. The Olympic officials didn't even recognize Ingemar after that for his second-place medal. The Swedish newspapers at the time felt Johansson had disgraced his country. For years Ingemar tried to erase that blot from his name and record. By becoming a professional and the European champion, he did. But still lingering in my mind was the remembrance of something I had never talked about, even after Johansson and I were signed to fight.

I had never in my life seen a man so scared in the ring as Johansson was in that fight against Sanders. I, like so many others, may have done Johansson an injustice, but first impressions are lasting, and that was mine.

I saw Johansson again for the first time since seeing him at Helsinki the day our fight was officially announced in a Swedish restaurant in New York City. He was bigger, just as handsome, and apparently very confident. When the newspapermen talked to him afterward, he talked about his right hand as though it were something mysterious. Edwin Ahlquist, Ingemar's advisor, described the punch as "toonder and lightning." Ingemar, himself, said it was so fast that it couldn't be seen when thrown. He said he saved it to throw it at the right time and even he didn't know when he threw it. It was like a button would be pushed in his brain, the right hand would lash out, and that would be it. I'd never know what hit me.

From a promotional point of view, that was fine, except that I guess I never quite believed it. As the training weeks went by, I tried to keep myself isolated from the stories of how Ingemar trained, what punches he threw when he boxed, the time he spent coming into New York to appear on television shows and to attend theaters and night clubs. It wasn't easy, though. Writers would come from Grossinger's to my camp, and I'd have to listen as they related that Johansson absolutely refused to let his right go when he sparred.

I remember once hearing how Ingemar even ignored Rosensohn when the promoter begged him to try to knock down a sparring partner because a show of such power would help the ticket sale, but Johansson wouldn't cooperate. Without realizing it, within myself, I wondered if he *could* cooperate.

I would never admit this to myself. Nevertheless, as the time for the bout approached, I found myself getting bored. Without appreciating how much the worm of my own disrespect for an opponent had begun to burrow into me, I was slowly losing my eagerness for the fight. It is a very hard thing to explain. Fighters understand the sense of anticipation that takes hold of them as a bout gets nearer and nearer. Your body can be in perfect condition. Your punches can be working hard and sharp. Your reflexes can be trigger-fine, yet there is a certain feeling which must go with all of it, and I didn't have that feeling. I kept telling myself it would come once I got into the ring. Never once would I allow myself to accept the fact that it wouldn't come. It would have been a dreadful thing for me to admit to myself that I had lost interest because I couldn't work up sufficient respect for Ingemar.

Not once in my entire career have I ever bragged before a fight to the press. Never have I predicted that I would win. The most I would ever say is that I would do my best. It had always been good enough, and this time with Ingemar discounted by the press as a four-to-one underdog, I kept telling myself I could not discount him, too. The worst of it all is that I believed in my own lies to myself. I deluded myself. I wanted so much to make this fight the one in which I'd become recognized not as a great champion but just a good one, that I would not accept my growing suspicion that I was beginning to take Johansson for granted.

Even as training came to an end, I could not throw off the feeling that something was missing. In my last sparring session, before a busload of newspapermen from all over the world brought up to camp by the promoter, I seemed as vicious as it was possible to be. My handlers obviously were satisfied with my "edge." The writers seemed impressed.

We broke camp the night before the fight and drove into New York City in a Cadillac provided by the mayor of Mount Vernon. A policeman drove the car and two detectives rode with us as a sort of bodyguard. Our destination was the Edison Hotel, where I was to stay overnight before the weighing-in ceremonies and until I went to the ball park for the fight.

That night I dreamed about the fight—not how it would take place, but about being home again with my family. When I realized that everybody at home was laughing and happy, I figured the fight had ended with me winning. There wasn't uneasiness in me, only impatience. I wanted to get it over with.

Unfortunately, rain postponed the fight one night. I had weighed in at 182, Johansson at 196. I had visited my old school, P.S. 614, and was back in the Edison when word came that the fight was off. "Can't they hire a man to wipe the seats?" I said. "Of all the days in the world it has to rain."

It rained part of the next day as well, but stopped about an hour before fight time. The seats were still wet for those who came. There was a mugginess in the air. With only 21,961 in the big ball park, there was almost a feeling of desolation. For so many months the promotion of the fight had been marred by law suits and other annoyances. The only way I can sum up my whole feeling, as we sat on our stools facing each other, is that I was bored and impatient and without the usual edginess that should precede the opening bell.

When the fight started, nothing happened to change my overconfident attitude. It seemed to me that Johansson was going to be satisfied to fight a completely defensive fight and be content to go the full fifteen rounds. He kept pushing his left jab out, not as an offensive weapon, but more defensive. It wasn't even a hard jab, just a flick, kind of. Every time I tried to come in, he'd jump back. It surprised me that, big as he was, he was so quick on his feet in retreat. But that only added to my feeling that it would be just a matter of time before I'd be able to close with him and put him away. That's all that was in my mind—my lazy mind, I should add, because I had no sense of caution in me. Every fighter should be a little afraid of what could happen to him, because fear makes your mind sharper. When you have nothing to fear, your mind becomes dull.

They tell me that in the first round Ingemar flicked out his left hand ninety-six times and one hundred seven times in the second, but I can honestly say I never felt one of them. They were just annoying. They were hardly more than brushes at me, but the more he did it the more impatient and disgusted I became. There were people in the ball park who paid one hundred dollars a seat at ringside, and some of them were already beginning to boo because there just wasn't any action in the fight. I could understand their dissatisfaction. It seemed a boring fight to me, and the burden was on me to make it a more interesting one.

The judges and referee gave me the first two rounds, but that wouldn't have mattered to me then, had I known it, nor does it matter to me now. What distressed me was that Ingemar showed no inclination to mix it. I couldn't get close enough to him to start my combinations or work on his body, because he'd always be jumping backwards. Once I leaped at him and threw a left hook, which he blocked, as he was retreating, by throwing up his right arm. Toward the end of the second round I got inside once, but instead of fighting, he just grabbed me in his big arms and squeezed me in a bear hug so that I couldn't punch.

At the bell ending the second round, I kind of scowled at him going toward his corner. I was disturbed with him for not making much of a fight; I must admit I was disturbed with myself as well. There had been one cautioning note in my mind that he could do me harm only by throwing his right hand. In the opening round he had thrown it once, but it didn't seem to me to be any more powerful than his left.

That was my miscalculation, because all along he apparently was trying me out, kind of testing my reaction to whatever moves he made. Three times, for example, he shoved out a left hand, and I found myself moving straight toward the right hand. I was directly in line with it, but three times he didn't do anything about throwing the right, and I said to myself, "He's not going to throw that right at all."

I was so positively sure that it would only be a matter of time before he'd make the big mistake. Then I would get to him, and then it would be all over for him. He seemed awkward and sloppy. Between the second and third rounds I'd more or less made up my mind I wasn't going to delay any longer. By that time I'd reached another conclusion. I was going to gamble by moving in on him, no matter what. Ordinarily I wouldn't risk anything like that so early, but it seemed to me that I'd given him chances, and he hadn't done anything about them. Therefore, one thing had to be true. He had never used his right hand in training because he didn't really have a right hand. Once I'd made up my mind to that, I was well on my way to getting bombed.

The result of my miscalculation wasn't long in coming. Soon after the third round started, Ingemar began to flick that left again. It was more a hook than the pushing jab this time, but I was moving in. I was not watching his right; I was watching the left, which I caught on my glove. I never saw the big punch come at me, which is what usually happens when you get hit hard. I have since seen the movies many times and know that the straight right penetrated through my hands held up toward my face in defense, but I didn't know it then. There wasn't any pain, just shock. That was the first of seven times Ingemar knocked me down, but I don't remember anything about going down the first two times.

The last recollection I had was of Ingemar starting to jump

back again and me starting to move in, and the next thing I knew I was hearing Referee Ruby Goldstein counting. I don't know what number he'd reached, but then the voice stopped counting and said, "Neutral Corner. Go to the farthest neutral corner." I assumed I had knocked Ingemar down. I didn't remember going down or getting up, so it had to be me who put him down.

As always when I go to the corner while the ref is counting, I started to take the mouthpiece out of my mouth. Suddenly I felt an impact on the back of my head and the side of my jaw. The one on the back of the head did the most damage. I remember being down then, but I don't remember going down. I saw the referee, but I was looking up at him. Then I knew it was I and not Ingemar who had been knocked down.

I had been down for nine twice, then for seven, six, seven and nine, before the referee finally stepped in and ended the bout. But the more I went down after the second knockdown, the more vividly I could remember what was happening.

I just couldn't believe it. I couldn't believe he had knocked me down and I was actually being beaten and being knocked around the ring. I think it was after the fourth knockdown, when I started to rise, that I looked right into the eyes of John Wayne, the movie actor, and I was more embarrassed than anything else. Here this famous man, whose movies I had watched so many times, had come to see me fight, and I was getting punched around and rolling on the canvas.

I got up and tried to give it everything I had, but with the first two knockdowns Ingemar had taken everything out of me. My legs and arms felt heavy. My head was clearing, but it still was groggy. When the referee stopped the fight, I sensed it more than I knew it.

Even at this late date, there are blanks about what happened next. I remember looking into Ingemar's corner, and the next thing I was aware of was being back in my own corner and

Buster was on my left side and putting a towel around me. Danny was on my right and throwing my robe around me, and Buster was saying, "Don't worry, we'll get him the next time."

I knew I had been beaten, but these words kept running around in my head, and I said to myself, "I've lost the championship." Things came to me, like in parts. It wasn't because of unconsciousness or blacking out or anything like that, but from thinking so deep within myself. I was crying inside, asking myself, "How did I lose? How did he get the right hand in? I never saw it."

From one period to the next, it was like my mind was a page of writing and somebody had cut a piece right out of the middle of it. I don't recall walking down the steps of the ring, but suddenly there was Sandra before me, her face wrinkled in distress, and she threw her arms around me and embraced me and said something which didn't touch my consciousness at all.

I must have walked from ringside halfway to the dressing room before I was aware that there were people all around me, shouting and yelling. As if a light was suddenly turned on, I can remember looking into one fellow's face, and he had a big smile on it, and he was yelling to another, "See, I told you. This guy can't fight." When we got into the dressing room, one of the commissioners was there. He was laughing aloud and he yelled at Danny, "So your boy finally got it." Danny had been holding me by one arm, but he let go and started for the commissioner. Buster grabbed him and stopped him.

There was no feeling in me—just a kind of despair and numbness. My mind grasped the fact that I was no longer the titleholder, but it hadn't grasped why. I don't even know how long I was allowed to sit in the dressing room with that blankness within me. I don't believe I even showered. Soap and water wouldn't wash away what had happened.

It's funny, but two thoughts are so clear. When I had dressed, I borrowed Buster's hat. I don't usually wear one, but maybe somewhere inside myself I felt that if I could pull the hat brim down over my eyes, people wouldn't be able to see the pain in them. When my wife, my mother, my mother-in-law and Mrs. November, the wife of my lawyer, finally were let in to see me, they all embraced me. They were so sympathetic. I hate sympathy. I didn't realize until then how much I do hate it. I didn't want to hear any more of what they were saying. What good was sympathy?

What good, too, was the meeting with the reporters? It took place in the large dressing room which the Yankees occupy during the baseball season. It had been partitioned off from the one I had used. They asked questions and I tried to answer, but I couldn't tell them much. I didn't know much about what had happened to me. I had already drowned. Words couldn't change whatever had happened, except to make me more confused.

I wanted to be alone. I wanted to think the whole thing out for myself and by myself, but I had to do something else first. I had to reassure my family that I wasn't hurt, although I had been thoroughly beaten. My brother Raymond drove Sandra and me to my family's home in Mount Vernon. We didn't stay there long. There was too much sympathy. In fifteen minutes Raymond was driving us back to my home in Rockville Centre.

My wife knows me. She knew I didn't want to talk about the fight, but she was worried. "How do you feel?" she asked, after we had driven awhile.

"How am I supposed to feel?" I said, looking at her curiously.

"I don't mean mentally," she said. "Are you in pain?"

"I've got a headache," I said, "but that's all."

Raymond was making a turn then. Sandra and I had been sitting apart; she had been looking at me intently, and I had been looking off into space. But the turn threw my body in her direction. I laid my head on her shoulder. She put her arms around me, and that was the way we rode home.

It wasn't so much being beaten—knocked out for the first

time in my career. There was so much more racing through my mind. Truly, I was thinking less of myself than I was of the others who were dependent upon me. My wife, my children, my brothers and sisters and mother. I thought Ingemar had smashed all my plans for them, all the dreams I had been building about their going to college and becoming something. I thought of my mother, who had never had a new dress until I began to make money in the ring. I wondered what would become of her. In those dark moments I did not believe I would get the opportunity to win back what I had lost, despite the return-bout clause in the contracts of the fight.

"Are you hungry, Floyd?" Sandra asked, once we were back home.

"I think I'll go right to bed," I said.

"I'll be right up, too," she said. "I'll bring you a cup of tea."

I went up to our room and got into my pajamas. I looked into the children's room. They were sound asleep. They didn't know the world had collapsed around their daddy's head. I got into my bed and pretended to be asleep when Sandra came up with the tea. She must have known I wasn't, but she didn't try to wake me. I don't know how long I lay there, but when I thought Sandra had fallen asleep, I quietly got out of bed and went downstairs to the den. Sandra's footsteps followed mine downstairs.

"Floyd," she said, "Floyd, what good will it do sitting down here in the dark thinking?"

"Will it do more good," I said, "lying up there in the dark?"

"You didn't drink your tea before," she said. "I'll heat up the water. We can have a cup together."

"How could it have happened?" I burst out. "How could he have hit me with that right hand?"

"It happened," she said, "and it will pass. Have faith."

The blinds were drawn, but through them the light was beginning to seep into the room. I had no idea of the time or how long we had been sitting there, but the dawn had come.

"The children," Sandra said, "will be getting up soon."

"You'd better go up and get an hour's sleep or so."

"Come up, too," Sandra said.

"I won't be able to sleep," I said.

"Don't let the children see you sitting here like that when they come down."

"I'll be up later. I'll try to get into bed before the children come down."

I must have dozed fitfully. I'd come awake with a start every so often, and it was like feeling that jolt again when Ingemar hit me behind the head. It must have been about eight in the morning when I opened my eyes with that growing feeling of uneasiness. There was Jeannie, my three-year-old, standing in front of my chair and staring at me. There was sadness in her face, which must have been reflecting the look in mine. I took her in my arms and held her on my lap with her head against my chest so that she couldn't look at me.

"She's only three," I said to myself. "How could she know about fighting? How could she know I've lost my title?"

"Floyd," Sandra said, coming into the den while I was moping that way, "you've got to go to bed."

I went up again, and this time fell asleep through sheer exhaustion. When I next opened my eyes, I saw Sandra standing beside the bed with a worried look on her face.

"What's wrong with your ear?" she asked.

"Just a pain," I said. "It was leaking a week ago and stopped, but I got hit there, and it must have started the leaking again."

"It's bleeding, Floyd," Sandra said. "The blood's all over the pillow."

There were blood stains on the pillow case where I'd twisted and turned in my sleep. "It'll stop," I said.

"No," she said. "You've got to see a doctor right away. I'll call the medical center."

"I don't want to go out," I said, horrified at the thought of how people would look at me.

"I'll drive you there," Sandra said. "It's only a few blocks."

We made an appointment to see Dr. Nathan Steinberg, an

ear, nose and throat specialist, who informed me that my left eardrum had been punctured by the force of Johansson's punch. It was nothing serious. It seemed the least of my worries. The deeper scars of the fight were all inside. The doctor asked me to come back again to see him in another week. By then the ear was almost healed. The other things that bothered me took so much longer.

It was late Saturday, long after we'd come back from the medical center and I'd had a few solid hours of sleep. I had discovered that sleeping was better than thinking. I was sitting in the den with the television turned on, but I didn't see what was on the screen. Sandra came into the room and turned off the set.

"You're not watching it, anyway," she said.

She sat down beside me. "This may be the time to give it up. Why don't you quit?"

"Quit?" I said. "Now? After one defeat?"

"We've got enough money," she said. "We can live. If necessary, I'll get a job."

"Definitely, this is not the time to quit," I said. "How could I live with myself? What would the fans think of me—running away because I was knocked out! Sandra, don't you understand that I've got to fight him again and prove something to myself?"

Chapter Sixteen

The blinds were down and the drapes were tightly drawn in all the rooms in my home. The sun shone brightly outside, but not inside or in me. Everybody walked softly, and those inside with me barely spoke, and when they did it was in hardly more than a whisper. More than once I thought to myself, "It's like a funeral parlor." I was mourning a death—my own as the heavyweight champion of the world.

One day my little Jeannie, who is a happy child who likes to laugh a lot and play, tiptoed into the den where I would hide away for most of the day and most of the night. The television set was on, but I wasn't watching it. I was lying on my back staring at the ceiling, hearing nothing, thinking about nothing, really, but inevitably my mind went back to the knockout and over and over again I'd cry out within myself, "Why? Why?"

The child spoke to me, but I didn't hear. She reached over and touched my arm, but I didn't move or respond. She could see my eyes open, almost transfixed.

"Mommy," she shouted in fright, running from the room. "Daddy's sick, Daddy's sick."

On the Sunday night following my knockout I was sitting in my accustomed place in the den with the TV set going. I wasn't aware of the program being on, when it went off, or when the new program started. I was just running away from everybody, and my fixation with television was just an excuse not to talk. Sandra came into the room and sat quietly on the couch.

Suddenly Sandra gasped. I looked at her and followed her eyes to the screen. By that time she was on her feet ready to turn off the program, but I had seen Ed Sullivan's face and with him was Johansson, his surprise guest for the night. "Wait," I said to Sandra. "Don't turn it off."

"I don't care if we don't watch it," Sandra said. "Let's get another program."

"No," I said more roughly than I intended. "Leave it on."

So I sat there watching the face of the man who had humiliated me. Then I saw him demonstrating the right-hand punch to Sullivan and the TV audience. I sat there and hated him. I had never felt that way before about anybody, an opponent in the ring or somebody I'd just met. He was laughing and joking with Sullivan, and I said to myself, "You're the champ. You've beaten me. What more do you want?"

Everything was so confused. It was to stay that way for such a long time while I stayed numb and despondent in what I thought were the ruins of my life. I had begun to doubt I would ever get a chance to win back the title from Johansson. I had begun to doubt myself. I couldn't keep the wild thoughts of skepticism out of my own mind. Had I ever been the champion, really? Had I ever deserved to hold that high place, when one punch and one loss could so destroy me? Was it just a fluke that I had licked Moore to win the crown—and then kept it because of inferior opposition until I was bombed by Ingemar?

I want so badly to be able to describe the blackness and despair I underwent for so many weeks. It was like being back hiding in the hole in the wall in the subway again. All the confidence, conviction and certainty was flowing out of me like blood from a wound in my soul.

For most of the day I would try to sleep. When I couldn't, I got up. I'd put on a pair of slippers and a robe and go down to the basement to hide, pretending to occupy myself with one thing or another. If I was in the living room or den and friends of Sandra's would come to call, I'd leave the room and go back upstairs or shut the door to the den. I didn't want to talk to anybody. I tried to eat, but I had no appetite. I tried to think of other things, but always my mind would come back to the only thing that seemed important.

At night when the rest of the family was asleep, I'd stay awake trying to analyze what had happened to me and what was happening. For three weeks I went out of the house only twice, both times to visit the doctor about my ear. I tried not to read papers or answer phone calls. I had my phone number changed several times during that period. Cus would come to the house, or Danny, or some of the others close to me, and try to tell me that I'd get my chance to prove the knockout was a fluke. But I either wouldn't listen or I wouldn't believe. Jackie Robinson and Howard Cosell came by to assure me of their friendship and their faith in me.

Then one day I received a letter from Archie Moore. I had knocked him out to win the title. I knew he would have an understanding of what I was undergoing. This letter I read. He's written to me eight or nine times, and I have all the letters. But this one is the one I remember best.

"Dear Floyd," he wrote. "The first bout is over. I know how you must feel. I hope you don't continue to feel bad. The same thing has happened to many great fighters. Of course, I hated to lose to you, and fate decreed it that way. Fate does strange-seeming things. If you are a believer in things that happen, happen for the best, listen to this and you can find your way out of a seeming tunnel.

"First, Johansson was not so great. You fought a stupid battle. Look at the film. Evaluate it. Never once did you lead

194

with a jab. All you did was move your feet and try to leap toward him. Now, this man was not like London. He could bang a little. You gave absolutely no respect to your opposition.

"But if he had been the banger the press said he was, he would have put you away with the left hook he hit you with your back turned. Well, if you concentrate on your jab and move around this guy, you will be the first one to regain the crown. You can do it. Your Friend, Archie Moore."

I was reading that letter and thinking about it as I sat in the living room, when I happened to glance up at the mantelpiece. On it was a crown set upon a base on which gold plaques were attached—one for each of my championship fights. But now I was no longer the champion. I stood up and took that crown off the base.

"Why are you doing that?" Sandra asked.

"Because I'm no longer entitled to it," I said. "Put it away somewhere until I win it again. Maybe I'll get the chance after all next September."

That was the first break in my moodiness. I was beginning to come out of the dumps, I thought, when I got a call from Danny to tell me about a story that had appeared in the *New York Journal-American* by sports columnist Jimmy Cannon. It was a cruel thing, which is all right if you want to hit a man when he is down, but what hurt most of all was that most of it was untrue. This is the way the story read:

> The saddest Patterson isn't Floyd, who was knocked out last Friday by Ingemar Johansson. He's Billy, Floyd's obscure brother, who trains with a purposeless dedication for a fight that will never be made. The pudgy middleweight, who hasn't spoken to Floyd for a year, although he was his brother's original trainer, is trying to convince the New York State Athletic Commission they should return his license. It was revoked because of a detached retina in 1950.

The big family is close, and even Billy concedes Floyd has been generous with the others. But Billy, disappointed, bitter and out of work, believes Floyd turned from him because Cus D'Amato, who manages him, influences him.

Billy, who was called Dickie by Floyd in their childhood, didn't see the Johansson fight. He didn't bother to listen to it on the radio. He feels that a man should send his brother a ticket when he is the champion of the world.

The last time Billy talked to Floyd, he ran a restaurant which was on the verge of bankruptcy.

"There was a little trouble," Billy said. "I needed money. I started to talk about how much I needed, but he said with the new house he was building and all, he couldn't give me none. It was a little bit to a champ. But to me it was everything. So I said forget about it. I haven't seen him since.

"Why should I bother to listen on the radio if he didn't bother to send me a ticket? We were close when we were kids but, afterwards, we argued. What can I do? Once Floyd offered me money, but it isn't enough to live on. I got to fight."

Danny knew, when he called me, how much this story would hurt me, but he also knew so much more about me and the relationship with my brother than anybody else, except my poor mother. How would she feel when she heard about the terrible thing one of her sons was saying about another?

Florio knew, too, how I helped to start Billy in a restaurant. Once I had to borrow a large sum of money from Danny to give to Billy. I had to repay the loan to Danny, but I never expected Billy to repay it to me. I was glad to be able to do something for him, because we were growing apart, and as I mentioned earlier, it seemed to me that Billy resented my success when I first began to achieve some fame in the ring.

Twice more after that first time, Billy asked me for money to help him out in business. Both times I gave it to him. He was part of my flesh, just as much as the others in my family whom I helped as I made more and more money. Once, I think it was

196

in August, 1958, I did something I'd never done before, just because my brother told me it would be a big favor for him.

Across the street from his restaurant, there was a saloon that sent its liquor customers into Billy's place for their food. I was in Billy's place this day. I'm not being vain when I say that my personal appearance at the restaurant helped pick up business. But after I was there awhile, Billy asked me to make a personal appearance in the saloon. Liquor makes me sick. The beer smell in a saloon turns my stomach, but I did what Billy asked just the same.

Well, maybe Billy had to give up his restaurant and try to get into boxing. Maybe he did ask me for money a fourth time to keep his business going, and maybe I did refuse, but if I did, it was because the others in my family needed help, too.

Anyway, when this story broke—I guess maybe I broke down with it again. I had my wife read my mail first, and she showed me only those letters that wouldn't add to my depression. I know she tried to keep all papers and magazines away from me which had pictures of me going down before Ingemar, but I wasn't helping Sandra much. I was no longer the champion, but I wasn't being much of a husband and father either. I wasn't easy to live with. Finally, I imagine, it was almost getting too much for Sandra.

"Floyd," she pleaded with me one night, "you just can't sit around this house moping any more. We've got to get out and do some things, be with people, talk to people."

"Who will I talk to?" I asked. "So many people are happy I lost. They act like it's a celebration."

"You have friends, honey, who believe in you. You've even had letters from people in Sweden saying you'll beat him the next time. Remember the way the people cheered you when we came out of Yankee Stadium that night? Think of all the people who have come past the house and looked at it. They know the champion lives here."

"The champion," I said, "doesn't live here any more. He

197

lives in Sweden. The people are coming by to look at a morgue."

"Floyd, you'll be the champion again," she said.

"I'd like to believe that," I said, "but it's hard."

"Let's get out," she said. "Let's go to a movie."

"All right," I said, "but not to New York. We'll go to one here in town."

I got out of my pajamas and robe and into some clothes. We drove a half mile or so into town. We parked the car in a lot around the corner from the theater and got out and walked to the movie house. As we turned the corner and could see the marquee over the street, I could feel Sandra slow up and flinch beside me. I stopped short and looked at her. Her face had suddenly gone sad again. Then I looked up at the marquee.

"JOHANSSON–PATTERSON FIGHT FILMS," the electric lights shone in the night.

Without saying another word, Sandra turned around and started walking back to the car, and I walked right with her.

"Do you want to find another show?" she asked after I'd started the motor.

"No," I said. "Let's just go home."

"You've got to see the picture sometime," she said.

"What picture?" I said, not understanding for the moment.

"The film of the fight," Sandra said.

"I'll see it when I'm ready for it," I said.

I couldn't see any point in seeing it yet. In the film I would be knocked down seven times. In my own mind I'd already been knocked down a hundred or more times. The pain was still there—a kind of embarrassment that I wondered if I'd ever get over. I couldn't help but know that in certain quarters of boxing and the press there was a great deal of satisfaction that I'd been beaten. Some of the writers were saying it was the best thing that could happen to boxing. Ingemar was popular. He was a handsome man who liked the spotlight, and I didn't. I liked what went with the title—the recognition on the street, kids coming to my door and asking for my autograph—and even that had come to a stop.

I truly don't remember exactly how many weeks or months went by while I gave into the black mood until I finally began to fight my way out of it. So many other things had happened and were happening, which were just as painful and embarrassing—and I'll go into them later on.

All this, together with the delays that took place before I was able to sign for my return match, made the year between the time I lost my title and won it back again a real nightmare. It was a bad time, a lost year. It was a time, I must admit, when I felt sorrier for myself than all the years I have lived. Adversity, they say, makes you tougher and more determined. I guess it did that for me, yet it was somebody else's bad luck that finally kicked me back on the right road. I use the word "kick," because it seems to be the only right one for what I mean. It was a jolt harder than Ingemar hit me, and it happened when I could have turned in on myself so badly that I would never have come out again.

This was very late at night. The house was still and quiet. Sandra and the children were asleep. I was in the den—where else?—with the television going, watching the "Late Late Show." I couldn't tell you now what I was watching. I couldn't have told you then. But suddenly I realized the show was over, because they were playing *The Star-Spangled Banner* and the channel was signing off for the night. I still wasn't sleepy, so I just sat there in the dark letting my mind wander.

Somehow or other I got to thinking of all the places I'd visited and all the things I'd been able to do as the champion. I'd been to Europe several times and to practically every state in the union. I lived well and traveled first class. For a kid who had grown up in the Bedford-Stuyvesant area, I'd even gotten accustomed to wearing a tuxedo. Once I even wore a white tie and tails.

Tails? Where was that? Yeh, Atlantic City. Now what was I doing there? Suddenly I remembered that Chico Vejar had fought somebody or other there, and it was a funny kind of a fight.

It was staged in a night club with an invited audience, all of whom had to be dressed up in evening clothes. As the champion, I had been invited to attend, and I'd been fitted out for tails by the evening-clothes manufacturer who had an advertising tie-in with the fight.

I recalled then that while I was in Atlantic City there were requests for me to visit various places, including a hospital. Sitting there in the dark, I could see it all clearly then. I had gone to a cancer hospital and gone through the wards talking to some of the patients. One of them was a little girl, who lay as still as death. Her body was shrunken. Her arms and legs were as skinny as toothpicks. I thought she was an infant, but the doctor with us told me she was five years old.

"What's the matter with her, Doctor?" I asked.

"The child has leukemia," he said.

"But she'll get better, won't she?" I asked.

"She may not live through the night," he said.

Such a sight is never pleasant. Such news can make you depressed, but you walk away from it and try to forget it. I had forgotten it—until that early morning mood when I recreated the hospital scene and that child in my mind. "She might have been my baby," I thought. "Her poor parents."

I watched the sun come up that morning—all the time giving myself a lecture about how lucky I had been to have been a titleholder, to have money in the bank, a house, a nice family and my children healthy.

"Who are you," I said to myself, "to sit there feeling sorry for yourself? So you lost a fight and lost your title. Now get up and start to fight back! Start to live again."

I pulled back the drapes and opened the blinds. I ran upstairs and shook Sandra awake. For the first time since the fight, she saw me smile.

"I'm going back into training," I told her. "I've had some thinking to do and I've done it and now it's over. Let's go to a show tonight."

"Uptown?" she asked.

"Uptown," I said.

That day I called Cus. I told him to get me a camp somewhere off in the woods. I told him I wanted to start working out again. It pleased him. He knew how down-in-the-mouth I had been. He was eager to get me going again, even if he was beginning to have considerable troubles of his own that I was only to learn about and begin to take seriously later. These troubles gave me many anxious moments, but for the time being, my problem was more basic. I had to get back into training. I had to prove to myself that I could fight well enough to recapture the title if I got the chance.

My first camp, if I can call it that, was at Roaring Brook in upstate New York. It was a little farm, which boarded a few people in the summer, and I could do some roadwork and take walks in the woods. After a couple of weeks, I had Wilson Hannibal, a sparring partner, come up. I figured we could fool around in the back yard with the big gloves. But after three weeks we had to leave there.

The weather was beginning to cool, and the place was closing for the fall. After searching around, we found a gym in Westport, Connecticut, which could be altered to our specifications. It was not as secluded as I could hope for, being in a wealthy section of Fairfield County, but it was good enough to start training in and to think about refitting. Cus moved into a motel nearby, and I started going around with real estate men looking for a place to rent for living quarters, but the people were asking ridiculous sums.

By this time the background of the promotion of the first fight had begun to fill the papers. The State Athletic Commission, the State's Attorney General, and New York's District

Attorney Hogan had begun an investigation into things I knew nothing about. When the name of Fat Tony Salerno, whom the papers identified as a mobster, came out as having been identified as a part owner of the promotion, I was horrified.

My feeling wasn't much worse than that of the people of Westport. One day I came to the gym and was shown the local paper. Its headline read: "Boxing Gangsters Invade Westport." I got out of there right that same day. I was no gangster. I wasn't going to be identified as such.

It was getting on into the late fall—and, remember, the return bout was supposed to have been fought in September, but no agreement of any kind had been reached yet—when we finally settled down in Newtown, Connecticut. Enric Madriguera, the band leader, owned the LaRonde, a roadhouse which had shuttered for lack of business, three miles outside of town. We rented the building and grounds on a monthly basis. We used the dance floor for the gym, setting up our ring in it. We installed our light and heavy bags, the mirrors for shadow boxing and the exercise mats. We stocked the abandoned kitchen with food and had five rooms upstairs for sleeping quarters for myself, Danny and the training staff.

You'll never know how anxious I was to box for the six weeks or so it took to outfit the gym properly. Meanwhile, I was chopping down trees, doing roadwork and working on the light and heavy bags, but all the time in my own mind was the wonder of whether or not I would be glove shy. Many veteran boxing men say a man knocked out the first time can't come back the same. The punch he took that put him away has to be on his mind. I thought that was ridiculous, but it had to be put to a test.

My first session finally came, and I was satisfied with myself. But I knew I could be fooling myself, too. It was only in the gym. I had to box and expose myself to being hit in front of people. I had Cus arrange a two-week exhibition tour in Canada for me. I boxed maybe ten times. Only then could I be certain that there was no aftermath of having been hit. A lot of people didn't believe it, but I proved it to myself with complete satisfaction by the time I had come home to rejoin my family just before Christmas.

There might still have been some reservations in the minds of those around me, even if there were none in mine. The thing that bothered them was that I still adamantly refused to look at the films of my fight with Johansson. Soon after we opened the camp, Danny and Buster wanted to begin studying the film. I said no. A few days later they asked again. "We got a lot of time. We can study it good," Danny said. "Why don't you want to look at it? When will you look at it?"

"Next week," I said. But I said the same thing the week after that and then again and again. I wasn't eager to see myself go down seven times. I just wasn't ready for it yet. Every few days they'd ask again. Once Buster said, "Floyd, do you mind if I look at them myself?"

"We'll all look at them at the same time, when I'm ready to," I said.

I had the film right there and a projector. All we had to do was load it and turn off the lights, but there was something much deeper in my delaying than Danny, Buster or even I knew then—and maybe know now. I've thought about it a lot. I thought about it in Göteborg, Sweden, when I visited there after knocking out Johansson to regain the title. Ingemar visited me and we talked about the third bout, and he looked me right in the eye. That puzzled me. I had to examine my own conscience about myself.

There was this time when Ingemar was still the champion, and he did a lot with the title. He appeared on Dinah Shore's show, and I didn't watch him. Then he appeared as an actor in the TV dramatization of Ernest Hemingway's *The Killers*. I knew the show was scheduled, but I had no interest in seeing it. I didn't think anybody in my camp would want to see it either.

The night the show was on, some of us were playing cards in

the kitchen. The game broke up and I came upstairs. Then I left the room, and while I was out, my brother Raymond turned on the set. I came back into the room, or maybe I was attracted back to it by the sound of the Swedish voice. I looked at the screen, and there was Ingemar lying on a bed.

"Who turned that on?" I asked. I must have sounded annoyed.

"I did," Raymond said. "I wanted to watch it. You want it off?"

"It's okay," I said. "Leave it on." But I started to leave the room. Then I walked back into the room and sat in a chair facing the set. At first I kept my head bowed so that I didn't see the screen.

"You might as well look at his face," I told myself.

I looked up and watched the rest of the show. Ingemar was a very good actor, but that bothered me. I've thought of it many times. I thought of it again, as I said, when I saw him after I had beaten him.

"Here he is happy and cheerful and friendly after I knock him out," I said to myself, "but I couldn't look at his face for a long time."

It wasn't fear. It was shame. During the winter after I lost and Ingemar was the champion, he and I were invited to the New York Boxing Writers' Dinner. He came, but of course, I didn't. I think the answer was that I didn't want to see him, not even later at the signing, until we were together in the ring again.

Of course, that couldn't be. I knew that sooner or later I'd have to look at the films of our first fight to study where I'd made my mistakes, to re-examine his strength and determine his weaknesses.

I just wanted it later, as late as possible. In my heart I knew that once I saw myself being beaten so badly, I'd build a viciousness in myself. I didn't want that feeling to come too soon. If I got the edge too fast, I might lose it before we got into the ring. A man can hold himself at an emotional peak only for so long.

When the time did come, finally, it wasn't my doing, really. It was in the first week in June, about three weeks before the bout. Louis Chantigny of the Montreal *Le Petit Journal*, one of my good friends among the newspaper people, visited my camp and stayed a few days. One evening after dinner he asked me if I'd seen the films yet. I told him I hadn't, but he asked a favor.

"Let me set up some still pictures as though you and I were watching the movie," Louis said.

I saw no harm in that. We set up the camera and put the film in it as Louis and I sat facing a screen.

"All you have to do, Floyd," Louis said, "is push the switch and then these pictures I want to take of you won't be false. It will help you, Floyd, more than it will help me."

"Why not?" I said. "It's about time anyway."

I pushed the button and the electric whirring of the machine began. I can truthfully say there was a whirring in my ears, too, that came from my heart. There I was on the screen, but it wasn't me at all. Buster and Danny and Louis began exclaiming about this, that, and the other thing . . . "You should have bobbed and weaved . . . You're letting his jab bother you, and it's no jab at all . . . You're letting him get set . . ."

I said nothing. As I went down time after time on the screen, I buried my head in my hands and groaned. "How could I be so bad?" I finally said.

It was a hard fight to lock the rest of my feelings inside myself. I couldn't wait for the second fight. I knew I could do better on my worst day. I saw so many openings before and even after I got hit. His head was up so straight, that if I threw a straight jab, I'd have been able to hit him. But I was in a low crouch and I couldn't reach him, while he could always reach me or, at least, flick that jab at me and bother me.

When the film had been run once, I had it rewound. "Play it again," I said. This time I watched it more intently. "I should

205

have looked at the picture a long time ago," I said. The film started up once more. When I hit the deck for the third time, I said, "That's enough."

It was as though nobody was listening to me. Nobody in the room went to the set to shut off the reminder of my disaster. I got up from my chair and yanked the plug out of the wall. I walked out of that room as angry as I've ever been—but the target for my anger was myself. Johansson would pay for my lost year. I made a vow to myself that I intended to keep.

I made up my mind to one other thing. Nobody went down with me those seven times that I went down to the canvas. A fighter walks alone and fights alone. If I could be successful the next time, I promised myself I'd be my own man. The mistakes would be mine, the decisions mine. I had to be defeated to learn that. I wouldn't forget it.

Chapter Seventeen

It's hard waking up to reality when you've been living in a kind of dream world, but life forces things on you that you've finally got to see when the morning comes.

That year between titles was the evening and the morning, and in between was a nightmare that became a time of decision for me. Ingemar did more than knock me out. He made me think for myself. That's an awfully painful thing, especially for somebody who always had somebody else to do his thinking for him.

Until Ingemar knocked me out, Cus was my mind, more or less. I had no reason to doubt anything he did or said, because every minute of my relationship with him I was like a son being guided by his father. Eventually, the son grows up. Inevitably he begins to think more and more for himself. Occasionally something happens that makes the boy become a man before it was intended. It is always a shock to the father, but after a while the father becomes resigned that that, too, is the way of life.

It seems to me that's about the most accurate way to sum up what has happened in my relationship with my manager. Nominally, at least, Cus continued to be what he always was, but actually I tried to show him that too many things had happened for me to allow myself ever to be completely in anyone's control again. I was Cus' boy, but in defeat and confusion I became my own man.

This is a difficult thing to discuss, because I never want to make it appear that I'm deliberately trying to hurt Cus. I was hurt, very badly, and maybe inadvertently by him, but whatever he did, I know he thought he was doing it solely for my benefit.

So let me try to retrace this subtle change, because I owe it to myself as much as I owe D'Amato a debt of gratitude. From the beginning Cus acted to protect me and instill the confidence in me that I didn't have. From the time he met me at the plane after I had returned from the Olympics until after I had become the champion the first time, everything he said or did I accepted as right. I believed in his crusade against the International Boxing Club because I believed in him. I had faith in the way he handled me, and it was borne out by my climb to the top.

Oh, there were irritations along the way, naturally, but Cus usually would have some kind of complicated explanation for them, and generally I'd accept what he said. Frankly, in the early days I didn't understand enough of what he was saying, and I'd just agree blindly, so as not to show my ignorance. Cus is a persuasive talker.

Once in a while I'd take a stand on something because I'd want it so badly, and then Cus would give in. For instance, in the days before I became the champ, but was moving up, I'd go off to camp by myself and I'd be lonely. I'd see somebody like Sugar Ray Robinson at Greenwood Lake with a big party of people around him all the time and ask Cus to let me have at least one guy to keep me company.

"You have to be careful about having people around you," Cus would warn me. "They'll take advantage of you."

For a long time I accepted that, but finally I wanted Buster with me. "What do you need him for?" Cus demanded angrily.

"I just want him with me," I said, arguing with Cus for the first time. "Besides, I want him to get something out of it."

I mention this only to show that now and then I'd stand up to D'Amato, but it was less a question of pitting my will against his or my inexperience in such things against his experience than it was learning to make decisions for myself. For a long time there were papers signed involving me in various business matters that I didn't know anything about. That was all right with me because I sincerely believed it was my business to fight and Cus' to manage. Some of these papers cost me money, and I didn't even mind that. Cus had helped me to make a lot of money. I couldn't even get sore at him in his maneuvering for the London fight and the change of promoters and site. It cost me a lot of money.

I wanted a warmup for Johansson, but I wasn't too proud of myself for what I did in Indianapolis. Neither was I proud of what came out after the fight. I could say this was kind of an alarm clock for me—the beginning of a sort of awakening that made me look at myself in relation to Cus.

Of all the fights I've had, this is the one about which I couldn't look in the mirror and tell myself I won it all by myself. I don't mean anything was wrong with it. I don't mean London was doped or whatnot, but to me it looked like we all won the fight, including London.

I was terribly embarrassed by that fight and all the circumstances surrounding it. First there was London being met at the airport in New York by D'Amato's representative and kept away from the newspapermen. That part I could understand. If the press had gotten to London before all the details of the fight had been straightened out, London might have talked, and the fight might never have come off.

But then London winds up doing his early training before going to Indianapolis at Cus' Gramercy Park Gym. He works out with my own sparring partners and is trained by Nick Baffi, who is a good boxing man but happened to be a friend of Cus' and a former business associate. Once when I was sparring at the gym, Cus came around to see me, and who should be with him, but the man who was going to be my next opponent.

We had guaranteed London his expenses and purse. Hardly had London returned to England when he told the newspapers there that Cus had originally guaranteed him a second shot at me if he would agree to let my manager manage him. I believed Cus when he denied that story. I still do. But only weeks before I was supposed to get into the ring with Ingemar the first time, another bombshell exploded, which Cus didn't try to deny.

In a book that was written for him in Sweden, Johansson claimed that to get his match with me, he had had to agree to take on an American manager suggested by Cus. It turned out to be a man named Harry Davidow, who used to be D'Amato's partner in the Gramercy Gym many years before I started fighting. Davidow, who had been out of boxing for fifteen years and was running a luncheonette in Brooklyn at the time, was to get ten per cent out of Johansson's purses and be allowed to select two opponents for him for the next five years, in the event he beat me.

Once the news of this undercover agreement broke, Cus explained he had no direct or indirect money interest in Ingemar. One paragraph in a three-page explanation was the following:

"I thought it would be better if Johansson had an American manager whom we both could trust. I recommended Harry Davidow, as a former associate of mine who knows the boxing business, as well as being thoroughly honest and reliable. The terms of the agreement are strictly Johansson's and Davidow's."

I can say this from the bottom of my heart. Those terms and any and every word in that agreement were not mine. I did not know Davidow. Until Johansson revealed the terms, I did not know such a man as Davidow existed or that such a contract existed.

When Davidow applied for a license before the New York State Athletic Commission on May 22, a little more than a month before my fight with Ingemar, it was disallowed.

I liked that decision. I didn't want any friend of my manager's being in Johansson's corner. I understood that Cus had acted to protect my interests, but I truly sympathized with Ingemar. It would have been a terrible injustice to him to have been forced to have Davidow. It was an injustice to me to have even a suggestion of that kind of a shadow fall across my reputation.

If I was concerned about my reputation before the fight, imagine what I must have thought of it afterward, when I not only was beaten but other things came out which made me wonder whether I'd ever get a second chance to prove myself. About the middle of July things began to appear in the papers that left me completely bewildered. At first I found them very difficult to believe. I assumed that now that I was down, some of Cus' enemies among the newspapermen were getting in their licks against him and me.

I'd never had what you'd call a "good press." Cus hadn't made too many friends among the newspapermen, and because a lot of them didn't like Cus, they'd get at him by giving me poor write-ups. So for a while, when names like Vincent Velella, "Fat Tony" Salerno, Frank Erickson and Gilbert Lee Beckley began showing up in the stories, I didn't believe them.

But then, before long, the District Attorney, Attorney General and New York State Athletic Commission came into the picture, and I began to see that at least some of it was true. Salerno was a gangster. Velella was his lawyer. Erickson and Beckley were gamblers with police records. I kept asking my-

211

self, "What could they have had to do with the fight or the promotion or with me or my manager?"

I began to ask Cus questions. "Is all of this true?"

"I was only trying to protect your interests," he'd tell me. "I had nothing to do with Salerno, Erickson and Beckley."

As the picture developed, I had to face it. Through Bill Rosensohn, who promoted the fight, Velella had become a partner in the promotion. Somewhere, somehow, Salerno had come into it. I began to see that maybe Cus had been taken by his friends. I didn't mistrust Cus then. I don't now, but I did begin to develop a mistrust of the people around him, for whom Cus always did favors.

The thing that bothered me most, of course, was that some of the dirt which had been uncovered about the promotion had to rub off on me. I had always kept myself out of negotiations, but I saw then that there was more to it than the mere signing of a paper. I made up my mind right then that if I ever got the opportunity again, nothing concerning me would ever be done without my knowledge and without my complete agreement.

When I talked to Cus about all these terrible things which I had so much trouble understanding, as they came out one after the other, I just formed my own answer. I also knew I had to take stock of how things had been between Cus and me. I had to weigh how much he had meant to me for so many years against the mistakes I realized he had made, and it got down to the conclusion that Cus had made some bad decisions, but also many good ones. It led me to thinking of other things that had happened along the way. "How many times before has Cus given me the same kind of answers?" I wondered. "How many agreements were there before that I didn't know about?" I thought about the time in California when I'd gone out there to train for the Harris fight and we'd brought José Torres, Cus' middleweight, along for sparring purposes.

As I wrote earlier, that was a terrible time for me, after almost a year's layoff. My reflexes were shot, my timing was off. I couldn't do anything right for a long time. Many days I sparred with Torres, and he made me look silly because he was so much faster than I; but there was one day that sticks in my mind. Torres threw a right hand. I jumped back to get away from it, and as I did, my legs became tangled and I began to fall to the canvas. At the same time Torres threw a left, which grazed my head as I was falling. I wasn't down because of a blow, but a slip. I jumped right back up and began to box him again.

After the workout, some newspapermen came into my dressing room. "Don't you feel funny about being knocked down by a middleweight?" one of them asked.

"Did it look like I was knocked down?" I asked.

Torres had come into the room. The same fellow said to him, "José, did you knock the champ down?"

Torres said, "No," with a smile on his face. And that would have been all right with me, as it should have been all right with the newspapermen. Except that, later, one newspaperman pursued the subject with Torres privately, and he had told another newspaperman that he actually had knocked me down but didn't want to embarrass me by revealing it publicly. The next day I got a call from my wife. "What's going on out there?" she asked me. "There's a big story you got knocked down by a middleweight."

The following day I got Torres in the ring in the gym, and I'm ashamed to say, I tried to show him up. I still wasn't right, but I had him hurt and I was trying to keep him hurt. Danny knew what had happened and he understood my feelings. He wouldn't call time, although Cus was on the ring apron waving to him frantically to stop the round. Danny finally did.

I never said anything to Cus about that incident, but I couldn't help concluding in my own mind that Cus should have made a greater effort to discourage a story from getting out that would embarrass me. I'm not saying Cus went along with it, but it did occur to me that maybe he felt the story would help to build Torres into a middleweight contender faster. I guess maybe the germ began developing in my own

213

mind then that I wasn't going to be used as a steppingstone for anybody else.

These were the things I kicked around in my mind in all those black months between the first and second Ingemar fights. In the meantime, I wasn't seeing Cus as often as I did before I lost the title. Maybe Cus understood that for a lot of that time I wanted to be alone. Much of the time, too, Cus was away for one reason or another. Maybe he had a lot to think about, too.

Certainly I gave him a few things to think about when I began to assert myself more and more. In the beginning he found it difficult to accept my new attitude. We argued a bit, but I explained to him that certain things were inevitable. Little by little I had to begin depending more upon my own decisions, and it just happened that the jolt of the Johansson defeat hastened the process.

By early fall there was a three-sided investigation into the background of the promotion of the Johansson fight. The District Attorney was talking to people involved in it. The Attorney General's office was looking into certain business aspects of it. The Athletic Commission, which had already suspended Rosensohn's license as a promoter, suspended Cus' as a manager. There's some legal business here that I really can't understand. Cus' license actually had expired and he hadn't bothered as yet to renew it. So you've got to wonder how anything that doesn't exist can be suspended. That's what the Court said, too.

In any event, the original date for the return bout, September 22, had passed, and I was worrying about whether or not there'd ever be a new date. The thing became further complicated by the possibility that the commission, which had brought some charges against Cus, would find him guilty and make it impossible for me to fight under his management in New York.

I should say here that Cus and I actually had no contract, other than our own personal bond for each other, at that point. Our contract had expired, and we hadn't taken the trouble to renew it. That's nothing to be excited about, of course, for during many years of our relationship there were no formal agreements between us. We still don't have a contract, but Cus gets, as he's always gotten, his 33⅓ per cent from the purses after all the expenses are taken off the top.

When I first tied up with Cus, we had no contract either, but as time went on and other people in boxing tried to move in and take me away from Cus, I finally told him that if we signed a formal contract, maybe all of that sniping would stop. We've had several such agreements, the longest for a period of three years.

Let me say here, too, so that nobody gets any other ideas, that as long as I keep fighting, Cus will continue to be my manager. I listen to any suggestions he makes, and if they're good, I accept them, just as I accept advice from my attorney, Julius November. A lot of people in boxing have concluded that November has replaced D'Amato as my manager. That isn't true.

Anyway, D'Amato's license was revoked on November 24, 1959. Many people wondered if I would or could be able to fight without Cus in my corner or advising me about the fight. This hurt, too. On the one hand, it made me appear to be kind of a puppet on a string in D'Amato's hands. On the other, it made me out to be kind of a fool.

From the moment Johansson beat me, all I ever had deep down in my consciousness was my desire to win the title back. From the moment D'Amato was de-licensed by the commission, there was no question in my mind that with or without Cus, I would face Ingemar anywhere to get my chance. Guys began writing that if D'Amato couldn't be with me, I would retire rather than fight without him. How stupidly can people think? As a matter of fact, long before any progress was made in the agreement for the second fight, I had hired a secretary who had only one real job. That was to clip out all the disparaging articles about me in newspapers and magazines and paste them into a scrapbook. A facing page was left blank for a definite purpose. I wanted all the bad things written about me to be right next to all the good things that would have to be written about me if I regained the crown.

Before that could be done, though, the promotional confusion had to be straightened out, and miraculously it was. In the agreement for our first fight there had been a return-bout clause. Rosensohn Enterprises thus owned the return-bout contract, but since Rosensohn himself had lost his right to promote and the commission would not recognize Velella, somebody else had to buy the contract from them.

First one group tried and failed. Then a group calling itself Feature Sports, with William Fugazy as its president and Roy Cohn as its counsel, bought up the shares owned by Velella and Rosensohn. That opened the way for the bout, which was set for June 20 at the Polo Grounds in New York City.

I signed for myself on April 21 in the commission's offices. By then I was deep in my training. Cus would call the camp at Newtown once or twice a week, and I would speak to him if there was anything I had to tell him, but most of the time he'd be satisfied to talk to Danny. Toward the end of the training period he came up to camp and spent a few days, but it was not like it had once been between us.

Two and a half weeks before fight time something happened that would have thrown D'Amato into a real tailspin had he been made aware of it. But I didn't want him to know it. He might have wanted the fight postponed. I didn't want anything to set the date back and cut into the fine edge I knew I was beginning to reach.

I was boxing with Julio Mederos, one of my sparring partners, when I felt a stabbing pain in my right elbow after throwing a long hard punch. I continued to box, but each time I repeated the punch, the pain became worse and worse. After the workout, I told Florio about it.

Danny and I drove to the Danbury Medical Center, a short distance away from my camp. An orthopedic specialist examined the arm and found that something really had gone wrong. The force of my punch had displaced bones in my forearm and upper arm. When these bones work normally, they hinge at the elbow. But the way they were working, the bones rubbed against each other instead of hinging.

The specialist said that I needed rest and some whirlpool treatment in hot water. I couldn't rest. If I laid off even for a couple of days, I would fall away from the peak of conditioning I was nearing. Once you lose that, there's hardly any chance at all of getting it back. I just had to take the chance of not resting, but concentrating on the whirlpool treatment.

We sent Buster to rent a whirlpool unit, and it was delivered in the darkness that night so that nobody could see it and then installed in my room where only those I allowed to enter could see the bath. The next day I went on with my training, but several times a day I gave the arm a fifteen-minute treatment. I discovered that if I shortened my punches and didn't put too much pressure on the elbow bones, I wouldn't have pain.

That satisfied me, except that right after I began taking the whirlpool baths I discovered that I seemed to be losing the strength in my right arm. If I held it up in my regular boxing position, the arm would start to feel weaker and weaker after a while, and I had to lower it or drop it completely. Florio, Buster and I talked about what it could be. One afternoon a thought hit me. "The water," I said suddenly.

Both of them looked at me as if I had gone crazy. "Don't you see?" I said. "We've been filling that tub with water as hot as my skin can stand without me getting burned. The doctor said hot water, and maybe we've been making it hotter than necessary. I've lost about two pounds every time I stuck my arm in it and kept it there for fifteen minutes."

It turned out that was the reason for the weakness. When

we dropped the water temperature, the arm stopped getting weak. We all breathed a sigh of relief, but on June 15, the day before I boxed for the last time in training, I was finishing up on the speed bag. I threw a hard, but high, left hand at it. Instead of landing on the bag, my hand hit the metal swivel on which the bag is attached. "My hand's broken," I thought immediately.

Again we kept it as secret as possible, but I couldn't hide it from my handlers. The bone wasn't broken, but the hand swelled at the third joints of the index and middle fingers and became extremely sore. Imagine how it was. Here I was training almost ten months, and the last few weeks of it I had to go and put all kinds of burdens on myself. However, nothing could stop me from getting into the ring with Ingemar at the appointed time at the Polo Grounds.

For over a year there had been all kinds of emotional, legal, financial, contractual and personal obstacles that had to be hurdled. If Cus had had his way early in the negotiations for the fight, there would have been no fight. When Ingemar demanded more than he was supposed to get, I told Cus, "Give it to him. Don't give him any excuse to delay the fight." Cus didn't want me to sign, but I told him, "I'm getting into the ring with him again, no matter what."

It's a funny thing, but the morning after the fight a press conference was held at the Hotel Commodore. One of the newspapermen in the crowd questioned me as to who had been the greater influence in my recapture of the title—Joe Louis, who had given me some advice on fighting Ingemar, or my manager.

As the question was asked, D'Amato, who stood behind me, leaned over. If he said something to me in my ear, I don't remember what it was. But I do remember most clearly what my answer was to that question.

"Floyd Patterson," I said.

Chapter Eighteen

During the many months of lonely training to win back my heavyweight title, I had three problems which had to be faced directly. The first, and perhaps the most important, was to prepare myself emotionally for what lay ahead of me. The second was to work up a defense for Ingemar's right hand. The third was my own offense against him.

The thing, it seemed to me, that made everything easier was the eventual appreciation that while I was the champion I didn't even feel like a champ. Not until I lost the title did I begin to understand properly how much it was that I had lost. It was less my belief in myself than the belief that others might have had in me. This is the thing that hurt, and as the months went on it became a real pain, driving me harder and harder toward the goal I was determined to achieve.

In January, 1960, for instance, Ingemar returned to this country to receive an award as "Sportsman of the Year." He was interviewed extensively by the newspapers, and in every article I read quoting him, it seemed to me that he went out of his way to disparage me. Whether or not he was quoted correctly or meant what he said, Ingemar's words helped to set me thinking along the right line. He claimed I still didn't know what hit me, but, he added, I would never forget it nor would

I ever recover from it. "It is a memory that must be terrible for him," Johansson was quoted.

It was a terrible memory, but it proved to me that Johansson was going to let himself be fooled by his first victory, just as I had let myself be fooled into defeat by my own indifference. I didn't want revenge, which is something I'd never seek, but I did want redemption more than I'd ever wanted anything else. Of course, I would remember the right hand that knocked me out and the first man who ever was able to do it, but not the way Ingemar thought I would. He thought less of me as a fighter because he'd won. I thought more of him, but no less of myself.

What Ingemar and so many others failed to realize as the time for the fight neared was that I was ready to be carried out again if necessary. I was going to respect his right hand, but not so much that there wasn't going to be any fight. Early in my training I found out I wasn't glove shy, but Ingemar apparently didn't believe it or didn't want to believe it.

When he talked to the newspapermen at his camp in Grossinger's, he could barely hide his disdain for me. He let them conclude that the first time he would look me in the eyes in the ring he would see fear in them. He even referred to me once as "a gymnasium fighter."

When the reporter who'd written those remarks came up to my camp at Newtown, I couldn't wait to get him alone and ask him whether Johansson actually had said all those things about me that had been written. "I happen to have my notebook with me in which I'd put down Johansson's remarks," he said.

He reached into a back pocket and took out one of those little brown dime notebooks. "Would you care to read the notes yourself?" he asked me.

"I don't think that's necessary now," I said. I had another reason added to all the others already stored up for fighting a completely different fight with a completely different attitude than I had had the first time. All of this built up a mental attitude in me, which actually was all the defense I felt I would need against Ingemar's right hand. I was developing a viciousness I had never felt before. There was a curtness and meanness in me that once would have been foreign to me but now seemed as normal as the nose on my face.

Only one thing still has to be explained, and that was my own decision to alter my style of offensive fighting which would nullify his style of defensive fighting. At first I was bothered by one little thing. I didn't seem fast to myself, certainly not as fast as I used to be. It's my practice to review films of my early fights. That way I can recall some of the moves I made that I liked and some that I didn't like. I guess it's the same way when they take motion pictures of baseball players at bat. They have them when the man's hitting good and then they take them when the man's hitting bad. He looks at himself at one stage and then he looks at himself at another. He can see right away how he's swinging differently, whether he's too anxious, or whether he's protecting the plate.

It was the same way with me. We'd show the movies of old fights, and I could see how fast I was. One night after watching one of these pictures, I said to Buster, "I've slowed down. I was real quick then. I'm not now."

I never saw Buster get so angry with me before. "You're fast now," he said, "only you're a heavyweight now, a real heavyweight. You didn't used to be. That's why you seem slower to yourself."

That was very true. I came in against Ingemar at 190, the heaviest I had ever fought in my life. Weight is supposed to rob you of speed, but the weight properly distributed in the right places gives you power, and that leads me to another of my preparations which led to my victory. If you remember, in the first fight Ingemar kept sticking his left hand into my face. It wasn't a hurting jab, just an annoying one. It spoiled my concentration, upset my timing, and together with my own doubt that he had any right hand, left me open for the punch which separated me from my senses and my crown.

But with the added weight and power on my side, Danny, Buster and I decided I should jab just as much as Johansson. My jab had become a hurting jab, so that it could be a real offensive weapon. At the same time, we figured that if I kept jabbing, Ingemar would be unable to throw that right hand, because in his style of fighting he didn't duck away from the jab, but picked it off with his right hand. If his right was kept busy on defense, he certainly couldn't be throwing it at my chin.

One other adjustment in my style had to be made. In the first fight I fought out of a crouch, from which I can bob and weave better, but from the crouch I could not reach Ingemar with a punch unless I closed with him. I'd be maybe six inches short, and this was proved to me by Danny. If I crouched less, I could be right on the target.

It all seems simple in the telling, and it turned out to be relatively simple in the doing, but there were months of sweat in the preparation and many more months of making all the little things fit together.

As we drove down the day before the fight from Newtown to the Governor Clinton Hotel in New York City, which would be my headquarters until I left for the Polo Grounds, I didn't have that feeling of mental laziness I had had the year before as I rode to my meeting with Ingemar.

There was a kind of contentment in me, born of the conclusion that I was as mentally, emotionally and physically prepared as I could be. Ingemar was favored this time, where I had been a five-to-one favorite the other time, but the odds meant little to me. What meant more than anything else is that I appreciated I had come through a bad year better for what had happened to me.

There was so much I had to make up for, not the least of which was my determination to prove that so many of the so-called experts had guessed wrong again. They had written some terrible things about me in the papers, some of which I'd read, some ignored. I suppose a fighter has to expect to have some harsh critics in the press, but it seemed to me that in so much of what was written about me there wasn't the objectivity that writers are supposed to have.

I imagine most of them supposed that I spent the night before the fight worrying about how I'd react the first time I'd get hit with Ingemar's right hand. At least, that's what they wrote. Well, some of them would have been real surprised to find that whatever concern I did have didn't interfere with my appetite at dinner that night. I ate heartily. I watched TV, including the films of the first fight in which I'd gone down so many times, and that was the final test for me. Those knockdowns didn't bother me at all.

I have no idea how Johansson spent the night, but I know that I played cards unconcernedly with my handlers, my attorney and Nat Epstein, a friend of Mr. November's who has become a friend of mine. In fact, just before I decided to go to bed, I'd won about $1.27 from Nat and we had a big laugh over the fuss he was making about me quitting the game when I was ahead.

"After the fight," I said, "I'll give you the chance to get even."

Then I went into the bedroom of the three-room suite my party occupied and went to bed. I fell asleep almost immediately, and I slept the sleep of the untroubled until the dream came, the dream which I spoke about on the first page of this story.

As I said then, I wouldn't let the dream finish because subconsciously there were two dangers. If I saw myself winning in the dream, then I might revert to my state of mind of a year before and underestimate him. If I saw Ingemar winning, it might be a sign of my own weakness. I never woke up that I know of, but the unfinished dream stayed with me all the next day, and before I knew it there I was in the ring with Johansson and the end of the dream developed far better than I possibly could have anticipated in any waking or sleeping moments.

If Ingemar expected me to be cautious, I gave him a quick surprise right at the start. There was an exchange of a couple of light jabs when I charged right after him and got in a hard left hook to his head which drove him into the ropes. I ripped a couple into his body. One of my hooks cut the skin under Ingemar's left eye, and the body attack had his left side an angry-looking red.

Right away I knew more about Johansson than I had been able to learn in our first fight. Once he threw the right hand at me, and I blocked it. I could see a look come into his eye. It was the look of a man who understood that things were going to be different this time. This time I meant business. I had the feeling that every time I connected with his head or face I was making him dizzy, and in the first fight I hadn't been able to hit him at all.

Now, before I had come out of my dressing room we had planned a little last-minute strategy. It wasn't spur-of-the-moment stuff because we had talked about it at camp. It was simply this. If Ingemar should land a solid right hand on me, I was to pretend to be hurt and retreat to make him think that what had happened in the first fight was happening again. Then, if he came at me as wide open as he did while I was floundering in the first fight, I would suddenly spring into action and catch him unawares.

Early in the second round that did happen. Ingemar hit me with the right, only this time I saw the punch coming, ducked a bit, and the blow landed too high on my head. Momentarily I was stunned, but not enough that I wouldn't know completely what was happening. My legs sagged and I staggered a bit. My immediate reaction when I'm hit is to go forward and retaliate, but then I remembered our plan and clinched.

Some people saw what happened next. As Ingemar and I came together in the clinch, I looked over his shoulder and looked right down into the worried face of Irving Kahn of TelePrompTer, which had the closed-circuit rights to the fight. Almost instinctively, I winked to let him know I was not as hurt as I looked.

When Referee Arthur Mercante broke us out of the clinch, I started to play coy. I back-pedaled, waiting for Johansson to come at me carelessly and winging, but maybe the idea had gotten across to him by then, too, that he wasn't fighting the same guy who had been so easy for him twelve months earlier. He didn't come to me.

Instead I could see another shadow pass across his eyes. I won't say it was fear, the kind he had said would have to be seen in my eyes because he had knocked me down seven times. But it certainly was something that kept him from coming to me when it seemed the opportunity was there.

So his chance passed, the only one he had for the rest of the bout. From that point on the only time he scored against me was when he flicked out his jab. From the third round some of those who were close enough to the ring to see our faces clearly have said there was a look of amusement, almost contempt, on mine. I was never amused. Fighting is a serious business. I never held Ingemar in contempt, although I knew with every feeling within me that it would be only a matter of time before I would force him to bring his guard down from his face and I would crash my fist against it again.

In the third I worked on the body hard. I was rushing him faster, getting inside so that he couldn't move away from me out of range before I could start pumping. Once he threw a right hand at me, but he was going away and it was short. Just before the round ended I got him with another left to the head and another one to the body. His strength was going out of him. I could feel it.

In the fourth round I was even hurting him with jabs,

which we had counted on happening. Midway in the round, Ingemar's eye, which I had cut in the first, began to swell, and it seemed only a matter of time before it would close. His corner must have thought so, too. During the rest period they applied an icebag to the eye.

I thought I could get him fast as we came out for the fifth. In the fourth he had put a sad smile on his face. Maybe the spectators thought he wasn't thinking too much of me even then, but I knew better. Only a hurt fighter or a silly one smiles when another man's trying to punch him. Ingemar wasn't silly, but he was hurt.

He tried to hold as we opened the fifth, but the ref broke him off me. I jabbed Ingemar a couple of times before letting go with a hard right to his body that caught him square. Johansson dropped his guard to protect his body, and I jumped in close and brought a left hook up to his jaw.

As soon as the punch was started, I knew he would be hurt if it landed. He took the count of nine on one knee. Inside me every bit of determination I could muster was stirring. I could hardly wait for him to come to his feet. I was on him as soon as the referee waved me in. He was clear-eyed, but he wasn't too steady on his feet.

My punches turned Ingemar around. In that moment of excitement I could have been excused if I had kept punching at him and maybe hit him on the back of the head or neck as he had hit me for the second knockdown of our first fight. Instead of doing that I spun him around and then let go with the final punch of the fight. People have since asked me if I have ever thrown a harder punch. I can't answer that. I know that I have never tried to throw a harder punch. It landed squarely on his jaw, and his head snapped to his left from the force of the blow. He went over backward, his feet flying in the air. I knew I was the champion of the world again, right then.

There was the matter of the count, though. When Ingemar

was in training he had said that if he hit me on the chin again, the referee could count one hundred over me, and I wouldn't get up. Nobody ever bothered to figure out how much the ref could have counted over him. I went to the neutral corner, but as the referee's hand tolled six and Ingemar still lay flat on his back without any movement to get up, there was no doubt the fight was over.

Actually, though, even in that greatest moment of my life, fear came back to me again. I was scared I had hurt him badly. As he lay unconscious on the canvas I could see blood trickling from the corner of his mouth, and his left foot was shaking like he was having a fit or something. I had knocked out men before, but I'd never seen anybody shake like that. I was frightened.

This I know. Nobody else could know it; yet for me it was a moment of greatly mixed and confused emotions. I know, too, that as the ref reached ten at 1:51 of the round, I turned to the fellows sitting in the working press and shouted down at them. It's been said I was gloating. But that isn't true. It was just the satisfaction of having proved myself to them.

That moment passed quickly. I ran to Ingemar, still lying on his back with his handlers, a doctor and the referee around him, and bent down over his quiet body. I don't know if he heard me. I don't imagine he did, because I read later that he was out on the canvas for four minutes, three more on his stool, and a long time later after he'd been taken to the dressing room.

However, I just had to say to him, "You definitely will get a third fight."

I wanted to give Ingemar the reassurance that he hadn't bothered to give me after he'd beaten me, and I went through all those long, lonely months of desolation without knowing. In fact, I repeated this same assurance to Ingemar in the ring once he had been returned to his corner. It was the least one fighter could do for another. It was more than a gesture to a man I had beaten, so far as I was concerned. Once the fight was over, all the viciousness that had been growing within me for so long, and had come to a boil in the ring, disappeared.

There was just one thing that took place on that historic night which disturbed me, and it shouldn't have, really, because I know that my wife feels her place is beside me even when I'm fighting. I guess she'd gladly take the punches I have to take to be the champion, because she's part of me and I'm part of her.

Anyway, after my handlers and I had left the ring, pushed our way through the wild crowd, and fought our way back into the dressing room, I remember laughing to myself that that part of it was tougher than the fight. In the dressing room, it was no better. The newspapermen, radiomen and television cameramen were jammed in there with the police and well-wishers, and it was so crowded I never did get a chance to shower at all.

Through all this I saw D'Amato coming toward me while I was trying to get into some clothes. For the first time in my career, Cus had not been in my corner, of course. He was unlicensed and therefore had to watch the fight from a ringside seat. Now as he came toward me I could see how pale he was.

"Sandra's here," he said.

"Where?" I said, not understanding for the moment.

"Outside the dressing room," Cus said.

For a moment I was dumfounded. "What's she doing here?" I said to myself. Before I had left the hotel to come to the Polo Grounds, I spoke to Sandra on the phone. She was at our home in Rockville Centre with some of the family and friends around her. She wasn't supposed to leave the house for one simple reason. She was pregnant and expecting our third child at any moment. The doctor had advised against her coming to the fight. We anticipated the crush, of course, and the doctor had warned that the excitement could be harmful to her, perhaps bring on the baby. Despite this warning, she had wanted to come, but I was dead set against it.

228

"She came for the fight?" I said.

"She was here," Cus said. "She saw it. She wants to see you."

"Please get her home," I said. "She should be in bed, not in this crowd."

Later I learned from Sandra that, although she had agreed with the doctor and me to stay home, she just couldn't. She prevailed upon some friends of ours to drive her to the fight, and she sat through it and saw it all. In the wild melee around the ring after I'd won, she became separated from our friends and tried to make her own way to my dressing room. Fortunately she bumped into Cus trying to do the same thing. Cus knew she was supposed to be at home, but he understood, as I do now, that she just couldn't stay there while I was going through the biggest moments of my life.

Understanding is one thing. What might have happened is another. Suppose I had lost? Or suppose the excitement of the night and the pushing around she took from the crowd had brought on the baby? I would have had one child born the night I won the title for the first time and a second born the night I became the first man in history to regain the heavyweight crown. Other things could have happened, too. I don't like to think of them.

The baby actually was born a little more than two weeks later, July 8. We named him Floyd II. After two girls, I had a boy. And after a year of derision between titles, I began to receive the kind of recognition and acceptance for which I had been searching all of my life. I don't mind confessing it was very pleasant.

The morning after the fight, for instance, there was a giant press conference at the Hotel Commodore. I'm still not much of a talker. It's a hard thing for me to expose myself to the questions of hundreds of newspapermen, all of whom have their own special way of asking questions. I've been the target at many press conferences, but I can't remember any I enjoyed as much as this one.

First I apologized for being a little late, but I explained

229

why it took me some time to get there. "I got up early this morning to read the articles written by you two or three weeks ago. I'm sorry that last night I disappointed so many of you."

The next few weeks following that morning after were hectic ones, of course. All kinds of engagements were being made for me. I made certain, though, that one day was kept open. Shortly after I regained the crown I made my usual appearance at the P.S. 614 graduation exercises. "I'm real proud," I told the students, "to bring back the championship to America and P.S. 614."

After that there was an official parade for me in Brooklyn in which I rode in the lead car from Grand Army Plaza to Borough Hall with Borough President John Cashmore. A few days later, Mayor Robert Wagner of New York City declared a "World Championship Day" and presented me with the city's medallion on the steps of City Hall.

On July 8, the people of Newtown, Connecticut, which had been my training base, held a reception for me at Town Hall, followed by another at the Carnival Grounds, and then a banquet in the Inn.

Don't let anybody tell you he doesn't like to hear speeches praising him, even if some of the words seem a little flowery. All of us want to be somebody, or at least think that other people think we are somebody. My friends in Harlem waited for a bright and sunny Sunday afternoon and then staged a two-hour parade in celebration of my victory. Then, on July 21, there was a huge testimonial dinner at the Hotel Commodore, co-chaired by Jackie Robinson and Ed Sullivan, with the proceeds going for the benefit of the Wiltwyck School. It had been planned that way—win, lose or draw.

It was the sort of evening the honored guest couldn't ever forget. On the dais to the right and left of me were the kind of people somebody like me would never have had the opportunity to meet if it hadn't been for boxing. There were Mayor

Wagner, Attorney General William P. Rogers and Justice Justine Wise Polier, James A. Farley and Branch Rickey, among others. My mother and mother-in-law, whom I regard as my second mother, sat with these people.

As I received a ceremonial robe sent to me by the president of Ghana, a cablegram expressing the blessings of His Holiness, Pope John XXIII, and a portrait of me painted by a "600" school student, I realized how far I had come from the scared youngster who would hide in the dark.

To top off that evening, D'Amato presented me with his own special gift. It was a fourteen-karat gold crown set with 174 diamonds, 248 rubies and sapphires and 250 pearls. They tell me it cost Cus $35,000. I can believe that, but I can't understand why he had to do it. Over the years he gave me a lot of presents, none of which was necessary, but all of which I naturally appreciated. One gift was sufficient. That was friendship.

Chapter Nineteen

When I went into training at the Spring Rock Country Club in Spring Valley, New York, for my third fight with Ingemar, the actual signing for the bout was many, many months away. Innumerable details, about which the public never knows, had to be worked out. For so much of my career I had never paid much attention to these details myself, but by this time I wanted to be informed about every one of them.

I had one other thing on my mind. I wanted to do a favor for a friend, and so I'll tell the whole story as it happened, because it will help to explain what being a fighter, winning the championship, losing it, and then regaining it has meant to me in addition to the money.

The friend is Mickey Alan, a singer who has become as dear to me as one of my own family. We first met in 1953, when I'd had only a handful of fights as a professional and Mickey was a singing waiter at a summer resort hotel called "The Riviera" in Tannersville, New York. This was one of my first training camps. I was a green and frightened kid, eager for companionship but wary of most people who made any effort to get close to me. Mickey, however, had one thing in common with me. He had tried fighting as a pro, but his heart was more in singing.

When he wasn't waiting on tables or studying his music, Mickey would do light sparring with me, and we'd take walks along the country roads or do roadwork together. I came to like Mickey and trust him. He was one of the few people my age, not of my race, with whom I was able to come to an understanding at that early age.

There was one time after I'd begun to move up in the rankings when Mickey asked me to visit him at his home in the Ridgewood section of New York. We spent a pleasant few days together, except for one unpleasant incident. We had gone out for a walk on this warm night to get a breath of air. On the way back to the house, Mickey stopped at a corner candy store to buy a paper. I waited for Mickey outside the store, not paying too much attention to three fellows standing on the corner, but I could tell they kept looking over at me and muttering to themselves. Just as Mickey came out of the store, I heard one of them say to the others, "What's a nigger doing in this neighborhood?"

I don't look for trouble, but I don't care for insults either. I was just starting toward them when Mickey said to me, "What's the matter?" He could see the anger welling up in my face.

"The three of them over there said something I didn't like," I said, and repeated the remark I had overheard.

"You stay put," Mickey said. He dropped his paper and headed for the three guys who thought they were tough. They saw him coming and got ready for him, but Mickey started swinging with both hands and knocked one flat on his back. The other two fled.

"It was my fight," I protested, "not yours."

"No," Mickey said, "it's everybody's fight. Besides, it's against the law for a professional fighter to go around hitting people outside of the ring."

"You're a fighter," I said.

"I'm a singer," Mickey said and then, more sadly, "if I ever get anywhere with it."

233

Through the years Mickey has stayed with his singing. He's been featured in small night clubs, but had never appeared before a national audience on television, which a singer really needs to hit it big. We've stayed close friends all this time, and Mickey is one of the few people whom I allow to live with me at camp when I'm training for a fight. He was with me for part of the time at Highland Mills, New York, where I went for my work leading up to my bout against Tom McNeeley last December 4 at Toronto.

Now, before my second meeting with Ingemar, the champ—as he was then—trained at Grossinger's. This is a famous resort hotel, and one of its most famous former employees is Eddie Fisher, the singer. Eddie worked at the hotel singing with the band and got his big break when he was discovered there by Eddie Cantor. While Ingemar was in training, Fisher came back to the hotel for a visit and they became friends. Just before our bout, Ingemar told Bill Fugazy, the promoter, that he wanted Fisher to have the honor of singing *The Star-Spangled Banner* as a prelude to our fight. Naturally enough, Fugazy said it would be all right.

I would have liked to do as much for Mickey. Something like that had been on my mind for a long time. For instance, for the first Johansson fight, I was invited to appear on Ed Sullivan's TV show. I was to be paid, naturally, but I set one other condition in addition to the price. I wanted Mickey to appear with me and be given the opportunity to sing before a national audience. The producers asked Mickey to audition. He did and sang so well that, even after I was knocked out, Sullivan still wanted Alan on the show. I lost, so I couldn't make that kind of an appearance, and when I didn't go on the show Mickey wouldn't either, although it would have been the greatest break in his life.

My feeling was that I had to make that up to him. After we'd finally signed for the Miami Beach bout, I attended a dinner at which Fugazy was present. "How was it," I asked the promoter, "that Eddie Fisher sang the national anthem for the last fight?"

"Ingemar asked me if it would be all right if Fisher sang," Fugazy said.

"If I asked you to let a singer friend of mine do the same thing, what would you say?"

"If you have a friend who is a singer and you want him to do this, then consider it done," Fugazy said.

"Just like that?" I said.

"Just like that," he said.

Later on I called Mickey and told him what arrangements had been made.

"You're kidding me," Mickey said.

"I wouldn't joke about a thing like that," I told him. "I mean it."

"What if I don't do well?" he said. "You'll look bad for recommending me."

"I know you can sing," I said, "and you know you can sing. Do you think I'd want you to be embarrassed if I didn't think you could do a good job?"

"I'll do a good job for you," Mickey said.

"You'll do a good job for yourself," I said.

As it turned out, Mickey did a far better job for himself than I did for myself. I trained so hard and so long for this third fight, but as I hit the canvas in the first round and looked up at Johansson I kept asking myself if I was going to be knocked down seven times again. I was disgusted with myself. After that I fought crazy, wild. I couldn't get myself together. I didn't know if I ought to press him, box him, or what.

I went out for that first round with my mind a blank. I survived the two first-round knockdowns and put him down in the same round himself. But between rounds, although I became more and more determined, I still felt bewildered.

"I can't find it. The style. I can't find the style to fight him," I cried to my handlers in my corner.

They were no great help, although they all tried to help me. Every one of them started to tell me something different. Their voices were coming at me, yet I felt all alone. To understand this you've got to appreciate what it is like when the lights go out all over the arena and then there are only you and your opponent in the center of the ring.

The way it was that night I had to reject everything that was being said to me. I had to be myself, yet I couldn't find myself. I fought with determination, but fought without skill, and when you feel that way the loneliness comes on you. You become a little afraid, and at the same time, because of the loneliness and the fear, you know you've got to strike out. You become—how can I put it?—almost an amateur. You go out and gamble. You take chances you wouldn't ordinarily take.

I guess when I made up my mind to gamble, take the chance of getting hit with his right hand in order to get to him, I reached a decision I had reached many, many years before at Wiltwyck.

There was this high wall. I climbed up on it and stood looking down at the ground, and the longer I stood there the higher I seemed to be off the ground and the more afraid I became. But the more my fear grew, the more I wanted to jump. I finally got my courage together, closed my eyes, and leaped off that wall.

I didn't close my eyes against Ingemar, but I did go in after him, taking punches I ordinarily would not and should not have taken. I fought badly, but I fought well enough to finally get to him. I had opportunities, but I didn't take advantage of them. I was happy to win, but I wasn't proud of the way it was accomplished.

The fight was bad, but the night was worse for me, because rolling around in a sleepless bed later on, I had only my thoughts to contend with. And I didn't like the way I had to think.

I couldn't forget the fight. I was low in spirit. It was one of my worst performances, and I had hoped it would be one of my best. The critics don't have to rate me. I rate myself. I put that third fight with Johansson in with the terrible one I made against Roy Harris.

I'm not the kind of a man who cries; at least I don't do it where anybody can see it. But why is it that you can get to a certain point where everything physical and your mental attitude seem to be perfect—then you get into the ring and do nothing? After that fight I went back to the house where I was staying, and all of a sudden I wanted to fight Ingemar again the next night. I knew it would be different. It was as if he had disregarded me and run over me in that first round.

What happened to me that night is that I discovered I am a moody fighter, which is something I didn't know before. I know now that every time I fight I must create a mood. My interest for Ingemar that night was almost at an all-time low, something like in the first fight when I took him for granted. It took me weeks to begin to understand that maybe that was the worst part of me against the best part of him. If that was the real him and it wasn't the real me, then I didn't do so badly.

However, once I reached that conclusion, I had to ask myself, "Which is the real me?"

Is it the man in the ring or the one outside of it? Is it the fighter who will isolate himself from his family for months on end while in training or the one who wants to watch his kids grow up more than he wants anything else? Is it the boy who once thought that if he had three hundred dollars in one piece in his pocket, he'd have anything any man could desire or the one who has learned the hard way what it costs a champion to live? Is it the one who would quit boxing tomorrow if the Catholic Church decreed against it or the one who knows how much he owes to a sport?

After the fight, I got to wondering about a lot of things. I wondered, for instance, why I'd gone through the trouble of getting Mickey the opportunity to sing the national anthem. It was more than friendship. It was the appreciation that there are people who can do many things. They've got the talent, but they just don't get the chance.

If I have to sum up my life, that would be as good a way as any. I got the chance and I became a champion. But being a champion isn't enough in itself. There are obligations that go with whatever position, wealth and celebrity I've attained. There are obligations to the sport, obligations to our country, obligations to my race, to my family and to myself.

I take every one of them seriously because I know what I still would be if the Lord hadn't pointed me toward the ring, given me the opportunity to do something with whatever natural talent I possessed, and allowed me to come in contact with the people who could bring that talent out of me. Boxing is supposed to be a dirty business, but it has made me clean and enabled me to do some good for others. If I was able to do nothing else in this world, I must say that seeing my mother the kind of woman she is today is enough to make me happy.

When I look at my children and realize the kind of life they will be able to lead, I know that all the time and effort I've put into being what I am has been worth it, and I would put in more if I had to to keep it that way. They'll go to school and live in nice places and meet nice people and not have to roam the streets as I did as a youngster. My many brothers and sisters will have advantages my poor parents could not have given them, as much as they wanted to.

I'm training my brother Raymond to be a fighter because he wants to be one, not because I am one. I'll manage him when he's ready to turn professional because I think I've learned enough about that side of the sport to let him benefit from my education in it. It would be nice if, for the first time in the history of boxing, one brother could succeed another as the heavyweight champion of the world, but if Raymond doesn't, it will not be because he didn't try hard enough or I didn't have my heart in his ambitions.

When I add up my own blessings, I know how far I have come from the darkness of the cellars and subways and the fears which used to haunt me and still haunt me now and then, but I'm no longer afraid, because I know now that nobody can do for me what I can do for myself. It may seem a small thing to some people who never had to worry about such things, but I take pride now in the way I'm able to speak and write and mingle with all kinds of people, although I was more nervous than at any time in my life when I had an audience with President Kennedy. I had a start toward an education, but I've never said to myself that I didn't have to learn any more once I was handed my diploma from P.S. 614.

I'm not ashamed to reveal it, but wherever I go these days I carry books with me, and one of those books is a dictionary. There was a time when somebody would say something to me and I'd pretend I knew what he was talking about when all along I didn't know the meaning of the words that were being said to me. That cost me—not alone in money, but in pride and shame.

Now when somebody says something to me, I ask the meaning of the word if I don't understand what is being said. For instance, when this book was being prepared, my collaborator, Milton Gross, used the word "introspective," in asking me a question about myself. I let the sentence pass for a while, but all the time I was thinking about what the meaning of that word was. Finally, I stopped talking in the middle of a sentence, knowing that I couldn't answer the question intelligently if I didn't grasp the full meaning of it.

"What is the meaning of that word—introspective?" I asked.

When it was explained to me, I realized how much it really applied to me, not just outside the ring, but inside it as well. Boxing is an outgoing business, but I do so much of my fighting inside myself. Let me be honest—I torment myself so much and so often because what I want above everything else now is what I wanted as a child. I want acceptance and I want commendation. I want people to say I've been a good champion. I want them to say I've been a good man and a thoughtful man. I would like the same sort of reception here that I received in Sweden when I went on my exhibition tour in August of 1960 and the people treated me as though I was somebody.

I must confess that those weeks spent touring twenty of Sweden's provincial districts, which are like the states of our country, were among the most satisfactory of my life. For the first time in my twenty-seven years of living as a Negro I really discovered what it might be like to live without a kind of iron curtain being raised between people because the color of their skin happens to be different. I have no intention of preaching a sermon this late in the story of my life, but it does seem to me that all people should be treated alike until you discover for yourself that one is better or more likeable or more honest or more decent than the other.

For myself, I approach everybody in one way. They all are 100 per cent, and I let them find their own level. Some go up to 110 per cent or more. Some drop down so much that before we're through they owe me some points. You can't like everybody, but you can't dislike everybody, either. And so far as hate goes, there aren't too many people in the whole world who are so bad that you must hate them.

There must be room in all of us for understanding. Coming from a fighter that may seem a strange thought to some people. Ours is the only business in which the fundamental idea is to knock the other guy unconscious, and if you follow that thought through to its logical conclusion, it is the only sport in which a man has a license to hurt another man.

Yet there isn't hate in any one of us. For myself, I can truthfully say I feel no differently inside if I'm fighting a white man or another Negro. I've got the title. The other man is trying to take it away from me. It's as simple as that. It's the way of life put into a ring surrounded by ropes, but before the fight neither one of us hates the other. During the fight we respect each other, and after it there's a kind of admiration and understanding which two men who have fought honestly can have for each other.

After the third fight against Ingemar, for instance, I went to him, threw my arms around him, and kissed him on the cheek. The press made a good deal of that act of mine the next day at a press conference. I realized it was a strange thing to do. I think I called it "girlish," when they asked me about it, but it was my expression of admiration for a man who had fought me well. That I beat him two straight after he had knocked me out was unimportant. The important thing is that he was a formidable opponent.

There is a lot about Ingemar which I admire, aside from his fighting ability. I like the way he handled himself when he was the champion and the kind of appearance he made to the public. He was on TV frequently and around the kind of places where people saw him a lot. After I defeated him the first time I resolved that I would try to be a lot like him in that respect, but I soon discovered that that kind of public life was not for me. I make some public appearances, but they're not the kind that Ingemar seems to be at his best at. He's more of an outgoing type of person than I am and no matter how much I would like to be, I just can't.

So I have to continue trying to be myself simply because I can't be anybody else. As long as I'm the champion—and right at this minute I still don't know how long I will continue to fight—I may continue being the champion nobody knows. At least, that's what a lot of newspapermen say about me. Sure, I go away to an isolated training camp and work hard there. But it's my business. I find that being alone I'm able to do more. I'd welcome the press to my camp while I'm training at any time, but I'd like them to know that there are times when it is necessary for a fighter to try things alone. At least it still is with me.

Funny thing, but I still admit to embarrassment when I'm attempting a new maneuver in camp and I miss and I get hit by a sparring partner. It still happens. I guess maybe it will always happen, but the way to train properly is to keep trying what you want to do until you get it. If people were around watching me, it's possible that I'd give up trying before I had accomplished what I set out to do.

But that's me and long ago I gave up fighting myself. Consequently, I prefer the isolated places such as Highland Mills, New York; Newtown, Connecticut; and Ehsan's where I've put in so many hours of my life to get where I am.

I know this hasn't been easy for my wife or my children. I'd like to be like other men, who put in eight hours a day in an office or at some other type of job and come home to spend the evenings with their families. I'd like Saturdays and Sundays and holidays at home, and more than anything else I'd like to be with my family and watch the children growing up.

But we talked this out long ago, Sandra and I. When I finally retire we'll have a lot of years together. We'll also have enough money so that we'll never want for a long time. The days, weeks, months and years we've given up for me to be the kind of champion I would like to be have been investments that will come back to us with interest.

A lot of my life has been lived in phone conversations between us. A lot of my enjoyment of my children has come only in snatches in the times I've spent at home. I've tried to make the most of those short hours, and I made a promise to myself long ago that I would make it up to them when all of it is over.

I like to keep my promises. I remember one I made that I was a little late in keeping, and I've regretted it ever since. That was in October, 1960, after I arrived at Idlewild Airport from my European tour. I went immediately to a phone to call a fifteen-year-old friend, Johnny Olsen, only to learn that the boy had died a few hours before my plane landed.

I had first learned about Johnny a year before then. He was sick with leukemia, and I was sick myself suffering from the aftermath of losing my title. I sent him an autograph, however, and a note that I would visit him at his home in Warren Township, New Jersey, as soon as I got back from a trip to Canada.

By the time I was able to get back to the United States, Johnny was terribly sick. His parents, Marian and Bob Olsen, didn't hold out much hope for their fading son. They told me Johnny had been inquiring about me every day since he'd gotten my note, and when I went to sit with him at his bedside, some of the spirit that was in his weakened body came into mine.

I believe I stayed with the boy about three hours that first night and thereafter, even when I went into concentrated training at Newtown, Connecticut, I'd called Johnny on the phone regularly. Whenever I could I'd visit him, and some of these times it wasn't any pleasure because the child had been sent to Memorial Hospital. His illness was terminal. In other words he was going to die, they told me.

I talked to Johnny just before the second Johansson fight and promised him my gloves whether I won or lost. I also sent him six tickets to the fight, hoping against hope he would take a turn for the better and be able to see me in the ring. The doctors told me he might not even live until fight-time.

There was spirit in that withered body, though. A couple of days after I'd regained the title, I went to the hospital and Johnny was alive. I gave him the gloves and it was only then that I learned that the child had no idea how ill he was. I suppose I should have realized that sooner, but I just struck the thought from my mind. I wanted this boy to get well.

The strangest thing is that Johnny did make a kind of recovery, enough to be taken home again. I rushed over to his home. With me I brought my deputy sheriff's badge from Rockville Centre and a gun, which I showed to him. He said he had to make something for me and began the next day to make a leather case for the pistol.

When my own son was born on July 8, Johnny kept himself busy making a hooked rug for my boy. He seemed so weak then, but he told me that when the rug was finished it would have a pair of boxing gloves woven into it. It was hard to keep from crying when I sat with Johnny. It was harder still when Mr. and Mrs. Olsen told me that my visits to their son and interest in him was helping to keep him alive.

I wanted to believe that, but when I heard over the phone that Johnny had died just a little while before I had arrived in this country from my European tour I kept thinking that maybe if I'd cut that tour short the boy might have had a few more hours on this earth. Johnny did what he said he would. He finished the rug before death took him, and in the middle of it there not only were two boxing gloves, but Floyd, Jr., my son's name.

Little Johnny Olsen thought of me and mine when he had every right in this world to think of everything else. I like to think I was able to offer some comfort, if not some help, to this child, because Heaven knows how much I needed comfort when I was a kid.

I really didn't begin to live until I was the age at which Johnny Olsen died. I believed in nothing, least of all myself. I was, you could say, kind of a stranger until I found myself and something worth striving for in the ring.

I have crowds with me now—a manager, trainers, sparring partners, lawyers and accountants. Some of them are still with me when I climb the four steps up into the ring and wait for the opening bell. But then it sounds, and they're out of the ring. The lights go out all over the arena, except for those that come on over the ring, and then you see the resin dust rising upwards and the man coming toward you from the other corner. And then it is only me against him. As I write this, I am the world's champion. But I am alone. Is there any other way?